THE ULTIMATE LIFE TOOLBOX

Discover the Secrets to a Confident and Peaceful Life

Vipan Kapoor

DEDICATION

To my love, whose presence in my life,
inspired me to create this book.

Special Thanks

To Neet Aujla, for suggesting insightful topics,
which significantly enriched the depth of this book.

-- Vipan Kapoor --

"If you want a thing done well, do it yourself"
Napoleon Bonaparte

CONTENTS

"The Ultimate Life Toolbox: Discover the Secrets to a Confident and Peaceful Life" is a practical guide designed to help you navigate life's ups and downs with ease and confidence. Whether you're dealing with stress, personal challenges, or just seeking more happiness, this book provides useful tools that can transform your everyday life. Each chapter offers a unique concept or practice that, when applied, can bring balance, growth, and clarity into your life. *Trust that some unseen forces have guided this book into your hands.*

The book is built on simple, powerful ideas that can help you live with more purpose and joy. Starting with **IKIGAI**, you'll learn how to find your true purpose and understand what truly makes you happy. This sets the foundation for the journey ahead. **Vision to Reality – Mapping Your Success** teaches you how to create a clear roadmap toward your dreams, setting goals that align with your passions.

In **Self-Reflection**, you will explore how to understand yourself better and identify areas for improvement. Building on this, **Journaling – Reflecting on Your Journey** introduces a simple yet effective tool for ongoing self-reflection, allowing you to track your growth and embrace the lessons along the way.

The **Gratitude** chapter shows you how powerful appreciation can be in shifting your mindset and enhancing your life. You will also dive into the connection between your physical and mental well-being in **Gut and Mind Connection**, discovering how taking care of your gut health can improve your overall mental clarity and emotional stability.

Positive Affirmations focuses on using positive thinking to build confidence and a positive mindset, while **Mindfulness and Prayer** explores simple techniques for connecting with your inner self and finding peace. In **Wabi Sabi**, you'll learn to embrace imperfections, seeing beauty in life's fleeting moments and embracing growth even in challenging times.

Life is full of change, and the chapter **Anicca (Impermanence)** teaches you how to accept it and use it as a tool for transformation. In today's world, **Digital Detox** is vital, and this chapter shows you how to reclaim your time and focus by stepping away from technology when needed.

You'll also learn the essentials of **Resilience**, **Time Management**, and self-care to enhance your physical and mental health. Learn **Emotional Intelligence** to improve relationships, and master mind mapping for better decision-making. The final chapter, integrates all concepts, guiding you to craft a personalized roadmap for success.

About the Book

This book is about applying practical tools to improve your life. Each chapter offers simple exercises and stories to guide you. Whether you're dealing with stress, personal growth, or career challenges, this book is for anyone wanting a more balanced, fulfilling life. With the tools inside, you'll be ready to create lasting change and begin your journey toward a more peaceful, purposeful, and joyful life.

This book is not meant to be read in one sitting. You can take your time with each chapter, exploring the ideas and trying the activities. Each tool is easy to understand and can be used right away. You will find stories, examples, and fun exercises to help you put the lessons into practice.

Join us on this journey to discover new ways to live with purpose, joy, and balance. Your adventure starts here!

HOW TO READ THIS BOOK

Welcome to *The Ultimate Life Toolbox*! This book is designed to be easy and enjoyable to read. Here are some tips on how to get the most out of it:

1. **Take Your Time**: You don't have to read the book all at once. Each chapter is short and focuses on one tool. Feel free to read one chapter at a time and take breaks in between.

2. **Choose What You Need**: You can start with any chapter that interests you. If you are facing a specific challenge, look for the tool that can help you with that situation.

3. **Try the Activities**: Each chapter includes fun exercises and activities. Make sure to try them out! These activities will help you apply what you learn to your life.

4. **Reflect and Take Notes**: As you read, think about how each tool relates to your life. You can write down your thoughts or keep a journal to track your progress and ideas.

5. **Share with Others**: If you find something helpful, share it with friends or family! Talking about what you've learned can make it even more meaningful.

6. **Be Open-Minded**: Some ideas may be new to you, and that's okay! Keep an open mind and be willing to explore different perspectives. It's all part of learning and growing.

7. **Use the Tools**: Remember, the tools in this book are meant to help you. Practice using them regularly in your daily life to see real changes.

8. **Come Back Anytime**: You can revisit any chapter whenever you need a boost or a reminder. This book is your personal toolbox, so feel free to use it as often as you like.

Enjoy your reading journey, and remember that every small step counts. Happy exploring!

ABOUT THE AUTHOR

Vipan Kapoor is an accomplished IT professional, software developer, and educator with extensive experience in the technology and education sectors. He is the Director and Founder of SkillHike Solutions (Website: www. skillhike.co.in), where he has dedicated his career to helping individuals and businesses enhance their skills, particularly in programming languages and digital technologies.

With a strong educational background, he has always been driven by the desire to share his knowledge and expertise with others. His commitment to personal and professional growth is evident in both his work as a trainer and his passion for continuous learning.

The Ultimate Life Toolbox marks **Vipan's debut as an author**. This book draws on his years of experience as a trainer and software developer, offering practical life strategies that help readers navigate challenges and lead more balanced, fulfilling lives. Vipan believes that the tools shared in this book can inspire positive change, just as he has seen in his own life and career.

As the recipient of the *Tech-Savvy Genius Excellence Award 2024*, Vipan hopes that readers find the same inspiration and practical guidance within these pages. He invites everyone to embark on a journey of self-discovery, personal growth, and transformation.

INTRODUCTION:

THE ULTIMATE LIFE TOOLBOX

Imagine you are handed a special toolbox at the beginning of your life. It's not a regular toolbox filled with hammers and screwdrivers, but one filled with essential tools to help you navigate through the ups and downs of life. These tools are not objects you can hold or touch but are powerful ideas, practices, and habits that support your mental and emotional well-being. Each tool in your life toolbox is designed to help you face challenges, grow, and get the most out of every day. They help you deal with stress, stay calm during difficult times, and help you understand what truly matters to you.

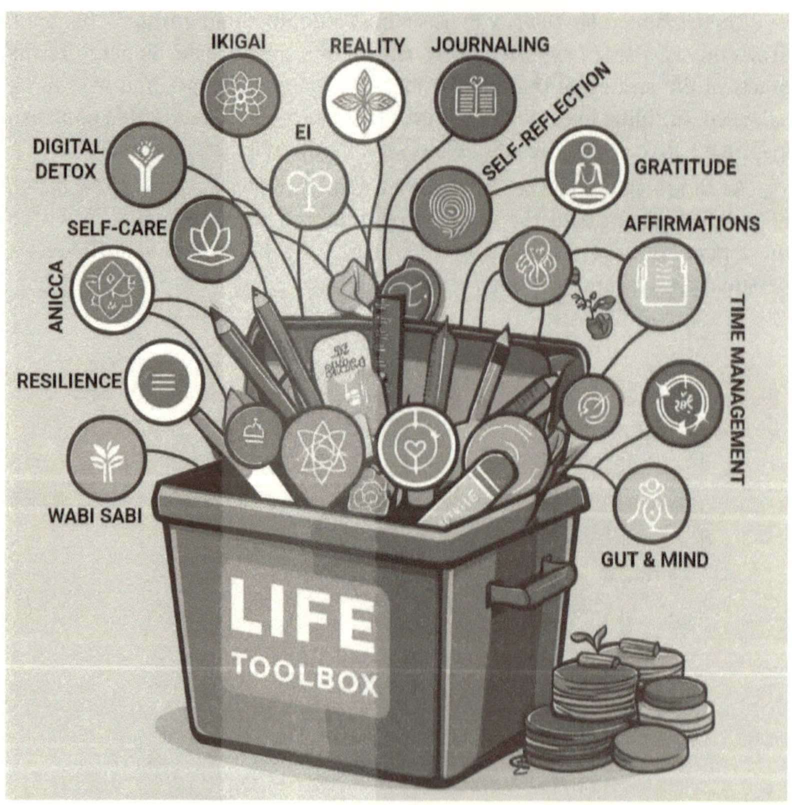

For young people today, these tools are especially important. Growing up in a fast-paced world can sometimes feel overwhelming. School pressures, family expectations, friendships, career decisions, and social media all contribute to stress and self-doubt. It's easy to feel lost or uncertain about the future. But, by using the right tools, you can manage these challenges more effectively. These tools will help you feel more confident, in control, and prepared to handle whatever life throws your way.

In this book, we'll introduce you to some of the most powerful tools you can add to your life toolbox. Each tool is designed to support you in building a strong, positive foundation for your life. We'll explore how to find your purpose, deal with change, practice mindfulness, develop gratitude, embrace imperfection, and so much more. These tools aren't meant to solve every problem right away, but they will help you handle them with a calmer, more positive attitude.

Why Start Building Your Life Toolbox Now?

You might be wondering why you should start building your life toolbox now, rather than later. The answer is simple: the earlier you begin, the better prepared you will be to face life's challenges. Think of these tools as steps that will lead you to a life that is stronger, more resilient, and more fulfilling. Each tool is a way to help you grow and adapt to life's ups and downs, whether it's coping with school stress, dealing with uncertainty about the future, or finding peace in your day-to-day life.

For example, if you often feel stressed about school or the pressure to meet expectations, tools like mindfulness and gratitude can help you manage those feelings. By practicing mindfulness, you'll learn how to stay present and calm, even when things are overwhelming. Gratitude will help you focus on the good things in your life, shifting your mindset toward positivity and contentment.

Tools like Ikigai—the Japanese concept of finding your life's purpose— can guide you when you feel uncertain about your future. Ikigai helps you explore what makes you happy and gives you direction, making it easier to set goals that align with your passions and values. Understanding your Ikigai will help you focus on what really matters and create a life that feels fulfilling.

These tools aren't meant to be quick fixes. Like learning any new skill, they require practice, patience, and a willingness to change. But with time, they will help you develop a mindset that is more positive, adaptable, and resilient.

How to Use This Book and Your Life Toolbox

This book is organized to guide you through each tool one by one. Every chapter introduces a new tool and explains how it works, why it's helpful, and how you can start using it in your life. Each chapter contains easy-to-understand explanations, relatable examples, and practical exercises that you can try out. You don't have to master each tool right away. Instead, focus on the ones that feel most useful to you. Over time, as you practice these tools, you'll build a toolbox that supports your mental and emotional well-being.

Take your time with each chapter. Reflect on how each tool connects to your life, and make a plan to incorporate it into your daily routine. Practice the exercises at the end of each chapter. Even small, consistent efforts can make a big difference over time. Remember, the goal isn't to get everything perfect but to create positive changes in your life that will last.

The beauty of this life toolbox is that it's personal to you. It's about discovering what works best for your unique situation and using the tools that resonate most with you. There's no rush—this is a journey of self-growth and self-discovery, and it's okay to go at your own pace.

So, are you ready to start building your life toolbox? Are you ready to create a foundation that helps you live a more fulfilled, balanced, and joyful life? Let's begin this journey together, exploring new ways to grow, adapt, and thrive, no matter what challenges come your way. It's time to unlock your potential and discover the power of the tools you already have inside you.

Chapter 1

IKIGAI

Finding Your Purpose

IKIGAI is a Japanese concept that means "a reason for being." It helps people find their purpose in life by combining four important aspects: what you love, what you are good at, what the world needs, and what you can be paid for. When these four elements come together, you can discover your Ikigai, leading to a happier and more fulfilling life.

The Four Key Parts of Ikigai

1. **What You Love**

   This part is about your passions and interests. It includes the activities that make you feel excited, happy, and fulfilled. Think about the things you enjoy doing in your free time. Ask yourself:

   - What activities do I look forward to?
   - What hobbies make me lose track of time?
   - What topics do I enjoy learning about?

Example: If you love gardening, that's a passion that brings you joy. You might find happiness in planting flowers, growing vegetables, or just spending time in nature.

2. **What You Are Good At**

This aspect focuses on your skills and strengths. These are the things you are naturally talented at or have developed through practice and experience. Consider:

- What skills do I have that others admire?
- What tasks do I find easy that others struggle with?
- What activities do I feel confident doing?

Example: If you are great at writing stories, that's a skill you possess. You might have a knack for creating interesting plots and characters, and people often compliment your writing.

3. **What the World Needs**

This part is about understanding the problems or needs in your community or the world that resonate with you. It involves thinking about how you can make a positive impact. Reflect on:

- What issues do I care about deeply?
- How can I contribute to my community or society?
- What changes do I wish to see in the world?

Example: You may notice that there are many stray animals in your neighbourhood that need help. You might feel a strong desire to support animal welfare and ensure that these animals receive care and shelter.

4. **What You Can Be Paid For**

This aspect explores career opportunities that align with your interests and skills. It's about finding ways to earn a living while doing what you love. Think about:

- What jobs match my passions and skills?
- How can I turn my hobbies into a career?
- What services or products can I offer that people would pay for?

Example: If you love baking and are skilled at making delicious cakes, you could start a small bakery or sell custom cakes for special occasions. This allows you to earn money while doing something you enjoy.

Let's look at a practical example to see how Ikigai works in real life.

Meet Ravi:

- **What He Loves**: Ravi loves playing music and teaching others how to play instruments. He feels most alive when he is performing or sharing his knowledge about music.

- **What He Is Good At**: Ravi has a talent for playing the guitar and has been praised for his ability to teach music. He finds it easy to explain concepts to beginners.

- **What the World Needs**: Ravi notices that many children in his community lack access to music education. He believes that music can positively impact their lives and help them express themselves.

- **What He Can Be Paid For**: Ravi thinks about starting a music school where he can teach children to play instruments. He knows there is a demand for music classes in his area.

Ravi's Ikigai:

By combining these four elements, Ravi finds his Ikigai: **He can pursue his passion for music, share his skills with children, fulfil a need in his community, and earn a living by teaching music classes.**

Another Example of Ikigai: Meet Ashwani

Ashwani's Story:

- **What He Loves**: Ashwani has a deep passion for cooking and trying out new recipes. He finds joy in experimenting with flavours and creating delicious meals for him friends and family. Every time He cooks, He feels happy and fulfilled.

- **What He Is Good At**: Ashwani is a natural in the kitchen. Him friends often say He has a gift for cooking, and He can make dishes that taste amazing. He enjoys sharing his cooking tips and techniques with friends, and they appreciate his advice.

- **What the World Needs**: Ashwani notices that many people in him community are too busy to cook healthy meals for themselves. He understands that cooking at home can help families eat better and save money. Ashwani wants to help people learn how to prepare quick and healthy meals.

- **What He Can Be Paid For**: Ashwani thinks about starting a meal prep service or cooking classes. He knows there are people who would pay for healthy meal plans or would be interested in learning how to cook.

Ashwani's Ikigai:

By combining these four elements, Ashwani discovers him Ikigai: **He can share him love for cooking, teach others how to prepare healthy meals, address a need in him community for better eating habits, and earn money by running a cooking class or meal prep service.**

Ashwani's Journey:

1. **Starting Small:** Ashwani begins by offering cooking classes in him community centre. He starts with a few friends, who invite others to join. Ashwani creates a fun and welcoming atmosphere where everyone can learn together.

2. **Gathering Feedback:** After each class, Ashwani asks for feedback. He learns what recipes him students enjoy the most and how He can improve him teaching. This helps him grow as a teacher and chef.

3. **Expanding Him Reach:** As him classes become more popular, Ashwani starts to think about offering online cooking classes as well. This way, He can reach even more people and share him love for cooking with a wider audience.

4. **Building a community:** Ashwani creates a social media page where him students can share their cooking successes, ask questions, and inspire each other. This builds a sense of community around healthy cooking.

Through this journey, Ashwani finds fulfilment and joy in him work. He is not only able to pursue him passion for cooking but also make a positive impact on him community by helping others learn how to eat healthier.

Ashwani's story shows how identifying your Ikigai can lead to a rewarding and meaningful life. It encourages young people to reflect on their interests and skills, and to think about how they can contribute to the world while also achieving their personal and professional goals.

Another Example of Ikigai: Meet Neeru

Neeru's Story:

- **What She Loves:** Neeru loves creating a warm and inviting home for her family. She enjoys decorating her space, organizing household items, and making her home a cozy place where everyone feels comfortable. She also loves planning family activities and making special meals for her loved ones.

- **What She Is Good At:** Neeru has a talent for interior design and organization. Friends often compliment her on her home's aesthetics and how well-organized everything is. She has a keen eye for colour combinations, space management, and creating beautiful arrangements. Neeru is also skilled at cooking and meal planning, ensuring her family enjoys nutritious and delicious meals.

- **What the World Needs**: Neeru notices that many families in her community are busy with work and life responsibilities and struggle to keep their homes organized and beautiful. She understands that a well-organized home can reduce stress and improve family life. Many people need guidance on how to create a comfortable living space without feeling overwhelmed.

- **What She Can Be Paid For**: Neeru considers turning her passion for home decoration and organization into a business. She thinks about offering home organization services, interior design consultations, or even cooking classes focused on meal preparation for busy families.

Neeru's Ikigai:

By combining these four elements, Neeru discovers her Ikigai: **She can share her love for creating a beautiful home, help others achieve an organized and inviting space, address a need in her community for support with home management, and earn money by providing her services.**

Neeru's Journey:

1. **Starting a Blog**: Neeru starts a blog where she shares tips on home organization, decoration ideas, and quick meal prep strategies. She posts before-and-after photos of her own home projects and shares her recipes.

2. **Hosting Workshops**: After gaining a following online, Neeru begins hosting small workshops in her community. In these sessions, she teaches participants how to declutter their spaces and offers practical decorating advice. She provides hands-on guidance and encouragement.

3. **Offering Personal Consultations**: As her reputation grows, Neeru starts offering one-on-one home organization and decorating consultations. Families book her services to help them transform their spaces, making them more functional and beautiful.

4. **Creating a Supportive Community**: Neeru forms a community group where families can share their home projects, exchange ideas, and support each other. This not only builds relationships but also fosters a sense of camaraderie among participants.

Through her journey, Neeru finds joy and purpose in her work. She transforms her love for home management into a fulfilling career while positively impacting the lives of other families. By helping others create comfortable living spaces, she finds her Ikigai.

Neeru's story illustrates how homemakers can identify their Ikigai by reflecting on their passions, skills, and the needs of their communities. It encourages others to think about how they can turn their talents and interests into meaningful work, even from the comforts of their homes.

Activities to Find Your Ikigai

Self-Reflection Exercise

Finding your Ikigai is a personal journey that starts with self-reflection. Spending time alone to reflect on your answers to the four elements of Ikigai – *What You Love, What You Are Good At, What the World Needs, and What You Can Be Paid For* – can reveal new insights about yourself. This exercise is designed to help you explore these areas deeply, guiding you to connect with your true purpose.

1. **What Activities Make Me Lose Track of Time?**

   When we engage in activities we genuinely love, we tend to lose track of time. This sense of timelessness is a strong indicator of something that resonates deeply with us. Here are some questions to guide you:

   - **What activities bring me pure joy?** Think of times when you felt genuinely happy, excited, or fulfilled. Was it while cooking, writing, helping someone, or creating something?

   - **What do I look forward to doing in my free time?** When you have a break, what do you naturally want to do? If you feel excited about certain activities on your days off, they might be connected to your passion.

   - **What am I doing when I forget to check the time?** When do you lose the urge to check your phone or watch? These activities can be powerful indicators of what you love to do and are worth exploring further.

2. **What Compliments Do I Receive Most Often?**

   Recognizing your strengths is an important part of Ikigai. Sometimes, others can see our strengths more clearly than we can. Pay attention to compliments and feedback from friends, family, and colleagues. Here are some questions to think about:

   - **What skills do people compliment me on?** Recall specific compliments from others. Do people tell you that you are a good listener, a problem-solver, or a creative thinker?

   - **What do people come to me for help with?** If people regularly seek your advice or help in certain areas, it likely means they see you as skilled or knowledgeable in those areas. Take note of these strengths as potential gifts you can use.

- **What makes me feel confident?** Think about tasks you complete with ease and confidence. Reflect on moments when you felt capable, appreciated, or proud of your work. These are strengths you can build upon.

3. **What Changes Do I Wish to See in the World?**

Considering the needs around you is a crucial part of Ikigai. Reflecting on what the world, your community, or even your family needs can help you connect with your purpose on a deeper level. Here are some guiding questions:

- **What issues or causes am I passionate about?** Are there social or environmental issues that matter to you? Think about things like education, mental health, sustainability, or equal opportunities. Identifying these passions can help point you toward meaningful work.

- **Who do I want to help or impact?** Do you feel a desire to help specific groups, like children, the elderly, animals, or the environment? By focusing on who you want to support, you can uncover ways to make a difference.

- **What positive changes do I hope to see in my community?** Sometimes, purpose is found close to home. Think about improvements you'd like to see in your neighbourhood or workplace. Perhaps you see a need for mentorship, skill development, or cleaner spaces. These changes can be a part of your unique purpose.

4. **How Can I Turn My Passions into a Career?**

Finding a way to be paid for what you love might be challenging but rewarding. Reflecting on how to make a living while doing something meaningful is essential for a balanced Ikigai. Consider these questions:

- **What services or products could I offer?** Think about the skills or passions you identified earlier. Could they be turned into a business, freelance work, or teaching opportunity? For instance, if you love cooking, you might consider becoming a chef, food blogger, or cooking teacher.

- **What careers align with my skills and interests?** Research jobs or businesses that involve the things you love and are good at. If you're a creative writer, look into freelance writing, editing, or content creation. If you're skilled at organizing, event planning or personal organizing could be a path for you.

- **Who would be willing to pay for my skills?** Identify potential clients, employers, or communities that need the talents you have. For instance, if you're good at helping people solve problems, consider consulting or coaching.

After going through these questions, take time to write down your answers. Review them and look for patterns. For example, if you notice that you love helping others and often receive compliments on your listening skills, you might explore careers in counselling, teaching, or social work.

This reflection process is not about rushing to find answers but about understanding yourself better over time. Keep revisiting these questions as you grow and change, and allow your Ikigai to evolve naturally.

Journaling Prompt: Imagine Your Perfect Day Living Your Ikigai

Journaling (writing down your thoughts, feelings, and experiences regularly) can be a powerful way to connect deeply with your thoughts and dreams. This activity will help you visualize a day in your life where you are fully living your Ikigai. Take time to describe your perfect day in as much detail as possible, imagining how each moment would feel. This vision can become your guide as you work towards finding and living your Ikigai.

Step 1: Prepare for Your Writing

Find a quiet space, free from distractions, where you can focus. Set aside around 15–20 minutes. Start by taking a few deep breaths, allowing yourself to feel calm and open-minded.

Step 2: Begin Writing About Your Perfect Day

Imagine a day in your life where you are completely fulfilled. This is a day where everything aligns with your purpose, where you feel a deep sense of satisfaction and happiness. Write as if you are experiencing it right now. Answer the following questions as you write:

1. **How does your day begin?**
   - Imagine yourself waking up. Where are you? Describe the room and the environment. Are you in a peaceful setting, like near a forest or beach, or maybe in a bustling city?
   - How do you feel when you wake up? Energized? Excited? At peace?
   - What is the first thing you do? Do you meditate, exercise, prepare breakfast, or simply sit quietly? Visualize this moment in detail.

2. **What are you doing that fulfils your Ikigai?**
   - Think about the main activity of your day. If your Ikigai involves teaching, imagine yourself giving a class. If it involves creating art, picture yourself painting, drawing, or crafting.
   - Describe the activity in detail. What tools or materials are you using? Who is with you? How does it feel to do this work? Does it make you lose track of time? How does it contribute to the world around you?
   - Think about how this activity brings out your best qualities and uses your strengths. Write about how you feel as you perform this work.

3. **How do you connect with others?**
   - Visualize the people around you on this perfect day. Are you working with a team, spending time with family, or meeting new people?
   - Describe the conversations you have, the connections you make, and the joy you feel in your interactions. How does your work positively impact those around you?
   - Write about any gratitude or appreciation you receive from others. How do they respond to the work you're doing?

4. **What moments of peace or relaxation do you experience?**
   - Imagine the breaks or quiet moments throughout your day. Where do you go to relax? How do you unwind?
   - Describe any places or activities that bring you calmness and help you recharge. Do you sit by the water, take a walk, or meditate?
   - Reflect on how these moments of peace help you stay balanced and grounded in your purpose.

5. **How does your day end?**
   - Picture the end of your perfect day. Where are you, and what are you doing as the day comes to a close? Do you spend time with loved ones, reflect quietly, or enjoy a hobby?
   - Describe how you feel at the end of the day. Are you satisfied, fulfilled, and ready for tomorrow?
   - Reflect on the gratitude you feel for this day, for the work you've done, and for the sense of purpose that guides you.

Step 3: Reflect on Your Writing

When you're finished, read through what you've written. Take note of any themes or activities that stand out. Think about how these moments and activities could fit into your real life. Even if you can't live this perfect day right now, you might start working toward small changes that bring you closer to it.

This exercise is not just about imagining a dream life – it's about discovering what truly matters to you. By understanding the elements of your perfect day, you can start taking small steps toward making your Ikigai a reality. Over time, revisit this vision, update it, and let it guide you on your journey.

Overcoming Challenges: Common Barriers to Finding Ikigai

Finding one's Ikigai, or true purpose, is an exciting journey, but it can also be challenging, especially for young people who may face unique barriers along the way. Below are some common challenges that many experience, along with practical strategies for overcoming them. Remember, discovering your Ikigai isn't always straightforward, and it's okay to face difficulties. The important thing is to keep moving forward.

Common Barriers to Finding Ikigai

1. **Fear of Failure**

   Many young people hesitate to pursue their interests or passions due to a fear of failure. They might worry about not succeeding or fear being judged if things don't go as planned. This fear can make them feel stuck, stopping them from taking that first step toward exploring their purpose.

2. **Societal Expectations**

   Society often has strong ideas about what a "successful" or "respectable" career looks like. Family, friends, or cultural expectations can make young people feel pressured to follow a particular path, even if it doesn't match their passions. This pressure can make it challenging to explore their true interests, as they may feel guilty or anxious about going against what's expected.

3. **Self-Doubt**

   It's common for young people to doubt their abilities and wonder if they're "good enough" to pursue what they love. Thoughts like, "What if I'm not talented enough?" or "Do I really have anything to offer?" can create a lot of self-doubt. This inner voice can stop them from trying new things or taking steps to discover their Ikigai.

4. **Lack of Clarity**

   Sometimes, young people simply aren't sure what they want to do or what makes them happy. They may feel confused about their interests or unsure about their strengths. This lack of clarity can be frustrating, and it can make the journey to finding Ikigai feel overwhelming.

5. **Comparing Themselves to Others**

   With social media and constant exposure to others' achievements, it's easy for young people to compare themselves to others and feel like they're not doing enough. Seeing others who seem to have their lives figured out can make them feel insecure or like they're falling behind, which can make it harder to focus on their own path.

Tips for Overcoming Barriers

1. **Start Small by Trying New Things and Exploring Different Interests**

   Begin by exploring activities that genuinely interest you, even if they seem small or unimportant. Trying out different hobbies, volunteering, or even taking on small projects can open doors to unexpected passions and skills. For example, if you enjoy drawing, consider joining an art class or creating illustrations in your free time. Remember, Ikigai often starts with simple interests that can grow over time.

   Takeaway: Don't pressure yourself to find your "life purpose" all at once. Instead, allow yourself to try new things, make mistakes, and enjoy the process of self-discovery.

2. **Seek Support from Friends, Family, or Mentors Who Encourage You**

   Surround yourself with people who believe in you and your journey. Talking to supportive friends, family members, or mentors can provide valuable insights and encouragement. They can help you recognize your strengths and offer guidance when you feel uncertain. Finding a mentor or coach can be especially helpful if you're struggling with self-doubt, as they can share their own experiences and guide you in navigating challenges.

   Takeaway: Reach out to people who uplift you. It's easier to face challenges when you have someone cheering you on and reminding you of your potential.

3. **Give Yourself Permission to Explore Without Judgment**

   Many young people feel they need to have everything figured out by a certain age. This pressure can lead to unnecessary stress and prevent them from exploring different paths. Give yourself permission to experiment without setting rigid expectations. Some of the best discoveries happen when we aren't afraid to try new things without worrying about the outcome.

Takeaway: Embrace curiosity and approach each new experience with an open mind. Remind yourself that you don't need to have everything figured out right away.

4. **Remember That Finding Your Ikigai is a journey, and It's Okay to Take Your Time**

Ikigai isn't something that appears overnight; it's a journey that requires patience and persistence. Understand that it's normal to feel lost or uncertain at times. Keep reminding yourself that every small step, even if it feels like progress isn't being made, brings you closer to discovering your true purpose.

Takeaway: Be patient with yourself and allow your Ikigai to develop naturally. Progress may be slow, but each step counts.

5. **Focus on Personal Growth, Not Perfection**

Many young people struggle with perfectionism, thinking they need to excel in everything to feel valuable. But Ikigai is not about being perfect – it's about finding what gives you joy and purpose. Allow yourself to grow gradually, recognizing that improvement happens over time and that every experience, whether successful or challenging, adds to your journey.

Takeaway: Instead of aiming for perfection, aim for growth. Each experience, whether it brings success or failure, is a step toward your Ikigai.

6. **Practice Self-Compassion and Kindness**

Being kind to yourself is crucial on the journey to finding Ikigai. When you feel discouraged, remind yourself that everyone has moments of self-doubt. Practicing gratitude for the progress you've made, no matter how small, can boost your confidence. Try to focus on your strengths rather than your shortcomings, and remember that you are capable of amazing things.

Takeaway: Be patient and gentle with yourself, especially during challenging times. Treat yourself with the same kindness you would offer a friend on their journey.

Embracing the Journey to Ikigai

Finding your Ikigai is like a lifelong adventure. It requires courage to explore, patience to keep going, and resilience to overcome setbacks. By taking small steps, seeking support, and giving yourself time, you can overcome the common barriers and gradually find the path that brings meaning, joy, and purpose into your life. Remember, your Ikigai is unique to you – trust in the journey, and allow it to unfold in its own time.

The Journey Continues

Finding your Ikigai—your unique purpose or reason for being—is a powerful step. But it's not a destination; it's the beginning of an ongoing journey. Your Ikigai will grow and shift as you do, adapting to the new experiences, lessons, and passions that emerge throughout your life. Embracing this continuous process means welcoming change and staying open to new possibilities.

Embracing Growth and Change

As you grow, so will your Ikigai. What fulfils you now may not be the same in the future, and that's completely natural. Life brings constant change, and every new phase, skill, or relationship can influence your purpose. Think of Ikigai as something flexible—something that evolves with your life's journey. Staying open to these shifts keeps you aligned with what truly matters to you at each stage of your life.

For example, if your Ikigai today centers around helping others through teaching, you might find that, in a few years, you want to support others in a different way, like mentoring or community work. Both are meaningful, but they reflect different aspects of who you are as you grow.

Exploring and Trying New Paths

The path to Ikigai isn't always clear, and sometimes it requires exploring different interests. By trying new activities, you can discover sides of yourself that you didn't know existed. Embrace each new experience as a chance to learn, even if it doesn't directly fit into what you initially thought was your purpose. These experiences add depth to your life and can provide valuable insights into what truly fulfils you.

Consider small steps—joining a club, learning a skill, volunteering, or starting a hobby. Each experience can guide you closer to the things that spark joy and bring meaning to your life.

Adjusting Along the Way

Sometimes, you may feel that the path you're on no longer feels right. When this happens, it's okay to pause, reflect, and adjust. Life changes, and so will your priorities and passions. If your work, relationships, or activities don't bring the joy or fulfilment they once did, take time to re-evaluate. Ask yourself if there's something new, you're drawn to or if there's a different way you could use your strengths. Making adjustments to stay aligned with your Ikigai keeps you true to yourself.

Embracing Setbacks as Part of the Journey

Challenges are natural, and they're an important part of finding and deepening your Ikigai. There will be times when things don't go as planned, or you may feel unsure of your path. Instead of seeing these moments as failures, view them as steps that guide you closer to your purpose. Each setback provides an opportunity to learn and grow, helping you gain resilience and clarity.

If a project or goal doesn't work out, reflect on what you learned. How did it make you feel? Did it reveal something new about your interests? These reflections can point you toward your next steps.

Staying Curious and Engaged

Staying curious is a powerful way to nurture your Ikigai. Keep exploring, learning, and questioning. Ask yourself often, "What brings me joy now? How can I contribute to others?" These questions will help you stay connected to your true self and your purpose.

Over time, you'll realize that Ikigai isn't about reaching a final destination; it's about enjoying and growing through the journey itself. Each day offers a new opportunity to understand yourself better, help others, and experience a fulfilling life. Embrace the journey with an open heart, and let your Ikigai unfold naturally as you go. Remember, every step is valuable—even if it's just one small step at a time.

Ikigai is all about finding what makes you happy and gives your life meaning. It's the combination of what you love, what you're good at, what the world needs, and what you can earn from. By focusing on these four parts, you can discover your unique purpose.

As you read about Ikigai, take notes on what stands out to you. Write down your thoughts on what you enjoy, your strengths, and how you can help others. Use these notes to create a simple plan, and try adding small actions into your daily life to feel more fulfilled. Remember, Ikigai is a journey—take your time, reflect, and enjoy each step.

The "10 Rules of Ikigai" offer a framework for a meaningful life:

1. **Stay Active** – Embrace work or hobbies that keep you engaged.
2. **Take it Slow** – Focus on living with patience and calmness.

3. **Don't Fill Your Stomach** – Eat in moderation, focusing on nourishing food.

4. **Surround Yourself with Good Friends** – Build relationships that support and uplift you.

5. **Get in Shape** – Prioritize physical health for a balanced life.

6. **Smile** – Maintain a positive attitude for mental and emotional wellness.

7. **Reconnect with Nature** – Spend time outdoors to foster calmness and clarity.

8. **Give Thanks** – Practice gratitude to appreciate life's gifts.

9. **Live with a Purpose** – Pursue activities that resonate with your deeper values.

10. **Accept Impermanence** – Embrace life's changing nature with an open heart.

These rules guide individuals toward well-being by aligning their actions with their inner purpose.

Key Notes on Ikigai

1. **Understanding Ikigai**: Ikigai is the Japanese concept of finding your purpose or reason for being, where passion, mission, vocation, and profession intersect.

2. **Four Elements**:
   - **What You Love**: Activities that bring you joy and fulfilment.
   - **What You Are Good At**: Skills and talents you possess.
   - **What the World Needs**: Opportunities to contribute positively to society.
   - **What You Can Be Paid For**: Ways to earn a living while doing what you love.

3. **Self-Discovery**: Take time to reflect on your interests, strengths, and values to identify your Ikigai.

4. **Activities to Discover Ikigai**:
   - Engage in new experiences to explore your passions.
   - Ask for feedback from others to understand your strengths.
   - Consider how you can contribute to the world around you.

5. **Self-Reflection Questions**:
   - What activities make you lose track of time?
   - What compliments do you receive most often?

- What changes do you wish to see in the world?
- How can you turn your passions into a career?

6. **Journaling**: Document your thoughts and feelings about your Ikigai journey. Describe what a perfect day living your Ikigai looks like.

7. **Overcoming Challenges**: Recognize common barriers like fear of failure and societal expectations, and adopt strategies to overcome them.

8. **The Journey Continues**: Finding your Ikigai is an ongoing process. Keep exploring and adjusting your path as you grow and learn.

9. **Implementation**: Create actionable steps based on your reflections to start moving towards your Ikigai.

10. **Encouragement**: Embrace the journey of self-discovery and remember that it's okay to take your time in finding your true purpose.

Chapter 2
Vision to Reality
Mapping Your Success

"Vision to Reality – Mapping Your Success" refers to the process of transforming your goals and dreams into tangible outcomes through careful planning, clarity, and action. This chapter or concept focuses on the importance of creating a clear vision, setting meaningful goals, and developing a roadmap to achieve those goals. It emphasizes the need for strategic thinking, persistence, and adaptability to turn a vision into reality, helping individuals align their efforts and stay motivated on their path to success.

What it means to set goals and why it's important

Goal setting is the process of identifying specific, achievable objectives that you want to accomplish within a certain time frame. It involves deciding what you want to achieve in different areas of your life, like personal growth, career, health, or relationships. When you set goals, you create a roadmap that gives you direction and helps you focus your energy on things that truly matter to you.

Why Goal Setting Is Important

Setting goals is important because it provides clarity about your priorities, motivating you to make progress in a meaningful way. Without clear goals, it's easy to feel lost or unsure about your path. Goals also help keep you accountable, so you can measure your progress and stay motivated, even when faced with obstacles. In essence, goal setting transforms ideas into achievable steps, guiding you toward success and fulfilment in both personal and professional aspects of life.

Purpose of Setting Goals: Direction and Motivation

Setting goals serves as a powerful tool for guiding our lives and fuelling motivation. Goals provide a clear direction, showing us where we want to go and helping us make choices that align with our bigger dreams and values. When we have goals, we're not just moving randomly through life but are instead focused on specific outcomes that we're excited about reaching.

Goals also keep us motivated by giving us something to work toward. Each small step we take toward our goals brings a sense of accomplishment and fuels our desire to keep going, even when challenges arise. This motivation can build momentum, making it easier to maintain progress and overcome obstacles. In short, goals not only shape the path we're on but also provide the energy and drive we need to stay on it, ultimately helping us reach our full potential.

The Role of Goals in Achieving Success: How Clear Goals Lead to Personal and Professional Success

Clear goals are essential for achieving success in any area of life, whether personal or professional. When we define specific, realistic goals, we create a clear path to follow, making it easier to focus on what's important and avoid distractions. Clear goals help us prioritize our time and efforts, so we spend our energy on actions that directly support our progress. This structure is like having a roadmap; it shows us exactly where to go and makes it simpler to measure how far we've come.

Setting and working toward goals also strengthens our skills and resilience. As we tackle challenges and celebrate achievements along the way, we build confidence and learn more about our abilities. Professionally, goals often lead to skill growth, better time management, and a stronger sense of purpose, all of which contribute to career success. In our personal lives, goals can support self-improvement, relationship growth, or even health and wellness.

Overall, goals give us purpose and direction, empowering us to accomplish more than we would without them. They act as stepping stones to success, helping us turn dreams into actionable plans and achieve lasting fulfilment.

The Benefits of Goal Setting

1. **Clarity and Focus**

   Setting goals provides a clear vision of what you want to achieve, helping you concentrate your efforts on what truly matters. With clear goals, it's easier to filter out distractions and focus on actions that lead directly to success. This clarity allows you to work efficiently, making each step count toward your desired outcome.

2. **Motivation and Accountability**

   Goals give you a reason to stay motivated because they remind you of what you're working toward. Breaking down larger goals into smaller milestones allows you to see progress, keeping you engaged and committed. Additionally, setting goals encourages accountability, as you can measure your progress and hold yourself responsible for completing each step.

2. **Personal Growth and Confidence**

Each time you achieve a goal, you gain confidence and a sense of accomplishment. This process fosters self-belief, showing you that with commitment and effort, you can make meaningful changes. Regularly setting and achieving goals also promotes personal growth, helping you refine skills, adopt new habits, and expand your comfort zone.

3. **Resilience and Adaptability**

Goals often bring challenges, and working toward them encourages you to solve problems and adapt when things don't go as planned. This helps develop resilience, as you learn to overcome setbacks and persevere even when things get difficult. Having goals allows you to stay flexible, adjusting your approach as needed while keeping your eye on the ultimate objective.

Overall, goal setting is a powerful tool for creating a structured, focused, and adaptable path toward both personal and professional success.

Types of Goals

1. **Short-Term vs. Long-Term Goals**
   - **Short-Term Goals:** These are smaller, more immediate objectives that can be achieved in a short period, usually within days, weeks, or months. Short-term goals provide quick wins and help build momentum for bigger goals. They serve as stepping stones toward achieving long-term goals.
   - **Long-Term Goals:** These goals take a longer time to achieve, often requiring years of effort. Long-term goals provide overall direction and purpose in life. They help you stay focused on big-picture outcomes, such as career aspirations or life dreams. Short-term goals help you make consistent progress toward these larger ambitions.

2. **Personal Goals**

Personal goals are related to improving various aspects of your life outside of work. These might include:
   - **Health goals:** Improving physical fitness, adopting healthier eating habits, or managing stress.
   - **Relationship goals:** Building stronger connections with family and friends, improving communication, or deepening romantic relationships.

- **Personal development goals:** Developing new skills, learning new things, or working on self-improvement and emotional well-being.

3. **Professional Goals**

Professional goals are focused on your career and business growth. These goals help you move forward in your job or business:

- **Career advancement goals:** Gaining a promotion, changing careers, or taking on more responsibilities at work.
- **Skill-building goals:** Acquiring new skills or certifications that help you advance in your profession.
- **Business objectives:** Growing a business, increasing sales, improving customer satisfaction, or expanding your network.

4. **Financial Goals**

Financial goals help you manage your money and create long-term wealth:

- **Saving goals:** Setting aside money for emergencies, travel, or big purchases.
- **Investing goals:** Building investments to generate future wealth, such as through stocks, bonds, or real estate.
- **Financial independence goals:** Achieving financial freedom by earning enough to cover your living expenses without relying on active employment.

5. **Creative Goals**

Creative goals are focused on expressing yourself or developing new talents:

- **Projects:** Starting a creative project, such as writing a book, painting, or creating a digital art portfolio.
- **Hobbies:** Pursuing new hobbies or refining your skills in existing hobbies, such as photography, music, or gardening.
- **Developing talents:** Working to become proficient in creative fields like design, writing, or performing arts.

By setting goals in various areas of your life, you create a balanced roadmap for success. These different types of goals work together to help you grow, both personally and professionally.

Effective Goal-Setting Techniques

1. **SMART Goals**

SMART goals are a powerful framework for setting clear, actionable, and realistic goals. Here's what each letter in SMART stands for:

- Specific: Your goal should be clear and focused. Avoid vague goals like "get fit." Instead, aim for "exercise 30 minutes, 4 times a week."
- Measurable: Define how you will measure success. For example, "save $200 every month" is measurable, whereas "save money" is not.
- Achievable: Ensure your goal is realistic and within your capabilities. While it's good to challenge yourself, setting an unachievable goal can lead to frustration.
- Relevant: Your goal should align with your values and long-term objectives. It should matter to you and contribute to your bigger picture.
- Time-bound: Set a deadline or time frame for your goal. This adds urgency and keeps you on track, such as "I will finish my book by December 31st."

2. **Setting Milestones**

Breaking a larger goal into smaller, more manageable milestones makes it easier to track progress and stay motivated. Milestones act as checkpoints that help you:

- Track progress step-by-step.
- Prevent feeling overwhelmed by focusing on smaller tasks.
- Celebrate small wins along the way, which boosts confidence and motivation.

Example: If your long-term goal is to run a marathon, your milestones could include:

- Running 5K, then 10K, and eventually 21K.
- Setting a training schedule for specific distances each month.

3. **Vision Boards and Visualization**

- **Vision Boards:** A vision board is a visual representation of your goals. By placing pictures, quotes, and images that reflect your dreams, you can keep them in sight and stay motivated. It's a way to make your goals tangible and real.
- **Visualization:** Regularly imagining yourself achieving your goals strengthens your commitment and mental focus. Close your eyes and visualize yourself accomplishing your goals, how it will feel, and the positive impact it will have on your life. This technique can reinforce belief in your ability to succeed.

4. **Prioritizing Goals**

Not all goals are equally important at any given time. Prioritizing ensures you focus on what matters most:

- **Recognizing Values:** Start by identifying your values (e.g., family, health, career, growth). Goals aligned with these values are more likely to bring fulfilment.

- **Long-term Vision:** Focus on goals that connect to your larger vision for the future, whether it's financial freedom, career success, or personal growth. It helps in making strategic decisions about where to focus your energy.

- **Daily Actions:** Choose goals that bring the greatest impact now, while keeping in mind your long-term goals, and balance short-term tasks with long-term aspirations.

Example: If career growth is your primary focus, prioritize goals related to learning new skills or taking on more responsibility at work over other activities that may not align with this vision.

These techniques help you create clear, actionable plans to achieve your dreams while staying organized and motivated.

Creating a Goal Roadmap

1. **Defining Your Starting Point**

Before setting out on your goal journey, it's essential to understand where you're starting from. This step involves assessing your current situation, resources, and any limitations that might affect your progress. Ask yourself:

- **What skills do I already have?** Identify your strengths and areas of expertise that can help you achieve your goals.

- **What resources are available to me?** Consider financial resources, support networks, time, or tools you have at your disposal.

- **What challenges or obstacles might I face?** Be realistic about potential challenges—whether it's time management, lack of knowledge, or external factors like family commitments. Knowing these in advance helps you plan for them.

Example: If your goal is to get healthier, assess your current exercise routine, diet, and time available for workouts. This helps in creating a plan that works with your existing lifestyle.

2. **Planning the Journey**

Once you've defined your starting point, it's time to plan your steps. Break down the goal into smaller, manageable tasks. Outline the actions you need to take, assign deadlines, and identify potential challenges. This detailed plan keeps you organized and focused on what needs to be done. Steps may include:

- **Research and Learning:** Identify any skills or knowledge gaps you need to fill.
- **Actionable Tasks:** Write down specific actions you need to take.
- **Deadline Setting:** Set realistic deadlines for each task, keeping in mind your other responsibilities.

Example: If your goal is to run a marathon, planning the journey could include:

- Finding a training plan.
- Scheduling weekly runs.
- Learning proper nutrition and recovery practices.

3. **Setting Timelines and Deadlines**

Creating a timeline helps you stay on track and adds urgency to your goal. Without a timeline, it's easy to procrastinate. Your timeline should be:

- **Realistic:** Avoid setting deadlines that are too tight, as they can lead to stress and burnout.
- **Flexible:** Allow for adjustments if things don't go as planned.
- **Action-oriented:** Set specific time frames for each action step so that you can measure progress.

Example: If your goal is to launch a business, set timelines for research, business registration, marketing plan creation, and launching. A timeline helps keep you accountable.

4. **Adjusting Goals as Needed**

Life is unpredictable, and sometimes, you may need to revise your goals or timelines based on changing circumstances. This flexibility is a key part of successful goal setting:

- **Reassess Regularly:** Periodically evaluate your progress and ask whether the goal still aligns with your values or if new challenges have emerged.
- **Revise When Necessary:** Don't be afraid to adjust your plan. Life changes, and your goals may need to evolve with it.

- **Stay Open to New Opportunities:** Sometimes, unexpected opportunities might lead you to refine your original goal.

Example: If you planned to save a certain amount of money for a trip, but a family emergency arises, adjust your savings goal or extend the timeline to accommodate the change.

By creating a clear roadmap with realistic steps and flexibility, you can navigate your goals effectively and stay on track for success. This approach ensures that you understand your starting point, have a clear plan, and remain adaptable to life's changes.

Real-Time Example: Divya's Journey to Starting a Small Business

Background: Divya, a digital marketing professional, has always dreamed of opening her own online retail store. She loves fashion and wants to sell affordable, trendy clothes for young women. However, Divya has never started a business before and has limited savings, which makes her hesitant about taking the leap. Despite these challenges, she decides to use goal setting and create a roadmap to make her dream a reality.

1. **Defining Her Starting Point**

   Divya begins by assessing her current situation. Here's how she evaluates herself:

   - **Skills:** She has a strong background in marketing and social media, which is helpful for promoting her online store. However, she lacks knowledge in managing inventory and setting up an e-commerce website.

   - **Resources:** Divya has a small savings account of Rs. 50,000, which she has set aside for her business. She also has a laptop, access to the internet, and a supportive family.

   - **Challenges:** Time is a significant challenge for Divya. As she works a full-time job, she's only able to dedicate a few hours a day to work on her business idea. Additionally, she's not sure how to manage finances and cash flow for her store.

   Self-Reflection: Divya realizes that her skills in marketing and her network of contacts will be beneficial, but she needs to focus on learning about inventory management tent and e-commerce platforms.

2. **Planning the Journey**

   With a clearer understanding of her starting point, Divya begins to plan her journey step by step. She breaks her goal of starting an online store into smaller tasks:

- **Research and Learning**:
  - **Task 2**: Research the best suppliers for clothing and how to manage inventory.
  - **Task 3**: Learn about managing business finances, including budgeting and profit margins.
- **Actionable Tasks**:
  - **Task 1**: Create a business plan that includes market research, target customers, and initial investment requirements.
  - **Task 2**: Design and set up her online store using Shopify.
  - **Task 3**: Develop a marketing strategy, including social media campaigns, email marketing, and influencer partnerships.
- **Deadline Setting**:
  - Task 1: Complete research on Shopify and suppliers by the end of the first month.
  - Task 2: Set up the website and finalize the first batch of inventory within two months.
  - Task 3: Launch the website in the third month and start marketing campaigns.

3. **Setting Timelines and Deadlines**

Divya now sets a timeline for each phase:

- **Month 1 (Learning Phase)**: Focus on learning the technical aspects of Shopify, e-commerce logistics, and finances.
  - **Week 1-2**: Complete an online course on Shopify setup and inventory management.
  - **Week 3-4**: Research suppliers and contact potential partners.
- **Month 2 (Setup Phase)**: Begin building the online store and sourcing inventory.
  - **Week 1-2**: Set up the website on Shopify, design the layout, and add product listings.
  - **Week 3-4**: Finalize the first order of clothing, test the purchasing system, and check the site for bugs.
- **Month 3 (Launch Phase)**: Launch the online store and start marketing.
- **Week 1**: Finalize the first batch of products, set up payment systems, and ensure logistics are in place.
- **Week 2**: Launch the website with a special promotion to attract customers.

- **Week 3-4**: Execute social media marketing campaigns and start email outreach.

Divya makes sure the timeline is flexible in case there are delays. She understands that sometimes things might take longer than planned.

4. **Adjusting Goals as Needed**

As Divya progresses, she encounters a few challenges that require her to adjust her goals:

- **Challenge 1**: During the research phase, Divya realizes that the suppliers she originally found have long delivery times, which could affect her ability to offer fast shipping. She decides to adjust by finding alternative suppliers who can meet her timeline.

- **Challenge 2**: While setting up her Shopify store, she struggles with understanding the complexities of taxes and shipping fees. She decides to extend her research on these topics and adds a couple of weeks to the timeline to ensure everything is set up properly.

- **Challenge 3**: A week before her planned launch, Divya experiences a sudden personal issue and needs to adjust her work schedule. She moves the launch date by one week but remains focused on the long-term goal.

Through these adjustments, Divya keeps her flexibility in mind, making changes to her plan without feeling discouraged. She learns to view setbacks as part of the process, rather than failures.

The Outcome

By the end of three months, Divya successfully launches her online clothing store. The website is functional, and she has received positive feedback from her early customers. She continues to improve her store, adapt her marketing strategies, and grow her inventory.

Reflection: Reflecting on her journey, Divya realizes how much she has grown. Not only has she launched her business, but she has also gained new skills in e-commerce, budgeting, and online marketing. Most importantly, she learned to stay patient, flexible, and committed to her goal, despite facing challenges.

Key Takeaways from Divya's Example:

1. **Clear Goal Breakdown**: Divya's goal was large, but breaking it into smaller, manageable steps allowed her to stay focused and make steady progress.

2. **Flexibility in Execution**: Divya adjusted her timeline and resources as needed, showing that being flexible and open to change is key to achieving success.

3. **Learning from Challenges**: Instead of feeling defeated, Divya used each obstacle as an opportunity to learn and improve.

4. **Celebrating Progress**: Divya took time to celebrate each milestone, whether it was launching her website or securing her first sale, which kept her motivated.

This real-time example demonstrates how effective goal setting, planning, and flexibility can lead to the successful realization of personal goals.

Staying Motivated and Overcoming Obstacles

1. **Maintaining Motivation: Techniques to Stay Committed, Even During Tough Times**

   - **Set Clear, Realistic Goals**: Break down large goals into smaller, achievable steps to make progress feel manageable.

   - **Visualize Success**: Regularly picture your end goal and remind yourself of the reasons you started.

   - **Establish a Routine**: Set aside dedicated time each day or week to work towards your goals, turning effort into a habit.

   - **Self-Reward System**: Create incentives for reaching milestones, giving yourself a reason to look forward to progress.

2. **Dealing with Setbacks: How to Handle Failure and Use It as a Learning Experience**

   - **Reflect and Learn**: After each setback, analyse what went wrong and identify changes you can make moving forward.

   - **Adopt a Growth Mindset**: View setbacks as opportunities for growth rather than personal failures.

   - **Stay Flexible**: Be open to adjusting your plans when needed, adapting to changes rather than feeling defeated by them.

   - **Stay Positive**: Remind yourself that setbacks are part of the journey and don't define your potential.

3. **Accountability: The Role of Friends, Mentors, or Tools to Stay on Track**

   - **Find an Accountability Partner**: Share your goals with a friend or mentor who can offer encouragement and check in regularly.

   - **Use Digital Tools**: Apps and online trackers can help monitor your progress and keep you motivated.

- **Join Supportive Communities**: Engage with groups or forums where people are working towards similar goals, providing mutual motivation and advice.
- **Regular Check-ins**: Set a schedule to review your goals, assess your progress, and make adjustments if necessary.

4. **Celebrating Small Wins: Recognizing Progress to Maintain a Positive Mindset**

- **Acknowledge Small Milestones**: Recognize even the smallest achievements as they contribute to long-term success.
- **Reward Yourself**: Take time to enjoy a treat, outing, or activity after reaching a milestone to boost motivation.
- **Reflect on Growth**: Look back at where you started to see how far you've come, reinforcing that you're making steady progress.
- **Stay Grateful**: Cultivate gratitude for each step forward, building a positive attitude towards your journey.

Tools and Resources for Goal Setting

1. **Journals and Goal Planners: Using Written Tools for Tracking Progress**

- **Journals**: A journal is a place where you can write down your goals and break them into steps. Writing helps you clarify what you want and track your progress over time.
- **Goal Planners**: These are special notebooks or templates designed to help you set goals, track milestones, and plan each step. They often include sections for deadlines, action items, and reflections, making it easy to stay organized.

2. **Apps and Technology: Digital Tools for Setting and Tracking Goals**

- **Goal-Setting Apps**: There are many apps, like Todoist or Habitica, that help you organize tasks and track your progress. These apps can remind you of deadlines, show your progress, and keep you motivated.
- **Calendars and Reminders**: Setting reminders on your phone or using a digital calendar can help you stay on schedule with your goals. This is useful for setting daily or weekly tasks that keep you moving forward.

3. **Books and Courses: Resources for Learning About Effective Goal-Setting Practices**

- **Books**: There are many books on goal-setting that provide strategies and techniques to help you succeed. Some popular books focus on setting realistic goals, staying motivated, and overcoming challenges.

- **Online Courses**: Many platforms offer courses on goal-setting, where you can learn step-by-step methods from experts. These courses often include exercises and examples to help you apply what you learn.

4. **Goal-Setting Communities: Online or Local Groups for Mutual Encouragement and Support**

- **Online Communities**: Many websites and social media groups bring together people who are working towards similar goals. In these groups, members share advice, celebrate wins, and motivate each other.

- **Local Groups**: In some areas, there are meetups or support groups for people with similar goals, like career development or fitness. Joining a local group can give you a sense of community and accountability.

These tools and resources make it easier to stay on track, stay motivated, and overcome obstacles in your goal-setting journey.

Success Stories: Real-Life Examples of Goal Achievement

1. **Stories of People Who Achieved Their Goals: Inspirational Examples of Goal-Setting Success**

- **Example**: A young woman, Sandhya, wanted to start her own small business selling handmade jewellery. She set clear goals, including researching her market, creating designs, and setting up an online store. Over time, she gained confidence and expanded her business. Today, she has a steady stream of customers and has even started teaching jewellery-making workshops.

- **Another Example**: Shiv, a working professional, set a goal to run a marathon. He started by running a few kilometres each day, gradually increasing his distance. He kept track of his progress, adjusted his training as needed, and stayed motivated. Eventually, he completed his first marathon, which gave him a great sense of accomplishment and improved his physical health.

2. **Lessons Learned: Key Takeaways from Individuals Who Reached Significant Goals**

- **Perseverance Pays Off**: Many people learned that staying committed to their goals, even when things got tough, was key to their success.

- **Flexibility is Important**: Successful goal achievers realized that it's okay to adjust goals and approaches along the way. This helped them overcome unexpected challenges without losing sight of the bigger picture.

- **Accountability Helps**: Having someone to check in with, whether a friend, mentor, or accountability group, gave them the support they needed to stay on track.

3. **How Goal Setting Changed Lives: Real Stories of Growth, Change, and Accomplishment**

- **Career Transformation**: Geeta was working a job she didn't enjoy and felt stuck. She set a goal to learn new skills in digital marketing and eventually transitioned into a role she loved. Setting and working towards this goal not only improved her job satisfaction but also gave her a sense of purpose and personal growth.

- **Health and Wellness**: Karan struggled with unhealthy habits but set a goal to improve his fitness. He started with small, manageable steps, like walking daily and cutting down on junk food. With time, his energy levels improved, and he developed a healthier lifestyle that positively impacted his family and overall happiness.

Through these stories, we see how goal-setting helped individuals achieve personal milestones, grow their confidence, and make meaningful changes in their lives. These examples demonstrate that setting clear goals and consistently working toward them can lead to positive transformation and success.

Keynotes

- **Importance of Goal Setting**: Goals give direction, motivation, and purpose, helping us focus on what matters most.

- **Benefits of Goal Setting**: Setting goals provides clarity, builds confidence, and encourages personal growth. It also enhances resilience by helping us adapt and overcome obstacles.

- **Types of Goals**: Recognize the importance of both short-term and long-term goals across different areas of life, such as personal, professional, financial, and creative.

- **Effective Techniques**: Use SMART goals, set milestones, prioritize, and use tools like vision boards to stay on track.

- **Overcoming Challenges**: Stay motivated, deal with setbacks constructively, and celebrate small wins along the way.

Encouragement for Goal Setting

- Setting clear goals can make a significant difference in achieving life success. Goals provide a roadmap to your dreams, making them more reachable and real. By taking small, consistent steps and staying committed, you're building a path toward personal and professional fulfilment.
- Remember, every goal achieved, no matter how small, contributes to your growth and brings you closer to your larger vision. Embrace goal-setting as a powerful tool for creating a life that aligns with your values and aspirations.

In conclusion, goal setting is a powerful practice that can shape a fulfilling and purpose-driven life. By setting goals with intention, we give ourselves direction and motivation, turning aspirations into achievable actions and helping us focus on what truly matters. Taking the first step on this journey may feel challenging, but it is also an opportunity for growth and self-discovery. Start small, build momentum, and stay committed, knowing that every step brings you closer to the life you envision. A clear, well-planned roadmap can be the difference between simply dreaming and truly achieving. When you have a strategy to follow, you're better equipped to overcome obstacles and stay on track. With each goal accomplished, you'll gain confidence, resilience, and a deep sense of satisfaction. Embrace goal setting as your pathway to a life of purpose, success, and happiness.

Chapter 3
Self-Reflection
Understanding Yourself

What is Self-Reflection?

Self-reflection is when you take time to think about your own thoughts, feelings, and actions. It's about looking at what you've done, how you've felt, and what you've experienced to better understand yourself.

Purpose of Self-Reflection:

1. **Self-Awareness**: It helps you understand your thoughts, feelings, and actions, so you know who you really are and what makes you tick.

2. **Personal Growth**: By thinking about what you've done in the past, you can learn where you're doing well and where you can improve.

3. **Emotional Intelligence**: It helps you understand your emotions and reactions, making it easier to handle your feelings and be kind to others.

4. **Better Decisions**: When you reflect on past experiences, you can make smarter choices in the future.

5. **Mindfulness**: Self-reflection makes you more aware of what's going on in your life right now, so you can live more intentionally.

6. **Problem-Solving**: Looking back at challenges helps you find better ways to solve problems in the future.

In simple terms, self-reflection helps you understand yourself better, make better choices, and grow as a person.

The importance of self-reflection in personal growth and self-awareness

Self-reflection is very important for personal growth and self-awareness because it helps you understand who you are, what you want, and why you act the way you do. Here's why it's so helpful:

1. **Understanding Yourself Better:**

    Self-reflection helps you look at your thoughts, emotions, and behaviours. By thinking about your past experiences, you start to understand what drives you, what makes you happy, and what causes stress or discomfort. This helps you get to know yourself on a deeper level.

2. **Identifying Strengths and Weaknesses:**

   When you reflect on your actions, you can see where you're doing well and where you might need to improve. Recognizing your strengths boosts confidence, and knowing your weaknesses allows you to work on them and grow.

3. **Making Better Choices:**

   By reflecting on past decisions, you can understand what worked and what didn't. This helps you make better decisions in the future. You'll also learn how to avoid repeating the same mistakes.

4. **Improving Relationships:**

   Self-reflection helps you understand your role in relationships. You can see how your actions or words may have affected others, and this awareness helps you improve communication and relationships with family, friends, and colleagues.

5. **Increasing Emotional Intelligence:**

   When you reflect on your emotions, you become better at understanding and managing them. This helps you stay calm in stressful situations and be more empathetic towards others.

6. **Setting Goals for Growth:**

   Self-reflection helps you figure out what you want to improve in your life. By thinking about where you are and where you want to go, you can set clear goals for personal growth and work towards becoming a better version of yourself.

In simple terms, self-reflection is like holding up a mirror to your mind and emotions. It allows you to see yourself clearly, understand your actions, and make changes that lead to personal growth and a more fulfilling life.

How self-reflection helps in understanding one's values, strengths, and areas for improvement

Self-reflection helps you understand your values, strengths, and areas for improvement by giving you the time and space to think deeply about yourself and your life. Here's how it works in simple terms:

1. **Understanding Your Values:**

   When you reflect on your experiences and choices, you start to notice what really matters to you. For example, if you always feel happiest when helping others, you may realize that kindness and generosity are important values for you. By thinking about what makes you feel proud or fulfilled, you can better understand your core values, like honesty, loyalty, or creativity.

2. **Recognizing Your Strengths:**

   Self-reflection helps you identify what you're good at. For example, when you think about situations where you've done well, like handling a tough project at work or being a supportive friend, you can spot your strengths, such as problem-solving, communication, or empathy. Recognizing these strengths boosts your confidence and encourages you to keep using them in your life.

3. **Finding Areas for Improvement:**

   Looking back at your actions and feelings helps you see where you could do better. For instance, if you notice that you often feel frustrated in certain situations or have difficulty with time management, self-reflection allows you to recognize these areas as opportunities for improvement. It helps you become aware of bad habits, negative thought patterns, or skills you may need to work on to become a better person.

Self-reflection is like taking a step back and evaluating yourself. It helps you see what you truly care about (your values), what you're good at (your strengths), and what you can improve (your areas for growth). By understanding these, you can make better choices, live more authentically, and keep growing as a person.

The Benefits of Self-Reflection

Self-reflection offers many positive benefits that can improve your emotional well-being, mental clarity, and long-term life satisfaction. Here's a simple breakdown of how self-reflection can help you:

1. **Emotional Benefits:**

   - **Enhanced Emotional Intelligence:** When you reflect on your thoughts and feelings, you get better at understanding your emotions and the emotions of others. This helps you manage your feelings more effectively, especially in tough situations.

   - **Stress Relief:** Taking time to reflect helps you process your feelings, which can reduce stress and make it easier to deal with difficult emotions. It allows you to step back, calm your mind, and see things more clearly.

   - **Resilience:** Self-reflection helps you learn from past challenges. When you understand how you overcame tough situations in the past, it makes you more resilient, or better able to bounce back, when facing future difficulties.

2. **Cognitive Benefits:**
   - **Improved Problem-Solving Skills:** Reflection helps you think more clearly about problems. By reviewing past situations, you can see what worked and what didn't, making it easier to come up with solutions in the future.
   - **Better Decision-Making:** By reflecting on your past choices, you become more aware of your decision-making process. This awareness helps you make better, more thoughtful decisions moving forward.
   - **Clarity of Thought:** Reflecting on your thoughts and actions helps clear mental clutter. It gives you a better understanding of what's important, so you can focus on what matters most in your life.

3. **Long-Term Benefits:**
   - **Stronger Sense of Purpose:** When you regularly reflect on your life, you begin to better understand what drives you. This helps you find a clearer sense of purpose and direction in life.
   - **Self-Acceptance:** Self-reflection encourages you to be kind to yourself. When you look at your life and see both your strengths and areas for growth, you learn to accept and love yourself as you are.
   - **Mindful Living:** Regular reflection helps you live more mindfully. By staying present and aware of your thoughts and actions, you can make intentional choices and live more consciously, rather than just reacting to situations.

Self-reflection brings many benefits. It helps you understand and manage your emotions, think more clearly, and make better decisions. Over time, it also leads to a stronger sense of purpose, self-acceptance, and a more mindful, fulfilling life.

Techniques for Self-Reflection

Self-reflection can be done in many ways, and different techniques can help you discover more about yourself. Here are some common techniques for self-reflection:

1. **Journaling:**
   - **What it is:** Journaling involves writing down your thoughts, emotions, and experiences regularly.
   - **How it helps:** Writing helps you organize your thoughts and uncover hidden emotions or patterns in your life. It's like talking to yourself on paper. By putting your feelings into words, you

can understand yourself better, discover what's going well, and identify areas for growth.

2. **Meditation:**

- **What it is:** Meditation is a practice where you sit quietly, focus on your breath, and observe your thoughts and feelings without judging them.

- **How it helps:** Meditation allows you to observe your inner world with a calm and open mind. It helps you become more aware of your emotions, reactions, and thought patterns, allowing you to understand your mind and body more deeply. Over time, meditation can help reduce stress, increase self-awareness, and improve emotional regulation.

3. **Visualization:**

- **What it is:** Visualization is the practice of imagining specific scenarios, such as achieving a goal or imagining how you would react in a certain situation.

- **How it helps:** Visualization helps you see your goals more clearly and understand how you might feel or behave in different situations. It can be a powerful tool for setting intentions, improving self-confidence, and gaining clarity on what you truly want in life. It helps you mentally rehearse situations and visualize success, which can make achieving your goals easier.

4. **Questioning:**

- **What it is:** This involves asking yourself deep, meaningful questions about your beliefs, motivations, and values.

- **How it helps:** Questioning helps you get to the root of your thoughts and behaviours. By asking questions like "What do I value most?", "What am I afraid of?", or "Why do I feel this way?", you uncover the deeper layers of your mind. This technique helps you understand your motivations and beliefs, and can reveal areas in your life that need attention or change.

These techniques—journaling, meditation, visualization, and questioning—help you explore your inner world, identify your thoughts and emotions, and understand what drives you. By using these practices regularly, you can gain deeper self-awareness, make better decisions, and lead a more intentional, fulfilling life.

Developing a Self-Reflection Practice

Building a self-reflection practice requires dedication and consistency. Here's how you can create a regular and effective practice for self-reflection:

1. **Setting Aside Time:**
   - **Tip:** Schedule regular time in your day or week for self-reflection. Even 10 to 15 minutes can be enough to get started.
   - **How to Do It:** Treat self-reflection as an important part of your day, just like any other task. You could set a specific time each day, like in the morning before starting your day or at night before bed. Make sure it's a quiet, peaceful time where you can focus on yourself without distractions.
   - **Why It Helps:** Regularly setting aside time for self-reflection helps make it a habit. The more you practice, the more you'll benefit from the insights you uncover about yourself.

2. **Creating a Comfortable Space:**
   - **Tip:** Choose a quiet, calm space where you feel comfortable and relaxed for your reflection time.
   - **How to Do It:** Find a place free from distractions like noise, technology, or other interruptions. This could be a cozy corner of your home, a quiet park, or even a café that makes you feel at ease.
   - **Why It Helps:** A peaceful environment allows you to focus and dive deeper into your thoughts without being disturbed. Your space should promote a sense of calm and openness.

3. **Choosing a Medium:**
   - **Tip:** Decide how you want to record your reflections. There are many ways to capture your thoughts, and it's important to choose the medium that works best for you.
   - **Options to Consider:**
     - **Journals:** Writing down your thoughts in a notebook or diary can help you process emotions and track your progress over time.
     - **Voice Notes:** If you find it easier to speak than write, you can use voice recordings on your phone or a recorder to express your thoughts.
     - **Digital Reflections:** Using a computer or app to type your reflections might be helpful for those who prefer digital platforms. You can even use mood or reflection apps designed for this purpose.
     - **Verbal Reflections:** Some people prefer to talk to a trusted friend, mentor, or therapist about their thoughts to gain clarity and perspective.

- **Why It Helps:** The key is to choose the medium that feels most comfortable and effective for you. Whether it's writing, speaking, or typing, this practice should feel natural and easy.

4. **Staying Consistent:**
   - **Tip:** The most important part of self-reflection is to make it a regular habit, even if you start small.
   - **How to Do It:** Start by setting a small, achievable goal, like reflecting for 5 minutes a day. Gradually increase the time or the depth of reflection as you get more comfortable. Remember, it's not about being perfect—it's about being consistent.
   - **Why It Helps:** Building a consistent habit of reflection helps you stay in tune with your thoughts, feelings, and goals over time. It takes patience, but over time, you'll notice the benefits as your self-awareness and personal growth deepen.

To develop a self-reflection practice, set aside dedicated time each day, create a comfortable and quiet space for focus, choose the reflection medium that works best for you, and be patient while building a consistent habit. With regular practice, you'll develop a deeper understanding of yourself, leading to personal growth and a more mindful life.

Self-Reflection Prompts (Signals) and Exercises

Self-reflection can be an incredibly valuable tool for personal growth and understanding. Here are some prompts and exercises that you can incorporate into your daily, weekly, and monthly practice to enhance your self-awareness and growth:

1. **Daily Reflections: Simple Prompts for End-of-Day Reflection**

   These prompts are designed to help you reflect on your day, capture important moments, and identify areas for improvement.
   - **What went well today?**
     Reflect on any positive experiences, achievements, or moments that made you feel good.
   - **What could I have done differently?**
     Consider any challenges or mistakes and what you can learn from them.
   - **How did I feel today?**
     Take note of your emotions throughout the day and try to understand why you felt that way.
   - **What am I grateful for today?**
     Gratitude is a powerful tool for fostering a positive mindset. List at least three things you're grateful for.

- **What is one thing I can improve tomorrow?**
  Set a small, achievable goal for the next day to focus on.

2. **Weekly and Monthly Reflections: Deeper Questions for Assessing Short- and Long-Term Goals**

These prompts help you take a step back and reflect on your progress over a longer period. They are especially helpful for goal-setting and assessing your journey.

- **What progress did I make this week/month toward my goals?**
  Reflect on the steps you've taken to achieve your
  short- and long-term goals.

- **What obstacles did I face, and how did I handle them?**
  Think about any challenges you encountered and how you dealt with them. Was there room for improvement?

- **What accomplishments am I most proud of this week/ month?**
  Celebrate even the small wins and acknowledge your hard work.

- **What's one area I would like to focus on next week/month?**
  Set a specific intention for the upcoming week or month, whether it's personal growth, a skill, or a goal.

3. **Values and Purpose Prompts: Questions to Uncover Core Beliefs and Life Direction**

Self-reflection is essential for understanding your values and purpose. These prompts help you explore your core beliefs and life direction.

- **What do I value most in life?**
  Reflect on the values that guide your decisions and actions. Think about what matters most to you, such as family, career, or personal growth.

- **What does a fulfilling life look like to me?**
  Define what success and fulfilment mean to you. This might include personal achievements, relationships, or contributions to others.

- **What motivates me to get out of bed each morning?**
  Think about what drives you to pursue your goals. Is it passion, financial stability, creativity, helping others, or something else?

- **Am I living in alignment with my values?**
  Reflect on whether your current actions, behaviours, and goals align with your core values. If not, what adjustments can you make?

4. **Growth Mindset Questions: Encouraging Self-Compassion, Resilience, and Adaptability**

    These prompts encourage a positive growth mindset, helping you approach challenges with resilience and compassion.

    - **What challenges did I face this week, and what did I learn from them?**
      Reflect on any difficulties and focus on the lessons they brought. How did they help you grow?

    - **What are my strengths, and how can I use them more?**
      Identify your strengths and think about ways to utilize them more in your daily life.

    - **How can I be kinder to myself?**
      Self-compassion is crucial for growth. Reflect on how you can treat yourself with more kindness and understanding during difficult times.

    - **What is one fear or negative belief I want to overcome, and how can I take small steps to do so?**
      Identify a limiting belief or fear that holds you back, and come up with a plan for confronting and overcoming it.

5. **Exercises for Deeper Reflection**

    In addition to prompts, here are some exercises that can help deepen your self-reflection practice:

    - **Mind Mapping:**
      Create a mind map to explore a topic or question that interests you. Write your central idea in the middle and branch out with related thoughts, feelings, and ideas. This helps you explore ideas in a non-linear way.

    - **Life Timeline:**
      Draw a timeline of significant events in your life and reflect on how they shaped who you are today. Look for patterns and learnings from each experience.

    - **Visualization Exercise:**
      Close your eyes and visualize your ideal future. What does your life look like in 5, 10, or 20 years? Use this exercise to help clarify your long-term goals and life direction.

By using daily, weekly, and monthly prompts, along with exercises for uncovering your values, purpose, and growth mindset, you can deepen your self-reflection practice. These tools help you stay connected with your goals, personal growth, and well-being, allowing you to move forward with intention and clarity.

Mind Mapping - A Tool for Creativity and Organization

Mind mapping is a visual method to organize ideas and concepts, reflecting the brain's natural way of processing information. It starts with a central idea and expands outward with branches representing related thoughts. Each branch may include keywords, symbols, or images to enhance understanding. This tool is widely used for brainstorming, problem-solving, planning, and studying as it enables clear visualization of relationships among ideas, promotes creative thinking, and enhances memory retention. Essentially, mind mapping acts as a "map for your thoughts," offering structure and clarity.

How Mind Mapping Organizes Ideas

Mind mapping structures scattered ideas visually, linking related concepts around a central theme. Key benefits include:

- **Big Picture Clarity:** It helps in identifying relationships among different ideas.
- **Enhanced Creativity:** Encourages exploration of new connections.
- **Focus and Clarity:** Keeps all information organized in one place.
- **Simplicity:** Breaks down complex ideas into manageable parts.

Benefits of Mind Mapping

1. **Creativity Boost:**
   - Encourages out-of-the-box thinking through visualizing connections.
   - Organizes chaotic ideas, making space for new insights.
2. **Problem-Solving:**
   - Breaks down issues into smaller components for easier resolution.
   - Reveals relationships and helps make informed decisions.
3. **Memory Enhancement:**
   - Visual elements like colours and symbols make information more memorable.
   - Logical structures improve recall and retention.

Core Elements and Structure

A mind map starts with a **central idea** and expands into:

- **Branches:** Representing key categories.
- **Keywords:** Summarizing key points.

- **Visuals and Colours:** Enhancing understanding and memory. This format mirrors the brain's associative and non-linear thinking style, making it a natural and efficient tool.

Practical Applications of Mind Mapping

1. **Personal Goals and Planning:**
   - Break down goals into actionable steps (e.g., fitness plans or budgeting).
   - Track progress visually using updates and markers.
2. **Project Management and Study:**
   - Outline stages of a project or coursework with branches.
   - Highlight deadlines and milestones to stay organized.
3. **Brainstorming and Problem-Solving:**
   - Explore ideas and solutions around a central problem.
   - Use connections to identify patterns and refine decisions.

Steps to Create a Mind Map

1. **Start with a Central Topic:** Place the main idea in the center.
2. **Branch Out:** Draw lines for major themes or categories.
3. **Expand with Subtopics:** Add specific details to each branch.
4. **Incorporate Visuals:** Use symbols, images, and colours to enhance engagement and recall.

Tools and Techniques for Mind Mapping

- **Traditional vs. Digital Tools:**
  - Pen-and-paper offers flexibility, while digital tools like MindMeister or XMind provide templates, collaboration options, and storage.
- **Best Practices:**
  - Use keywords, avoid clutter, organize branches clearly, and focus on relationships with connecting lines and arrows.

Everyday Uses and Real-Life Examples

Mind mapping is versatile:

- **Students:** Organize study material with branches for subjects, subtopics, and key points.
- **Entrepreneurs:** Outline business strategies by categorizing ideas like marketing, budgeting, and growth areas.

- **Problem-Solvers:** Map causes, solutions, and potential outcomes to analyse challenges effectively.

By leveraging mind mapping, users can visualize complex information, encourage creativity, and enhance memory. It is a practical tool adaptable to personal, academic, and professional contexts.

Overcoming Challenges in Self-Reflection

Self-reflection can be a powerful tool for personal growth, but it's not always easy. At times, it can bring up difficult emotions, lead to overthinking, or make you feel overly critical of yourself. Here are some strategies to overcome common challenges in self-reflection:

1. **Facing Discomfort: How to Approach Difficult Emotions and Realizations**

   When reflecting on your life, you may encounter uncomfortable feelings or realizations that you'd rather avoid. These can include regret, guilt, or sadness. The key to handling this discomfort is to approach it with compassion and openness.

   - **Acknowledge the Emotion:** Instead of avoiding or suppressing difficult emotions, allow yourself to feel them. Acknowledge them as part of your experience without judgment.

   - **Embrace Vulnerability:** Being vulnerable in your self-reflection allows for deeper growth. Understand that it's okay to feel discomfort, and it's a sign that you're engaging in meaningful self-reflection.

   - **Use Self-Compassion:** Remind yourself that it's okay to make mistakes and feel uncomfortable. Practice being kind to yourself, as you would to a friend going through a difficult time.

   - **Shift the Focus to Growth:** Use discomfort as an opportunity to learn. Ask yourself, "What can I learn from this emotion? How can this help me grow?"

2. **Avoiding Overthinking: Balancing Self-Reflection Without Becoming Overly Critical**

   It's easy to fall into the trap of overthinking while reflecting, which can lead to self-doubt and unnecessary worry. Overthinking can make the process unproductive and stressful, so it's important to find balance.

   - **Set a Time Limit:** To avoid overthinking, set a specific time for your reflection practice. For example, give yourself 10–15 minutes to reflect on a specific question or event. This prevents you from dwelling too long on one thought or idea.

- **Focus on Solutions, Not Just Problems:**
  When you face a challenge, don't get stuck thinking only about what went wrong. Once you know the problem, start thinking about how you can fix it or what steps you can take to move forward.

- **Limit Negative Self-Talk:** Overthinking often brings up negative thoughts. Challenge these thoughts by asking, "Is this true? Is this helping me? What's a more positive way to think about this?"

- **Take Breaks:** If you start feeling overwhelmed by your thoughts, take a break and return to your reflection later. Sometimes, stepping away for a moment helps clear your mind.

3. **Staying Objective: Techniques to Observe Without Self-Judgment**

It can be hard to reflect without becoming self-judgmental. We tend to be our own harshest critics, which can cloud the objectivity needed for productive self-reflection.

- **Adopt the Role of a Neutral Observer:** Try to look at yourself as if you're observing someone else. Ask yourself, "What would I say to a friend who went through this?" This can help you detach from your emotions and look at the situation more objectively.

- **Practice Non-Judgmental Awareness:** When reflecting, try to stay neutral and avoid labelling your thoughts or actions as "good" or "bad." Simply notice your thoughts and emotions without judgment. This approach is often used in mindfulness and helps create space for growth without criticism.

- **Focus on the Facts:** Stick to the facts of the situation instead of making assumptions or jumping to conclusions. For example, instead of saying, "I'm a failure because I didn't achieve my goal," say, "I didn't achieve my goal, and here's why that happened."

- **Use Positive Language:** Reframe negative language in a more positive, constructive way. Instead of saying, "I'm not good enough," try, "I'm learning and improving every day."

Self-reflection isn't always easy, but it's an important practice for personal growth. To overcome challenges:

- Face difficult emotions with openness and self-compassion.
- Avoid overthinking by setting time limits, focusing on solutions, and limiting negative self-talk.
- Stay objective in your reflection by adopting a neutral observer role, practicing non-judgmental awareness, and focusing on facts and positive language.

By using these strategies, you can make your self-reflection practice more productive and less overwhelming, helping you grow in a balanced and healthy way.

Self-Reflection and Relationships

Self-reflection doesn't only benefit personal growth; it also greatly impacts our relationships with others. When we understand ourselves better, we communicate more effectively, build empathy, and develop healthier connections. Below are ways in which self-reflection enriches relationships, along with exercises to help you understand relational dynamics in friendships, family, and partnerships.

1. **How Understanding Oneself Improves Communication and Empathy**

   When you reflect on your thoughts, emotions, and behaviours, you gain insight into why you react the way you do in relationships. This awareness can lead to clearer, more compassionate interactions.

   - **Improved Communication:** Understanding your needs, boundaries, and triggers helps you express yourself more clearly. For example, if you recognize that you feel overwhelmed when someone interrupts, you can communicate this boundary politely and directly.

   - **Increased Empathy:** Self-reflection often increases empathy because it helps you understand your own challenges and insecurities. When you're aware of your vulnerabilities, it's easier to empathize with others and recognize that they may have similar struggles.

   - **Reduced Misunderstandings:** Reflecting on your assumptions and beliefs can help reduce misunderstandings. Instead of jumping to conclusions about someone else's behaviour, self-reflection helps you stay open-minded and ask clarifying questions.

2. **Reflecting on Relationship Patterns, Boundaries, and Values**

   Taking time to reflect on relationship patterns, personal boundaries, and core values can be transformative in all types of relationships. It helps you identify recurring behaviours, establish healthy limits, and ensure that your relationships align with your beliefs and priorities.

   - **Relationship Patterns:** Reflect on the dynamics of your relationships. Are there recurring patterns that need to be addressed? For instance, if you notice that you often avoid confrontation, you may decide to work on healthy assertiveness.

- **Boundaries:** Clear boundaries are essential for healthy relationships. Self-reflection helps you identify which boundaries you need in different types of relationships, such as how much time or energy you're willing to invest.

- **Values:** Reflect on your values and how they align with the relationships in your life. When you understand what's most important to you, such as honesty, trust, or kindness, you can strengthen connections with people who share similar values.

3. **Exercises for Self-Reflection in Relational Contexts**

   These exercises encourage thoughtful exploration of your interactions in friendships, family, and partnerships.

   - **Friendship Reflection:** Think about a close friendship. Ask yourself, "What do I value most about this friendship?" and "How do I show appreciation to my friend?" This can help you nurture meaningful connections.

   - **Family Reflection:** Reflect on your family dynamics and your role within the family. Consider questions like, "What boundaries would help improve my relationship with my family members?" or "How do I balance my own needs with family expectations?"

   - **Partnership Reflection:** If you're in a partnership, think about your communication style. Ask, "How well do I communicate my needs?" or "What patterns do I notice in how we handle conflicts?" Recognizing these patterns can lead to more supportive, resilient partnerships.

   Self-reflection is a valuable tool for understanding how you relate to others. By reflecting on your communication style, empathy, patterns, boundaries, and values, you can create healthier and more fulfilling relationships. Regularly engaging in reflection exercises can help you strengthen connections in friendships, family, and partnerships, fostering trust, respect, and understanding.

Tools for Enhancing Self-Reflection

Incorporating tools and resources can deepen your self-reflection practice, making it more engaging and productive. Here are some effective ways to support your journey of self-discovery:

1. **Apps and Technology**

   Using technology can make self-reflection more accessible and convenient, especially for those who prefer guided assistance or digital journaling.

- **Guided Self-Reflection Apps:** Apps like **Headspace** and **Insight Timer** offer mindfulness practices that encourage self-awareness and reflection. **Reflectly** and **Day One** are journaling apps with prompts to help you uncover your thoughts and emotions.

- **Digital Journaling Tools:** If you prefer digital journaling, apps like **Evernote** or **Notion** allow you to organize your reflections and revisit them over time. These platforms often offer templates for goal-setting, gratitude logs, and more.

- **Meditation Aids:** Meditation apps with guided reflections, such as **Calm** or **Breethe**, can enhance self-reflection by creating a peaceful space to observe thoughts without judgment.

2. **Books and Resources**

Reading books focused on self-discovery and personal growth provides a wealth of ideas, exercises, and insights to guide self-reflection.

- **Recommended Books:**

- *"The Gifts of Imperfection" by Brené Brown* explores self-acceptance and authenticity, which can aid in self-reflection.

- *"Atomic Habits" by James Clear* helps in understanding habit formation and self-improvement.

- *"The Power of Now" by Eckhart Tolle* encourages mindfulness and living in the present, which are essential for reflective practices.

- **Workbooks and Journals:** Books with exercises, like *"The Self-Compassion Workbook" by Kristin Neff*, provide structured reflection prompts, while guided journals like *"The Five-Minute Journal"* encourage daily introspection.

3. **Feedback from Others**

Constructive feedback can act as a mirror, offering perspectives you might not see on your own. Using feedback thoughtfully can highlight strengths and areas for growth, enriching self-reflection.

- **Seeking Feedback:** Approach trusted friends, family, or colleagues for honest feedback on areas like communication, empathy, or work habits. Choose people who offer supportive, balanced insights.

- **Self-Reflection on Feedback:** After receiving feedback, set aside time to reflect on it. Ask yourself, "What did I learn from this feedback?" and "How can I use this insight to improve?"

- **Incorporating Professional Support:** Sometimes, a mentor, counsellor, or coach can provide feedback and guidance that deepens self-awareness. They may offer tools, exercises, or insights that encourage growth.

Self-reflection can be enhanced through tools and resources that support thoughtful, consistent practice. Apps and technology provide accessible ways to track and guide reflections, books and workbooks offer structured insights, and feedback from others adds valuable outside perspectives. By integrating these tools, you can make self-reflection more engaging, impactful, and sustainable.

Success Stories: Real-Life Examples of Self-Reflection

Self-reflection has helped many people overcome difficulties, make positive life changes, and discover new paths for themselves. Here are a few simple, real-life examples of how self-reflection made a difference in people's lives:

1. **Pooja – Overcoming Job Dissatisfaction**

   Pooja was feeling stuck and unhappy in her job. She spent some time each evening writing in a journal, exploring what exactly made her feel this way. Through self-reflection, she realized that she craved more creativity and independence in her work. This led her to pursue a career change to graphic design, something she had always been passionate about. Self-reflection helped Pooja recognize her true interests and gave her the courage to switch careers.

2. **Sahil – Improving Personal Relationships**

   Sahil noticed that he often had arguments with close friends and family members. Through self-reflection, he began to understand that his quick temper and impatience were affecting his relationships. Sahil started practicing mindfulness and taking a few deep breaths before responding during tense moments. Over time, his relationships improved, and he felt closer to his loved ones. Self-reflection allowed Sahil to see his behaviour clearly and make positive changes.

3. **Neha – Building Self-Confidence**

   Neha often felt insecure and doubted her abilities. She decided to keep a self-reflection journal, where she noted small accomplishments each day, like completing a project or helping a colleague. By reflecting on these achievements, Neha began to see her strengths more clearly. Over time, her confidence grew, and she felt more motivated to take on new challenges at work. Self-reflection helped Neha focus on her strengths and build a stronger sense of self-worth.

4. **Rishi – Finding Life Purpose after Retirement**

   After retiring, Rishi felt lost and unsure of what to do next. He used self-reflection to explore what gave him meaning and joy. He realized he missed teaching and helping others, so he decided to start volunteering at a local school. This brought Rishi a new sense of purpose and happiness. Through self-reflection, Rishi discovered what truly mattered to him and found a fulfilling way to spend his time.

These examples show how self-reflection can guide us through challenges, lead to positive changes, and help us understand ourselves better. By taking time to reflect, people can uncover what they truly want, make thoughtful decisions, and find greater satisfaction in life.

Practical Tips for Making Self-Reflection Part of Daily Life

Here are some simple ways to make self-reflection a regular part of your day. Starting small and staying consistent can help you discover meaningful insights over time.

1. **Start Small with Simple Reflections**
   - Begin with just a few minutes each day. You don't need to dive deep right away; start by asking yourself a simple question at the end of each day, like "What went well today?" or "What could I improve tomorrow?"
   - Write down a quick note or a few sentences if you can. Over time, this habit will feel easier and more natural.

2. **Use Self-Reflection Alongside Affirmations and Goal-Setting**
   - Pairing self-reflection with positive affirmations or daily goals can help you stay focused on your growth and mindset.
   - For example, after doing affirmations, take a moment to ask yourself how you feel about them or how they might align with your current goals.

3. **Reflect in the Morning or Before Bedtime**
   - Choose a time of day that works best for you. Many people find it helpful to reflect in the morning to set intentions or in the evening to review their day.
   - Making it part of a routine—like having a cup of tea or a few quiet minutes before bed—can make self-reflection easier to stick with.

4. **Celebrate Small Wins and Progress**
   - Recognize any positive changes, no matter how small. Did you react more calmly in a challenging situation today? Or make a choice that aligns with your values? These are all things worth celebrating!

- Acknowledging growth builds confidence and makes self-reflection feel more rewarding.

5. **Keep a Journal or Use Digital Tools**

- Journals are a great way to keep track of your reflections. Writing things down can make your thoughts feel more organized and real.

- If you prefer digital tools, try using notes on your phone or apps that remind you to pause and reflect. Find what feels easiest for you.

6. **Stay Patient with Yourself**

- Self-reflection is a journey, and sometimes it takes time to see patterns or changes. Be gentle with yourself and remember that it's okay if some days feel more reflective than others.

- Over time, small, consistent efforts can add up to powerful insights and positive changes.

By keeping these tips in mind, you can build a self-reflection practice that feels meaningful and manageable in your everyday life.

Keynotes

- Self-reflection is a powerful tool for personal growth and self-awareness.

- It helps in improving emotional intelligence, decision-making, and problem-solving skills.

- Regular self-reflection allows you to track progress, set goals, and adjust your approach to life.

- Techniques like journaling, meditation, visualization, and questioning enhance the self-reflection process.

- Overcoming challenges such as writer's block, vulnerability, and self-judgment is part of the journey.

- Self-reflection improves relationships by fostering better understanding and empathy.

- Tools such as apps, feedback from others, and reflective prompts can support the self-reflection process.

- **Consistency is key**: Make self-reflection a habit for long-term personal development.

Self-reflection is a powerful tool for personal growth, helping us understand our thoughts, feelings, and behaviours on a deeper level. By taking time to look inward, we become more aware of our values, strengths, and areas where we can improve. This practice not only enhances emotional intelligence and clarity but also builds resilience and encourages a stronger sense of purpose.

Making self-reflection a regular part of life can open doors to meaningful personal development. When we actively work to understand ourselves, we gain the ability to make better decisions, improve relationships, and live more authentically. Integrating self-reflection into our daily routines helps us stay connected to who we are and who we want to become.

Embracing self-reflection means embracing the journey of self-discovery. By being patient and gentle with ourselves, we can foster a greater sense of self-acceptance and mindfulness. This commitment to understanding ourselves brings us closer to a more fulfilled, balanced, and purposeful life.

Chapter 4
Journaling
(Writing Dayri) Reflecting on Your Journey

What Journaling Is and Its Purpose

Journaling is the act of writing down your thoughts (Writing Dayri), feelings, experiences, or anything that's on your mind. It can be as simple as keeping a notebook where you jot down what happened during the day, or as detailed as exploring deeper questions about life and your emotions. Some people journal to organize their ideas, others to vent their feelings, and many to gain a better understanding of themselves.

The purpose of journaling goes beyond just recording events. It's a way to make sense of our experiences and connect with our inner thoughts. When we write about our day or our emotions, we create a space where we can reflect, process, and work through our feelings. It helps us slow down and look at things from a new perspective, which can be especially helpful during tough or confusing times.

Journaling is also great for personal growth. By regularly reflecting on our thoughts and actions, we can see patterns in our behaviour, recognize what's working well in our lives, and identify areas where we'd like to grow or change. Over time, these small insights can help us make better decisions, build confidence, and stay on track toward our goals.

For example, if someone feels stressed about work, they might journal about what's causing that stress, which helps them understand it better. They might even realize that their stress isn't just about work but also about a need for more balance in their life. With this insight, they can then start making small changes to feel more at ease.

Overall, journaling is a valuable tool for both self-reflection and self-improvement. It gives us a safe space to express ourselves without judgment and helps us build a stronger, healthier relationship with our own thoughts and emotions.

The Importance of Self-Reflection and Personal Growth

Self-reflection and personal growth are essential for developing a better understanding of ourselves and leading a more fulfilling life. When we take time to reflect, we look back on our thoughts, actions, and experiences, helping us see things more clearly and gain valuable insights.

Self-reflection is like a mirror for our mind. It allows us to pause, think about our choices, and understand why we feel a certain way. For example, if someone often feels stressed at work, self-reflection might help them realize the root of the stress, like a heavy workload or a lack of time for self-care. This kind of awareness is the first step toward making positive changes, as it helps us identify what's working well in our lives and what needs improvement.

Personal growth is the natural result of regular self-reflection. When we understand our thoughts and actions better, we're able to learn from our experiences and become more aware of what truly matters to us. Personal growth doesn't mean we become perfect; instead, it's about continually improving ourselves and becoming the best version of who we are. It can include things like building confidence, improving relationships, or working toward our dreams and goals.

For example, by regularly reflecting on our daily experiences through journaling or thoughtful conversations, we might notice we feel happiest when helping others. This realization could guide us toward choosing a career path, a hobby, or volunteer work that aligns with that value, making our lives more meaningful.

In short, self-reflection and personal growth help us better understand who we are, what we value, and how we can lead a life that feels true to us. This journey of self-discovery can lead to greater happiness, resilience, and a deeper sense of purpose.

How Journaling Complements Other Practices Like Affirmations and Meditation

Journaling works well with practices like affirmations and meditation because it adds depth and insight to our personal growth journey. Each practice has its unique benefits, and when combined, they create a balanced approach to self-care and self-awareness.

1. **Journaling and Affirmations: Building Positive Thoughts**
    - Affirmations are positive statements we repeat to ourselves to develop a confident mindset, like saying, "I am capable and worthy." However, sometimes repeating affirmations alone might feel superficial, especially if our deeper thoughts don't fully agree.
    - Journaling can help bridge this gap by allowing us to explore the emotions behind our affirmations. For instance, if we're struggling to believe we're "worthy," journaling about why we feel this way helps uncover any hidden doubts or past experiences.

Writing down our feelings can give us insights that make our affirmations feel more authentic and believable.

- Additionally, we can use journaling to record positive changes or progress in our mindset, which makes affirmations feel more grounded in real growth.

2. **Journaling and Meditation: Gaining Clarity and Inner Peace**
   - Meditation is all about finding calm, focus, and presence in the moment. It trains us to observe our thoughts without judgment, helping us manage stress and find inner peace.
   - Journaling complements meditation by providing a space to record any thoughts, emotions, or insights that surface during or after meditation. For example, if meditation brings up feelings of stress or restlessness, writing these down can help us understand why they're there and what we might do about them.
   - Journaling also lets us set intentions before meditation or reflect on the experience afterward, deepening our understanding of our mental and emotional state. This can create a feedback loop where journaling enhances meditation, and meditation brings clarity to our journaling.

3. **Together, Journaling, Affirmations, and Meditation Create a Full Circle**
   - When used together, these practices offer a well-rounded approach to self-care. **Meditation** helps us calm our minds and become aware of our thoughts, **affirmations** guide our thinking toward positivity, and **journaling** lets us reflect, process, and build self-awareness.
   - For instance, after a day of meditation and affirmations, we can journal about any positive feelings or challenges that arose. This way, we track our growth, become more aware of our progress, and feel more connected to our goals and values.

In essence, journaling, affirmations, and meditation each work in unique ways to nurture our minds and spirits. When practiced together, they help us become more mindful, positive, and in tune with ourselves, creating a strong foundation for lasting inner peace and growth.

Benefits of Journaling

Journaling is a powerful tool with numerous benefits that positively affect our emotional and mental well-being. It also has long-term advantages that help us see progress in our lives, achieve our goals, and grow personally.

1. **Emotional Benefits**
   - **Stress Relief**: Writing down our thoughts and feelings allows us to release any pent-up stress or anxiety. When we put our worries on paper, we often feel lighter and more in control.
   - **Clarity of Emotions**: Journaling helps us identify and understand our emotions better. By writing freely, we can express our true feelings without judgment, which can lead to valuable insights about why we feel a certain way.
   - **Self-Awareness**: Regular journaling encourages self-reflection, making us more aware of our thoughts and behaviour patterns. This increased self-awareness often leads to more mindful decision-making in everyday life.

2. **Mental Benefits**
   - **Improved Focus**: Journaling helps clear mental clutter, which allows us to concentrate better. By organizing our thoughts on paper, we free up space in our minds to focus on other tasks.
   - **Enhanced Problem-Solving**: When faced with a challenge, writing about it can help us think through solutions. The act of putting thoughts into words can reveal new perspectives and ideas we might not have considered before.
   - **Organized Thoughts**: Journaling organizes the many ideas that come to mind, making it easier to structure our thoughts logically. This is especially helpful when we're overwhelmed by too many things to think about or accomplish.

3. **Long-Term Benefits**
   - **Tracking Growth**: Journaling provides a record of our experiences and personal growth over time. Reading past entries shows us how much we've learned and changed, reminding us of our resilience and progress.
   - **Goal Achievement**: By recording goals and tracking progress, journaling keeps us motivated. We can revisit our goals, adjust them, and celebrate each small step we take toward achieving them.
   - **Identifying Patterns of Personal Development**: Over time, journaling helps us notice patterns in our thoughts, emotions, and behaviours. This awareness allows us to make positive changes in areas where we see recurring issues, which helps us grow consistently.

In summary, journaling offers a simple yet effective way to support our emotional and mental health while also helping us grow and move toward our goals over time. These benefits make it a valuable daily habit for anyone looking to understand themselves better and improve their quality of life.

Types of Journaling

Journaling can take many forms, each with its own unique focus and benefits. Here are some popular types of journaling that serve different purposes, from daily check-ins to creative expression.

1. **Daily Journaling**
   - **Purpose**: Daily journaling involves writing short, regular entries that capture your thoughts, feelings, or reflections on the day.
   - **Benefits**: This type of journaling provides a quick emotional release and a way to track your day-to-day experiences. It can also help you stay grounded and aware of your mental and emotional state.
   - **Example**: Each night, you might jot down a few sentences about something that went well, something that didn't, or anything noteworthy from the day.

2. **Gratitude Journaling**
   - **Purpose**: Gratitude journaling focuses on listing things you're thankful for, helping you to appreciate the positives in life.
   - **Benefits**: Regular gratitude journaling cultivates a more positive mindset, helps reduce stress, and can boost overall happiness.
   - **Example**: Each morning, write down three things you're grateful for, like a supportive friend, a good meal, or a moment of peace.

3. **Reflective Journaling**
   - **Purpose**: Reflective journaling involves exploring specific events, situations, or challenges in detail to gain insight and process your feelings.
   - **Benefits**: This type of journaling helps you learn from experiences, work through difficult emotions, and develop greater self-awareness.
   - **Example**: After a challenging day, you might write about what happened, how it made you feel, and any lessons you learned.

4. **Goal-Oriented Journaling**
   - **Purpose**: Goal-oriented journaling focuses on setting, planning, and tracking progress toward personal or professional goals.

- **Benefits**: This method keeps you organized and motivated, helping you to visualize success and stay accountable for your goals.
- **Example**: Write down your goals, create an action plan, and check in regularly to document your progress, celebrate wins, and adjust as needed.

5. **Creative Journaling**

   - **Purpose**: Creative journaling combines writing with artistic expression, using sketches, poetry, or free-form writing to capture your thoughts.
   - **Benefits**: This type of journaling encourages creativity and can serve as a stress-reliever, allowing you to express yourself freely without structure.
   - **Example**: Create a journal entry that includes a doodle of something that represents your mood, along with a few descriptive words or a short poem.

6. **Guided Journaling**

   - **Purpose**: Guided journaling uses prompts or questions that help you dive deeper into specific areas of your life, thoughts, or emotions.
   - **Benefits**: Using prompts can help you explore areas you might not consider on your own and lead to new insights and self-discovery.
   - **Example**: Use a prompt like, "What is something I learned about myself recently?" and spend a few minutes writing your response.

Each type of journaling offers unique ways to support personal growth, self-awareness, and emotional well-being. You can mix and match these methods depending on your needs, or try different types to discover what resonates most with you.

Getting Started with Journaling

Starting a journaling habit can feel challenging, especially if you're new to it. Here are some simple steps to help you ease into journaling and set yourself up for success.

1. **Tips for Overcoming Initial Hesitation or Fear of Writing**

   - **Start Small**: Begin with a few sentences or bullet points rather than aiming for long entries. This helps you get comfortable without feeling pressured to write a lot.

- **Let Go of Perfection**: Remember, your journal is private, so there's no need for perfect grammar or polished thoughts. Write freely, and focus on expressing yourself honestly.

- **Set a Time Limit**: Give yourself 5-10 minutes to write, rather than thinking you need hours to journal. This makes it feel manageable and removes the pressure of time.

- **Use Prompts**: If you're unsure where to start, prompts like "Today I feel…" or "One thing I'm grateful for is…" can give you a simple starting point.

2. **Choosing a Journal Type or Format that Fits Your Needs (Digital vs. Physical)**

   - **Digital Journals**: Digital journaling is convenient if you prefer typing or using a device. Apps like Notion, Google Keep, or dedicated journaling apps let you write anytime, anywhere. It's also easy to organize and search through past entries.

   - **Physical Journals**: Writing by hand in a notebook or journal can be a more personal experience, which some find relaxing and grounding. Choose a notebook that you enjoy and feel comfortable using, whether it's lined, blank, or a bullet journal.

   - **Combination**: Some people use both formats, keeping a physical journal for in-depth reflections and a digital one for quick notes or on-the-go thoughts. Experiment to see what works best for you.

3. **Creating a Comfortable and Consistent Journaling Space and Routine**

   - **Find Your Space**: Choose a place where you feel relaxed, whether it's a cozy chair, your desk, or a quiet corner. Creating a dedicated space can make journaling feel like a special time for yourself.

   - **Set a Time**: Establish a regular time each day or week to journal, like in the morning to set intentions or in the evening to reflect on your day. Consistency builds habit and helps make journaling a natural part of your routine.

   - **Bring Comfort Items**: Enhance your journaling experience by adding things that make you comfortable, like a warm drink, soft music, or a favourite pen. This adds to the ritual and can help you feel more motivated to journal regularly.

By taking small steps, finding the right format, and creating a cozy, consistent routine, journaling becomes an enjoyable and fulfilling practice. It's all about making it easy, personal, and something you look forward to.

Effective Journaling Techniques

There are several journaling techniques you can use to make your practice more effective, helping you explore your thoughts, emotions, and experiences. Each technique offers a different approach, so you can experiment with different methods to see what resonates with you.

1. **Free Writing**
   - **What It Is**: Free writing is all about letting your thoughts flow onto the page without any filters or judgment. You don't worry about spelling, grammar, or structure. The goal is simply to write for a set amount of time, letting whatever comes to mind spill out.
   - **Why It's Effective**: This technique helps to release pent-up emotions, clear mental clutter, and discover hidden feelings or ideas. It's a great way to kickstart your journaling practice when you're not sure where to begin.
   - **How to Practice**: Set a timer for 5-10 minutes and just write. If you get stuck, repeat the last word you wrote until new thoughts come to you. Don't stop until the timer goes off.

2. **Prompt-Based Journaling**
   - **What It Is**: Prompt-based journaling involves answering specific questions or reflecting on particular themes. This could include prompts like "What am I grateful for today?" or "What challenges did I face and how did I overcome them?"
   - **Why It's Effective**: Prompts help to focus your thoughts and guide your writing. They are especially useful if you feel stuck or don't know what to write about. Prompts can also deepen your reflection and encourage you to think more critically about your experiences.
   - **How to Practice**: Choose a prompt (either from a list or create your own) and write a response to it. Spend a few minutes reflecting and writing without rushing. Some great prompts include:
     - "What am I most proud of right now?"
     - "What lesson did I learn today?"
     - "What do I want to achieve in the next week?"

3. **Stream of Consciousness**
   - **What It Is**: Stream of consciousness writing is a method where you write without pause, letting your thoughts flow freely and unedited. This technique allows you to dig deeper into

your subconscious mind and discover underlying emotions or patterns.

- **Why It's Effective**: It helps uncover hidden thoughts and feelings you might not be aware of. By writing continuously, you allow yourself to bypass your usual thought filters and tap into deeper insights about yourself.

- **How to Practice**: Start writing non-stop for 10-15 minutes. Don't worry about making sense or being coherent. Just write down whatever comes to mind, even if it seems unrelated. The goal is to let your thoughts spill out and uncover what's on your mind.

4. **Reflection and Analysis**

- **What It Is**: Reflection and analysis involve looking back at previous journal entries to identify patterns, recurring themes, and insights. You can reflect on how you've grown, what you've learned, and how your mindset has changed over time.

- **Why It's Effective**: Revisiting past entries helps you track your personal growth and gain perspective. It allows you to see progress, identify recurring challenges, and celebrate achievements. Analysing your journal can also highlight areas where you may need to shift your mindset.

- **How to Practice**: Every few weeks or months, go back and read your past journal entries. Take note of any recurring thoughts, patterns in your emotions, or significant breakthroughs. You might also ask yourself questions like:
  - "How have my goals changed over time?"
  - "What have I learned about myself?"
  - "What obstacles have I overcome, and what do I need to focus on next?"

By incorporating these journaling techniques into your practice, you'll be able to reflect more deeply on your thoughts and emotions. You can mix and match these methods to suit your mood or what you're working on, ensuring that your journaling remains fresh and meaningful.

Journaling is a powerful tool for fostering personal growth by helping you set goals, track progress, identify limiting beliefs, and cultivate a more compassionate relationship with yourself. Here's how to use journaling effectively to support your journey toward self-improvement and inner growth.

1. **Setting Intentions and Goals Through Journaling**

- **Purpose**: Writing down intentions and goals gives you clarity and a sense of purpose. It encourages you to articulate what you want to achieve in different areas of life, whether it's personal, professional, or spiritual.

- **How to Practice**: Start by reflecting on what truly matters to you. Set goals that are specific, measurable, achievable, relevant, and time-bound (SMART goals). For example, if you want to improve your health, your goal could be "I will exercise for 20 minutes three times a week." Write these goals in a dedicated space in your journal and review them regularly.

2. **Tracking Progress and Celebrating Milestones**

- **Purpose**: Tracking your achievements and celebrating small wins reinforces your motivation and keeps you moving forward. Noticing your progress, even when it feels slow, helps build confidence.

- **How to Practice**: Dedicate a page or section of your journal to record small victories and progress toward your goals. For example, if your goal is to meditate daily, note each time you complete a session. Reflect on how these actions are helping you move closer to your larger goals. Celebrate milestones by acknowledging your efforts and writing a few words of self-congratulation, such as "I'm proud of myself for staying consistent."

3. **Recognizing Negative Patterns or Limiting Beliefs and Working to Overcome Them**

- **Purpose**: Journaling can reveal self-sabotaging thoughts or behaviours that may be holding you back. When you write honestly, you can spot recurring negative patterns or beliefs that need attention.

- **How to Practice**: Regularly review your entries and look for patterns in your thoughts. For instance, you might notice phrases like "I can't" or "I'm not good enough." Challenge these thoughts by questioning their validity. For each negative belief, write a counter-belief, such as "I am capable and open to growth." Over time, practicing this shift in mindset can help you develop a more positive self-image.

4. **Practicing Self-Compassion and Self-Acceptance Through Reflective Entries**

- **Purpose**: Reflective journaling encourages you to show kindness toward yourself. By practicing self-compassion, you acknowledge your feelings without judgment and treat yourself as you would a close friend.

- **How to Practice**: After writing about a challenging experience, add a few lines of self-compassion, such as "It's okay to make mistakes" or "I'm learning and growing every day." Reflect on what you would say to someone else in your situation, and direct those kind words toward yourself. Journaling in this way builds self-acceptance and encourages you to embrace your imperfections.

By using journaling for personal growth, you create a roadmap for self-improvement, develop greater awareness of your strengths and weaknesses, and cultivate a kinder, more supportive relationship with yourself. This practice helps turn your journal into a meaningful space for both reflection and transformation.

Overcoming Common Journaling Challenges

Journaling can be a deeply rewarding practice, but it often comes with its own set of challenges. Here are some common obstacles and strategies to help you move past them, so you can fully embrace the benefits of journaling.

1. **Writer's Block: Tips for Breaking Through Mental Blocks**
   - **Challenge**: Sometimes, staring at a blank page can feel intimidating, and you might not know where to start or what to write.
   - **Solutions**:
     - **Start Small**: Begin with a single word or phrase that describes how you feel at that moment. This can help kick-start your flow.
     - **Use Prompts**: Prompts provide direction. Questions like "What am I grateful for today?" or "What is something new I learned?" can inspire thoughts and ideas.
     - **Free Write**: Set a timer for five minutes and write whatever comes to mind without judgment. This loosens up thoughts and clears away any mental clutter, often leading to more meaningful entries.

2. **Consistency: Creating Habits to Make Journaling a Regular Practice**
   - **Challenge**: Many people start journaling with enthusiasm but find it hard to stick to a regular routine.
   - **Solutions**:
     - **Set a Time and Place**: Choose a specific time and comfortable place for journaling. This can help make journaling feel like a natural part of your daily routine.

- **Start Small and Build Up**: Commit to writing for just five minutes a day. Gradually increase this as it becomes a habit.
- **Use Reminders**: Set a daily reminder or alarm on your phone. You could also leave your journal in a visible place, like your bedside table, as a prompt to write.
- **Celebrate Small Wins**: Acknowledge each day you journal as a success. Over time, celebrating these small wins will make the habit more rewarding and reinforce consistency.

3. **Vulnerability: Addressing Discomfort with Self-Reflection and Personal Honesty**
   - **Challenge**: Journaling can bring up uncomfortable emotions or thoughts, making it hard to write with full honesty.
   - **Solutions**:
     - **Remind Yourself It's Private**: Remember, your journal is a safe, judgment-free space. You don't have to share it with anyone, so allow yourself to write freely without worrying about others reading it.
     - **Start with Positives**: If vulnerability feels overwhelming, start by writing about things you're comfortable with, like positive experiences or things you're grateful for. Once you feel more comfortable, you can gradually explore deeper topics.
     - **Practice Self-Compassion**: Approach your feelings with kindness. If you uncover difficult emotions, reassure yourself that these feelings are valid and part of the human experience.
     - **Use Prompts for Difficult Emotions**: Prompts like "What are some things I've learned from past challenges?" or "What do I need to let go of?" can help you reflect with a focus on growth rather than self-criticism.

By overcoming these common challenges, you can make journaling a valuable, regular practice that supports your personal growth and emotional well-being. It may take time to find what works best, but the key is to keep experimenting, be patient with yourself, and enjoy the journey of self-discovery.

Journaling Prompts for Self-Discovery and Growth

Journaling is a powerful tool for self-reflection, personal growth, and understanding oneself on a deeper level. Here are some prompts that can guide you through various aspects of self-discovery, including reflection, gratitude, goal-setting, emotions, values, and aspirations.

1. **Prompts for Self-Reflection, Gratitude, Goal Setting, and Personal Growth**
   - **Self-Reflection:**
     - What are three qualities I appreciate about myself?
     - What recent experience taught me something valuable?
     - What habits or routines make me feel my best?
   - **Gratitude:**
     - What are five things I'm grateful for today?
     - Who has positively impacted my life recently, and why?
     - How can I show more gratitude to myself and others?
   - **Goal Setting:**
     - What are my top three goals for the next month?
     - How do I envision my life in five years?
     - What is one step I can take today to move closer to my dreams?
   - **Personal Growth:**
     - What do I need to let go of to grow?
     - How have I changed in the last year?
     - What lessons from the past am I now ready to apply to my life?
2. **Questions for Exploring Emotions, Values, and Dreams**
   - **Exploring Emotions:**
     - How do I feel today, and why?
     - What emotions have I been avoiding, and why?
     - How can I express my emotions in a healthy way?
   - **Exploring Values:**
     - What are the three most important values in my life?
     - How do my actions reflect my core beliefs?
     - Are there any values I want to embrace more fully?
   - **Exploring Dreams:**
     - What did I dream of as a child, and does it still inspire me?
     - If I could do anything without fear or limitation, what would I choose?
     - What legacy do I want to leave behind?

3. **Ideas for Prompts to Explore Past Experiences and Envision Future Goals**
   - **Exploring Past Experiences:**
     - What is a challenge I overcame, and what did it teach me?
     - What's a memory that makes me feel proud?
     - How has my past shaped who I am today?
   - **Envisioning Future Goals:**
     - What are three things I want to accomplish in the next year?
     - What does my ideal day look like five years from now?
     - How can I make choices today that align with my future self?

These prompts can serve as a roadmap for self-discovery and growth, helping you reflect on your experiences, emotions, and aspirations. Remember, there's no right or wrong way to answer these questions—your responses are a reflection of your unique journey.

Real-Life Examples of Journaling Practices

Journaling is a simple but powerful tool that people use in many areas of their lives. Here are a few real-life stories that show how journaling can help people grow personally and professionally.

1. **Harry's Story: Using Journaling to Reduce Stress and Stay Focused**
   - **Background:** Harry is a teacher who feels overwhelmed by her busy schedule.
   - **Journaling Practice:** Every evening, she writes down three things that went well during her day and three things she's grateful for.
   - **Benefits:** By focusing on positive moments, Harry feels calmer and more in control. She notices that her stress levels have decreased, and she now sleeps better at night.

2. **Gopi's Story: Gaining Career Clarity Through Goal Journaling**
   - **Background:** Gopi works in marketing and often feels uncertain about his career path.
   - **Journaling Practice:** Each week, he sets aside time to write down his career goals and reflect on his progress.
   - **Benefits:** This practice has helped him stay focused and build confidence in his work. By reviewing his entries, Gopi sees his growth over time and feels more motivated to pursue his goals.

3. **Varun's Story: Tracking Fitness Goals for Motivation**
   - **Background:** Varun wants to lose weight and improve his health, but he struggles to stay consistent with his workouts.

- **Journaling Practice**: He keeps a fitness journal, where he records each workout, what he ate, and how he felt afterward.
- **Benefits**: By tracking his progress, Varun can see the changes in his body and mindset. This motivates him to keep going, and he's proud of how much he has achieved.

4. **Bhumi's Story: Building Confidence with Gratitude Journaling**
   - **Background**: Bhumi is a college student who often feels anxious and self-critical.
   - **Journaling Practice**: She writes down things she appreciates about herself each day, like her kindness, resilience, and creativity.
   - **Benefits**: Over time, Bhumi has become more positive and self-assured. She now feels better equipped to handle challenges and has noticed a big improvement in her confidence.

These stories show how people from all walks of life use journaling to build better habits, understand their emotions, and achieve their goals. By spending just a few minutes each day reflecting on their experiences, they're able to make meaningful, positive changes in their lives.

Enhancing Your Journaling Practice

Once you're comfortable with regular journaling, you can deepen your practice by integrating it with other techniques and tools. Here's how to make journaling even more impactful and engaging.

1. **Integrating Journaling with Mindfulness, Affirmations, and Meditation**
   - **Mindfulness**: Start or end your journaling session with a brief mindfulness exercise, like deep breathing or a body scan. This helps you become more present and aware, allowing you to write with greater clarity and focus.
   - **Affirmations**: Use your journal to write down positive affirmations. Affirmations are powerful statements, like "I am confident and capable," that reinforce a positive mindset. Writing them down daily can increase your confidence and self-belief.
   - **Meditation**: After a meditation session, take a few moments to journal any insights or thoughts that came up. Meditation can often help you uncover deeper emotions and thoughts, and journaling them can provide a sense of release and understanding.

2. **Using Tools like Planners, Bullet Journals, and Mood Trackers**

- **Planners**: A planner can help you track daily tasks and goals, keeping you organized. Combine it with journaling by writing reflections on your day or noting progress toward your goals. This blend helps you stay both productive and reflective.
- **Bullet Journals**: A bullet journal is a flexible system where you use bullet points and symbols to organize tasks, ideas, and reflections. Many people use it as both a planner and a journal, allowing for creativity and personalization.
- **Mood Trackers**: A mood tracker lets you log your emotions each day, helping you see patterns over time. Pair it with journaling by jotting down notes about what may have influenced your mood. This can help you identify habits or situations that impact your emotional health.

3. **Experimenting with Different Journaling Techniques to Keep the Practice Engaging**
   - **Prompt-Based Journaling**: Use different prompts for variety, like "What is one thing I am grateful for today?" or "What did I learn from today's challenges?" Prompts keep your journaling fresh and help you explore new topics.
   - **Art Journaling**: Add sketches, doodles, or even collages to your journal. Visual elements can express emotions and thoughts in ways that words sometimes cannot.
   - **Storytelling**: Occasionally, write about your day or an experience as if it were a story, using rich details and narrative style. Storytelling makes journaling feel more creative and can help you look at situations from a new perspective.

Enhancing your journaling practice with these techniques can make it more enjoyable and rewarding. By combining journaling with mindfulness, adding helpful tools, and experimenting with new methods, you can turn journaling into a meaningful, personalized routine that supports growth, relaxation, and self-awareness.

Keynotes:

1. **Purpose of Journaling**: A tool for self-reflection, emotional clarity, and personal growth.
2. **Benefits**:
   - Emotional: Reduces stress and boosts self-awareness.
   - Mental: Enhances focus and organizes thoughts.
   - Long-Term: Tracks growth, goals, and personal patterns.

3. **Types of Journaling**:
   - Daily, gratitude, reflective, goal-oriented, creative, and guided.
4. **Getting Started**: Choose a format, create a routine, and overcome initial hesitation.
5. **Techniques**:
   - Free writing, prompt-based, stream of consciousness, and reflective review.
6. **Growth Applications**: Set intentions, track progress, recognize patterns, and practice self-compassion.
7. **Challenges**: Overcome writer's block, build consistency, and embrace vulnerability.
8. **Prompts**: Use questions for gratitude, goal setting, and exploring values.
9. **Enhancing Practice**: Combine with mindfulness, affirmations, and tools like planners.
10. **Final Takeaway**: Journaling supports self-discovery and intentional living through reflection and tracking.

Journaling is a simple yet powerful tool for self-reflection, personal growth, and emotional balance. By writing down thoughts, emotions, and experiences, you create a dedicated space to explore your inner world, understand yourself better, and build habits that support your well-being. Journaling has numerous benefits, from reducing stress and clarifying emotions to helping you track progress toward personal goals and gain insight into patterns in your life.

Making journaling a part of your daily routine is a valuable step toward self-discovery. With just a few minutes each day, you can unlock your thoughts, build self-awareness, and experience the positive shifts that come from intentional reflection. Through journaling, you're also better equipped to face challenges, set goals, and celebrate milestones, providing a meaningful path to navigate life's ups and downs.

In the end, journaling is about more than just putting words on paper. It's a way to live with greater intention and purpose, continuously learning and growing from each day's experiences. By committing to this practice, you're investing in a deeper understanding of yourself—your values, dreams, and strengths—paving the way to a more mindful, fulfilling life.

Chapter 5

Gratitude

The Power of Appreciation

What is Gratitude?

Gratitude is the quality of being thankful and showing appreciation for the good things in life. It involves recognizing the positive aspects of our experiences and the kindness of others. Gratitude is not just a fleeting feeling; it is a deeper emotional response that encourages us to acknowledge and appreciate what we have, rather than focusing on what we lack.

At its core, gratitude involves two main components:

1. **Recognition of Positivity**: Gratitude requires us to notice and appreciate the positive experiences, relationships, and moments in our lives. This can include simple things like enjoying a beautiful sunset, receiving help from a friend, or savouring a delicious meal.

2. **Acknowledgment of Others**: Gratitude often involves recognizing the contributions of other people in our lives. This could be thanking someone for their support, kindness, or efforts that have positively impacted us. It emphasizes the interconnectedness we have with others and the importance of acknowledging their role in our happiness.

Gratitude can be expressed in various ways, including verbal thanks, written notes, or acts of kindness. It is a powerful emotion that can improve our overall well-being, foster positive relationships, and enhance our outlook on life. Practicing gratitude regularly can lead to a more positive mindset, greater life satisfaction, and improved mental health.

Why Gratitude is Important

Gratitude is especially important for young people as it plays a crucial role in their emotional and social development. Here are some key reasons why practicing gratitude is beneficial for them, along with examples:

1. **Enhances Mental Health**: Practicing gratitude can significantly improve mental well-being. Young people often face stress from school, social pressures, and personal challenges. Regularly reflecting on what they are thankful for can reduce feelings of anxiety and depression. For example, a teenager who keeps a gratitude journal

may find that writing down three things they appreciate each day helps them feel more positive and less overwhelmed.

2.   **Builds Resilience**: Gratitude fosters resilience by encouraging young people to focus on the positive aspects of their lives, even in difficult situations. When faced with challenges, such as poor grades or conflicts with friends, a grateful mindset helps them see the silver lining. For instance, a young student might be disappointed by a bad test score, but by reflecting on the support from their teachers and friends, they can find motivation to improve and learn from their mistakes.

3.   **Strengthens Relationships**: Expressing gratitude helps build and strengthen relationships. Young people who regularly thank their friends and family create a positive atmosphere, which encourages stronger bonds and mutual respect. For example, a child who regularly thanks their parents for their support or a friend who expresses appreciation for shared experiences fosters deeper connections and encourages others to reciprocate.

4.   **Promotes Positive Behaviour**: Gratitude encourages kindness and generosity. Young people who practice gratitude are more likely to engage in prosocial behaviours, such as helping others and volunteering. For instance, a teenager who feels thankful for their community might choose to organize a charity event or help at a local shelter, spreading positivity and encouraging others to do the same.

5.   **Increases Life Satisfaction**: Practicing gratitude helps young people appreciate what they have, leading to greater life satisfaction. Instead of constantly comparing themselves to others, they learn to value their unique experiences and achievements. For example, a young athlete might focus on their progress in sports rather than obsessing over not being the best player, leading to greater enjoyment and fulfilment in their activities.

Gratitude is essential for young people as it enhances their mental health, builds resilience, strengthens relationships, promotes positive behaviour, and increases overall life satisfaction. By cultivating gratitude, they can navigate the challenges of youth with a more positive and hopeful outlook.

Understanding the Power of Appreciation:

The Benefits of Practicing Gratitude

Practicing gratitude is a simple yet powerful way to improve overall well-being and happiness. When people appreciate what they have, rather than focusing on what they lack, they experience a range of emotional, social, and physical benefits. Here's a closer look at why gratitude can be transformative and the specific benefits it brings:

1. **Improves Mental Health**: Gratitude has been shown to reduce stress, anxiety, and depression. When people take time to reflect on things they're thankful for, they shift their focus from negative thoughts to positive experiences. This change in mindset can boost their mood and help them manage stress more effectively. For example, someone who writes down three things they're grateful for each day is likely to feel a lift in their spirits and greater resilience against stress.

2. **Enhances Physical Health**: People who practice gratitude often report better physical health and even improved sleep. The positive emotions generated by gratitude can lead to reduced blood pressure, a stronger immune system, and better sleep quality. Feeling thankful and satisfied reduces mental strain and allows the body to relax, which promotes better rest and overall health.

3. **Strengthens Relationships**: Expressing gratitude fosters stronger social bonds and trust. When people regularly thank and appreciate those around them, it creates a positive atmosphere that encourages closeness and understanding. Friends and family who feel valued are likely to reciprocate, resulting in deeper and more meaningful relationships. For example, regularly expressing gratitude to a friend can make the friendship more resilient and enjoyable.

4. **Increases Resilience**: Gratitude can help individuals cope with challenging situations. By focusing on what they're grateful for, people can find hope and strength even in tough times. For instance, someone who reflects on the support they receive from loved ones may feel more capable of handling a difficult situation. Gratitude helps people to see the good amidst the bad, encouraging perseverance and resilience.

5. **Boosts Self-Esteem**: Gratitude helps people value themselves and their unique experiences without comparison to others. By focusing on personal achievements and the positive aspects of life, individuals can develop greater self-worth and confidence. Rather than comparing themselves to others, they can feel content and satisfied with what they have, leading to a healthier self-image.

6. **Encourages Positive Actions**: People who are grateful tend to be kinder and more helpful. The feelings of appreciation can inspire them to give back, volunteer, or simply spread kindness. Gratitude can lead to a "pay-it-forward" mentality, where acts of kindness are passed along to others, creating a ripple effect of positivity.

In short, gratitude is a powerful practice that enhances mental and physical health, strengthens relationships, builds resilience, and boosts self-esteem. By cultivating gratitude in daily life, individuals can create a positive foundation that enriches all areas of life.

How Gratitude Impacts Mental and Emotional Well-Being

Gratitude has a profound effect on mental and emotional health, helping people to experience more happiness, peace, and resilience. Here's how practicing gratitude can uplift mental and emotional well-being:

1. **Boosts Positive Emotions**: Gratitude shifts focus to the positive aspects of life, allowing people to savor the good moments. By regularly reflecting on what they are thankful for, individuals can boost their sense of joy and contentment. Positive emotions like joy, love, and hope become more frequent, creating a happier, more balanced outlook.

2. **Reduces Anxiety and Depression**: Studies have shown that practicing gratitude can reduce symptoms of anxiety and depression. When people focus on things they appreciate, they train their minds to notice the good, reducing the tendency to dwell on worries or negative thoughts. This shift in focus can ease feelings of sadness and improve mental clarity.

3. **Enhances Self-Esteem**: Gratitude helps individuals feel valued and capable, which can strengthen self-esteem. By appreciating their achievements, relationships, and unique qualities, they foster a healthier self-image. This reduces self-doubt and creates a feeling of confidence and worthiness, even in the face of challenges.

4. **Promotes Resilience**: Grateful people tend to be more resilient when facing difficult situations. Gratitude helps individuals see challenges as temporary and manageable. For example, someone going through a tough time may feel stronger by focusing on support from friends or personal strengths. This perspective fosters courage and persistence, allowing them to face adversity with greater confidence.

5. **Encourages Mindfulness and Reduces Stress**: Gratitude brings awareness to the present moment, similar to mindfulness practices. By focusing on things, they appreciate here and now, people experience calmness and peace, which reduces stress. Instead of worrying about the past or future, gratitude helps them stay grounded, giving their minds a much-needed break from stress.

6. **Creates a Positive Mindset**: A gratitude practice rewires the brain to notice and emphasize the positives. Over time, people who regularly

practice gratitude become more optimistic, seeing opportunities rather than obstacles. This positive mindset can uplift moods, create hope, and encourage a proactive approach to life.

7. **Fosters Emotional Stability**: Gratitude helps people to process emotions and balance negative feelings with appreciation for the positives. By recognizing what is going well in their lives, they feel more grounded and less overwhelmed by temporary setbacks. This stability promotes overall emotional health, allowing people to better manage ups and downs.

In essence, gratitude nurtures a healthy, balanced mindset that strengthens mental and emotional well-being. By integrating gratitude into daily life, people can reduce stress, cultivate positivity, and build resilience, creating a foundation for greater happiness and peace.

Real-Life Examples of Gratitude

Gratitude can change lives in powerful ways, making people feel happier, more at peace, and ready to face challenges. Here are some personal stories showing how gratitude can make a difference.

1. **Appreciating Small Blessings – Bhumi's Story**

    Bhumi is a college student who feels overwhelmed by exams, projects, and endless assignments. Every day seems stressful and rushed, and she often finds herself worrying about the future. One day, her teacher suggests trying a gratitude journal to manage her stress.

    Bhumi decides to give it a try. Each night, she takes just a few minutes to write down three things she's grateful for. Sometimes it's as simple as a warm cup of tea her mother made, a friend's encouraging text, or the sunlight streaming through her window. She doesn't write big things; she just notes small comforts and happy moments in her day.

    Slowly, Bhumi begins to feel more positive. She notices how these small, good moments make her days feel easier. By focusing on what's going well, she stops stressing as much about what might go wrong. She realizes that even during hard times, there are moments to be thankful for. This simple habit helps her feel calm and balanced, even when exams are tough.

2. **Finding Strength During Hard Times – Sahil's Story**

    Sahil had been working at his job for many years, but suddenly, he was let go because his company had to make cuts. At first, Sahil felt lost and scared. He worried about how he would support his family and what he would do next. He felt a heavy weight on his shoulders.

Instead of giving up, Sahil decided to look for the positives in his life. He reminded himself of his supportive family, the friends who were there for him, and all the skills he had learned over the years. Every day, he tried to focus on these things instead of just his fears.

By practicing gratitude, Sahil started to feel stronger and more hopeful. His positive mindset helped him stay calm and gave him the courage to look for new job opportunities. His gratitude even helped him build better relationships with his family and friends, who saw him as a strong role model.

Eventually, Sahil found a new job that suited him well. He believes that focusing on gratitude helped him through one of the toughest times in his life.

3. **Learning to Appreciate Health – Meera's Story**

Meera is someone who rarely thought about her health until she fell seriously ill. During her recovery, she felt weak and frustrated, but she realized how much she missed simple things like going for a walk or cooking her favourite meal. This experience made her start appreciating her health more than ever.

When Meera finally recovered, she began to value every healthy day. She started to express gratitude for her body and for being able to do everyday things she once took for granted. Her attitude changed, and she became more positive and caring toward herself.

4. **Gratitude for Relationships – Ravi's Story**

Ravi used to take his family and friends for granted. He was always busy and didn't spend much time with them. One day, a close friend moved to another city, and Ravi realized he hadn't even spent much time with him before he left. This made him realize the importance of relationships.

Ravi decided to change. He started showing gratitude for his loved ones, calling them regularly, and spending quality time with his family. His relationships became closer, and he felt happier than before. He learned that showing gratitude for people in our lives brings deeper connections and joy.

5. **Finding Joy in the Present – Yogita's Story**

Yogita used to worry a lot about the future. She would stress over her job, money, and things she couldn't control. But then, a friend introduced her to the idea of gratitude and encouraged her to start noticing the good things happening each day.

Yogita began small. She started by appreciating her morning coffee, the fresh air during her walk to work, and the support of her coworkers. Soon, she realized that her mind was calmer and her heart was lighter. By focusing on what she had instead of what she lacked, she found more joy in the present. This shift helped her enjoy life more and worry less.

These stories show that gratitude is a powerful tool. No matter what challenges you face, focusing on things to be grateful for can lift your mood, improve relationships, and give you strength. Practicing gratitude is simple, but it brings real happiness and peace into everyday life.

Ways to Cultivate Gratitude

Practicing gratitude daily can bring a positive change to our lives by helping us focus on the good things we already have. Below are a few simple methods to incorporate gratitude into your day-to-day routine.

1. **Daily Gratitude Practices**

   Creating a habit of gratitude takes just a few minutes each day, but it can significantly shift your perspective. Here are some popular methods:

   - **Gratitude Journaling**: Keep a small journal where you write down a few things you're grateful for each day. It could be something as simple as enjoying a nice cup of tea, a good conversation, or a moment of peace. Over time, you'll see how many positive things happen in your life, no matter how small.

   - **Gratitude Lists**: Similar to journaling, making a gratitude list can be an effective way to remind yourself of the good things in life. At the end of the day, write a list of three things that went well or things you appreciated. This habit can help end your day on a positive note.

   - **Gratitude Letters**: Sometimes, writing a letter to someone you appreciate can be a powerful act of gratitude. You can write to a friend, family member, teacher, or even someone who did something kind for you. Share why you're grateful for them and the positive impact they've had on you. You don't always have to send the letter, but writing it helps you acknowledge the people who enrich your life.

   - **Expressing Thanks in Person**: Don't overlook simple verbal gratitude. Saying "thank you" directly to someone can be powerful and uplifting for both you and the person you thank. For example, thanking a colleague for their hard work or expressing appreciation to a family member can strengthen your relationships and build positivity.

2. **Mindfulness Techniques to Enhance Appreciation**

   Mindfulness can help deepen our sense of gratitude by encouraging us to live in the present moment and fully experience life. Here are a few mindfulness practices that can enhance your appreciation:

   - **Mindful Observing:** Take a few moments to notice the world around you—nature, people, sounds, or colours. This practice helps you become aware of things we often take for granted. Observing a beautiful sunset, feeling a breeze, or hearing birds chirping are all moments to appreciate. By tuning in, you may feel a stronger sense of gratitude for the beauty that surrounds you daily.

   - **Breathing Exercises:** Slow, deep breathing helps calm your mind and center your thoughts. Take a few minutes to close your eyes and focus on your breathing. As you breathe, think of something or someone you're grateful for with each breath in. This can help you cultivate a sense of appreciation and peace.

   - **Savouring Moments:** Instead of rushing through your day, try savouring simple moments. Enjoy a cup of tea slowly, take a mindful walk, or spend a few extra moments with family. Savouring these moments allows you to appreciate the experience, which helps in nurturing a grateful mindset.

   - **Body Scan Meditation:** A body scan involves focusing on each part of your body from head to toe, noticing any sensations or tension. As you do this, appreciate each part for what it allows you to do—seeing, hearing, walking, or even resting. This practice helps you acknowledge and appreciate your body and all it does for you.

By incorporating these daily gratitude practices and mindfulness techniques, you can make gratitude a natural part of your life. These small acts of appreciation can improve your mood, build resilience, and help you handle challenges with a positive outlook. Gratitude is like a muscle—the more you use it, the stronger it becomes, making it easier to appreciate both big and small blessings.

Gratitude in Relationships

Gratitude plays a powerful role in building and strengthening our relationships. When we express appreciation to the people around us, it creates a positive cycle of kindness, empathy, and understanding that brings us closer together.

How Expressing Gratitude Strengthens Connections with Others

Expressing gratitude in relationships shows others that we value and appreciate them. This can be as simple as saying "thank you" for a small favour, acknowledging a friend's support during tough times, or complimenting a family member for their efforts. These gestures may seem small, but they make others feel seen, valued, and loved.

For example, if you thank a friend for always being there for you, they feel appreciated and will likely continue to support you, knowing their presence matters. Gratitude reminds us not to take people for granted, and by sharing our appreciation, we create deeper, more meaningful bonds with those around us.

In a family setting, expressing gratitude strengthens connections by reducing conflicts and misunderstandings. It builds a supportive and positive environment where everyone feels important. Regularly sharing appreciation in small ways—like thanking a sibling for their help or showing love to parents—creates a warm atmosphere where kindness flows naturally.

The Role of Gratitude in Fostering Empathy and Kindness

Gratitude also helps us develop empathy—the ability to understand and share the feelings of others. When we practice gratitude, we start to see the good in people and the efforts they make for us. This understanding helps us connect with their experiences and emotions, making us more compassionate and willing to support them in return.

For example, when a colleague stays late to help you with a project, expressing gratitude not only shows you appreciate their help, but it also opens your heart to their efforts and sacrifices. Recognizing this builds a sense of empathy and inspires you to be there for them when they need it.

When people feel appreciated, they are often more willing to show kindness and patience in return. This cycle of appreciation leads to stronger and more resilient relationships. Over time, expressing gratitude encourages us to be kinder and more forgiving, reducing negative feelings and creating a positive ripple effect in our communities.

In short, gratitude is like glue in relationships; it brings people closer and strengthens bonds. By appreciating the small and big ways that others make a difference in our lives, we build a foundation of love, kindness, and trust that can withstand the ups and downs of life.

Overcoming Challenges to Gratitude

Sometimes, feeling grateful isn't easy, especially when we're dealing with stress, negativity, or tough times. Yet, gratitude can be even more valuable in difficult moments. Here, we'll discuss some common barriers to gratitude and offer tips to help cultivate it during challenging times.

Common Barriers to Feeling Grateful

1. **Stress and Anxiety**: When we're stressed or anxious, our minds tend to focus on problems or worries. This focus can make it difficult to appreciate positive things, as we're preoccupied with handling challenges.

2. **Negative Experiences or Loss**: Facing hardship, such as a loss or a painful event, can make gratitude feel out of reach. In these times, it may be hard to see the good in life or even want to acknowledge it.

3. **Comparison with Others**: Social media and daily interactions often lead to comparisons, which can make us feel like we lack something others have. This mindset shifts our focus away from appreciating what we have and instead fosters feelings of inadequacy or envy.

4. **High Expectations**: Sometimes, we have high standards or expectations of ourselves, our lives, or those around us. When reality doesn't meet these expectations, it can lead to disappointment and make us less likely to feel grateful.

Tips for Cultivating Gratitude in Difficult Times

1. **Start Small**: Even in challenging times, there are small moments or things to appreciate. Try noticing just one small positive thing each day—a warm cup of tea, a call from a friend, or even a good meal. Starting small helps build a habit of gratitude, which can gradually grow over time.

2. **Reframe Negative Thoughts**: Instead of focusing solely on the negative aspects, try looking for a small silver lining. For example, if you're dealing with a busy schedule, you might appreciate the growth it brings or the support of those helping you. Reframing can help you see something positive even in challenging situations.

3. **Practice Self-Compassion**: Being grateful for yourself and your resilience is essential. Instead of being hard on yourself during tough times, take a moment to appreciate your strengths, the lessons you're learning, or the support you give yourself.

4. **Find Gratitude in Small Acts**: In difficult times, small acts of kindness can go a long way. Offering gratitude to others, even in small gestures like saying "thank you" or complimenting someone, can help lift your own spirits. Gratitude often grows when we give it freely.

5. **Focus on the Present Moment**: When life is tough, worrying about the future or dwelling on the past can make gratitude hard to find. Practicing mindfulness can bring your attention back to the present, helping you notice the small, good things around you right now.

6. **Keep a "Gratitude Anchor"**: Having an item, photo, or journal as a reminder of things you're grateful for can serve as an anchor in difficult times. This could be a small object or note that brings you comfort and reminds you of the positives in your life.

7. **Express Gratitude Out Loud**: Talking about what you're thankful for with others can make it feel more real and genuine. Even in challenging times, sharing these thoughts with a friend or family member can bring positivity to your mindset.

By recognizing and addressing these barriers, you can build resilience and make gratitude a supportive tool, even in life's harder moments. Remember that gratitude doesn't mean ignoring challenges—it's about finding strength and positivity within them.

Gratitude as a Tool for Personal Growth

Gratitude is more than just a feeling—it can be a powerful tool for personal growth and development. When we practice gratitude, we create positive changes in our mindset that can help us build resilience, stay motivated, and move toward our goals. Let's explore how gratitude leads to personal growth and strengthens our ability to face challenges.

How Gratitude Can Lead to Positive Changes and Personal Development

1. **Increased Positivity and Happiness**: Practicing gratitude regularly shifts our focus from what we lack to what we already have. This shift promotes a positive mindset, helping us feel happier and more content with our lives. Over time, this positivity can improve our overall outlook and give us a stronger foundation for growth.

2. **Enhanced Self-Reflection**: When we take time to be grateful, we also become more aware of ourselves and our lives. This awareness helps us reflect on what's important to us, what we value, and what we want to improve. It encourages us to appreciate our journey and celebrate our progress.

3. **Motivation to Reach Goals**: By focusing on the positives, we feel more motivated to set and achieve our goals. For example, gratitude helps us recognize our strengths, the support we receive from others, and the opportunities available to us. This recognition builds confidence and reminds us that we're capable of moving forward, even if the path is challenging.

4. **Better Relationships and Support Networks**: Practicing gratitude also strengthens relationships, as we naturally appreciate and value the people around us. Stronger relationships mean we have a solid support network, which is essential for personal growth. Friends, family, and mentors who feel appreciated are more likely to offer support, encouragement, and guidance as we pursue our goals.

5. **Greater Sense of Purpose**: Gratitude reminds us to appreciate small successes and stay connected to what truly matters. This can help us develop a sense of purpose, as we become more mindful of the things that bring us joy and fulfilment. With a sense of purpose, we're more likely to focus on meaningful goals and work toward them with determination.

The Connection Between Gratitude and Resilience

1. **Finding Strength in Challenges**: Gratitude helps us see challenges from a different perspective. Instead of being overwhelmed, we learn to look for positive aspects even in difficult situations—whether it's a lesson learned, a skill gained, or support from others. This perspective makes it easier to adapt and find strength in adversity.

2. **Encouraging a Growth Mindset**: Resilience requires a growth mindset—the belief that challenges can help us grow. Practicing gratitude supports this by helping us see setbacks as opportunities rather than roadblocks. With gratitude, we're less likely to view failures negatively; instead, we view them as stepping stones to growth.

3. **Emotional Stability**: In tough times, gratitude can serve as a grounding force, helping us stay calm and balanced. This stability gives us the resilience to handle stress and uncertainty more effectively. We become less reactive to temporary hardships and can focus on long-term goals.

4. **Developing Patience and Endurance**: Building resilience isn't always easy; it takes patience and endurance. Gratitude fosters both by encouraging us to appreciate small steps and progress rather than expecting instant success. This patient approach to life helps us keep going, even when challenges arise.

5. **Boosting Self-Compassion**: Being grateful also means being kind to ourselves. When we practice self-compassion, we're more forgiving of our mistakes and less harsh on ourselves during tough times. This self-compassion adds to our resilience, allowing us to stay motivated and hopeful even in difficult situations.

By incorporating gratitude into our daily lives, we not only become more positive and motivated, but we also build a strong foundation for resilience. Gratitude encourages us to grow, adapt, and become the best version of ourselves. It teaches us that every challenge, big or small, can be a valuable step on our journey to personal development.

Activities to Practice Gratitude

Practicing gratitude doesn't have to be complicated—it can be as simple as paying attention to the positives around you. Here are some easy exercises to help incorporate gratitude into daily life, as well as group activities for sharing gratitude with others.

Simple Exercises to Incorporate Gratitude into Daily Life

1. **Daily Gratitude Journal**: Spend a few minutes each day writing down three things you're grateful for. This could be something as simple as a good meal, a conversation, or even a moment of peace. Keeping a gratitude journal helps you focus on positive experiences, lifting your mood and improving your outlook over time.

2. **Gratitude List**: Start your day by listing things you appreciate about your life. You can keep this list on your phone or notebook, adding new items as you think of them. Looking back at your list on difficult days can be a great way to boost your spirits.

3. **Thank-You Notes**: Take a moment to write a short thank-you note or message to someone who has helped or inspired you. It could be a friend, teacher, family member, or even a coworker. Expressing gratitude not only makes them feel good but also deepens your relationship with them.

4. **Mindful Gratitude**: While doing everyday tasks, like eating or walking, try to mindfully focus on something you're grateful for in that moment. For example, while eating, think about the people who made your meal possible—the farmers, the cook, and even the person who served it. This mindfulness can increase your appreciation for small things we often overlook.

5. **Evening Reflection**: Before going to bed, think of one positive thing that happened during the day. Reflecting on this small success or joyful moment helps end your day on a positive note, setting you up for a peaceful sleep and a positive outlook for the next day.

Group Activities for Sharing Gratitude with Others

1. **Gratitude Circle**: Gather friends or family and form a circle. Take turns sharing one thing you're grateful for. Hearing each other's

responses often brings smiles and laughter, reminding everyone of the good things in their lives and building stronger connections within the group.

2.   **Group Gratitude Jar**: Place a jar in a common area and encourage everyone to write down something they're thankful for each day on a small piece of paper. After a week or month, open the jar together and read through the notes. This is a fun way to celebrate positivity and appreciate each other's contributions to the group.

3.   **Thankful Thursdays**: Pick one day a week, like Thursday, and make it a gratitude-focused day with family, friends, or coworkers. Each person shares something they're grateful for, and you can even make it a regular habit by sharing over a meal or meeting.

4.   **Gratitude Partner**: Pair up with someone and agree to check in with each other once a week. Share things you're both grateful for and encourage each other to stay positive, especially during challenging times. Having a gratitude partner helps keep you both accountable and motivated.

5.   **Random Acts of Kindness**: Plan a group activity where everyone performs a small, random act of kindness, such as writing a thank-you note to a teacher, helping a neighbour, or complimenting a friend. Afterward, gather to share your experiences. This practice creates a cycle of gratitude and spreads positivity to others as well.

These activities are easy to incorporate into daily life and can help you experience the power of gratitude firsthand. Whether practiced alone or with others, they encourage a mindset of appreciation that makes life more fulfilling and joyful.

Key Notes on Gratitude

Here's a quick summary of the main ideas discussed in this chapter, along with some actionable insights to help you start practicing gratitude in your everyday life.

1.   **Understanding Gratitude**: Gratitude is about recognizing and appreciating the positive aspects of life, no matter how small they may seem. It involves focusing on what we have rather than what we lack.

2.   **Importance of Gratitude**: Practicing gratitude has a positive impact on mental and emotional well-being. It can reduce stress, improve relationships, and boost resilience, making us better able to face challenges.

3. **Gratitude in Relationships**: Expressing gratitude strengthens connections with others. When we show appreciation for the people around us, it fosters empathy, kindness, and a sense of belonging.

4. **Overcoming Challenges to Gratitude**: It's natural to struggle with feeling grateful during tough times, but overcoming barriers like stress or negativity can help you find a silver lining in any situation.

5. **Gratitude as a Tool for Personal Growth**: Embracing gratitude encourages personal development and resilience, helping you focus on growth and positivity even in difficult moments.

Actionable Insights for Practicing Gratitude

1. **Start a Daily Gratitude Journal**: Dedicate a few minutes each day to writing down three things you're grateful for. This helps you develop a habit of appreciating positive moments regularly.

2. **Express Appreciation to Others**: Tell friends, family, and coworkers what you appreciate about them. A simple "thank you" or a thoughtful note can go a long way in strengthening your relationships.

3. **Create a Gratitude List**: Keep an ongoing list of things you're thankful for. When you're feeling down, revisiting this list can remind you of the positives in your life.

4. **Practice Mindful Gratitude**: Throughout the day, try to be aware of little things that bring joy or comfort—such as a good meal, fresh air, or a kind interaction. Pause to acknowledge and appreciate them.

5. **Engage in Group Gratitude Activities**: Try gratitude exercises with friends or family, like sharing what you're thankful for during meals, or creating a gratitude jar that everyone contributes to.

6. **Overcome Challenges to Gratitude**: If you find it hard to feel grateful, start small and try focusing on one positive thing each day. Surround yourself with positive people and remember that it's okay to take time to build the habit.

These simple yet powerful actions can help you cultivate a mindset of gratitude. Remember, gratitude isn't about ignoring difficulties—it's about finding value in the positive aspects of life and building resilience to face challenges. Implementing these practices will lead to a more fulfilling, connected, and joyful life.

In *The Ultimate Life Toolbox: Discover the Secrets to a Confident and Peaceful Life*, we have explored the transformative power of gratitude. Gratitude is not merely a polite gesture; it is a vital tool that can significantly enhance our mental and emotional well-being. It shifts our focus from what is lacking in our lives to what is abundant, fostering a sense of appreciation for even the simplest joys.

As we wrap up this chapter on gratitude, it is important to recognize that cultivating a grateful mindset is essential for a fulfilling life. By actively practicing gratitude, we can strengthen our relationships, foster kindness, and enhance our overall resilience. These practices are not just fleeting moments of appreciation; they are foundational habits that contribute to our growth and happiness.

I encourage you to integrate gratitude into your daily life as outlined in this book. Start by keeping a gratitude journal, expressing thanks to those around you, or simply taking a moment each day to reflect on the positives in your life. Each small step you take in embracing gratitude can lead to profound changes in your outlook and experiences.

Remember, the journey to living a life filled with appreciation is continuous. By embracing gratitude, you open the door to a more fulfilling existence, where every day offers something to celebrate. Let *The Ultimate Life Toolbox* serve as a guide, reminding you that with gratitude, you can navigate life's challenges with a lighter heart and a more joyful spirit. Embrace gratitude, and allow it to illuminate your path as you journey through life.

Chapter 6

Gutt and Mind Connection
Gut Health & Mental Well-Being

What is the Gut & Brain Connection?

The **Gut-Brain Connection** refers to the two-way communication between the gastrointestinal system (gut) and the brain. This complex relationship is mediated through the **vagus nerve**, a critical part of the nervous system that transmits signals between the gut and the brain. The gut is often referred to as the "second brain" because it contains millions of neurons, similar to the spinal cord, which play an essential role in regulating emotions, thoughts, and behaviours.

The gut-brain axis affects various aspects of health, including mental well-being. The gut is home to a large number of microorganisms, also known as the **gut microbiome**, which produce neurotransmitters (like **serotonin**) that influence mood, anxiety levels, and cognitive function. Disruptions in this microbiome can lead to mental health issues such as anxiety, depression, and stress.

Additionally, the brain can influence gut health. Chronic stress, for instance, can upset the balance of the gut microbiome, leading to inflammation, digestive issues, and further mental health challenges. The **gut-brain axis** plays a role in conditions such as **Irritable Bowel Syndrome (IBS)** and **depression**, which are often interconnected.

The gut and mind connection has been discussed in various lectures and podcasts, emphasizing the important relationship between gut health and mental well-being. Key points include:

1. **Gut-Brain Communication**: The gut and brain are linked through the vagus nerve, affecting emotional and mental health. Imbalances in the gut microbiome can lead to mood swings, anxiety, and depression.

2. **Gut's Role in Mental Health**: A healthy gut microbiome is vital for maintaining a positive mental state, affecting neurotransmitters like serotonin that regulate mood.

3. **Impact of Stress**: Chronic stress disrupts the gut-brain connection, leading to gut imbalances and affecting mental clarity and stability.

4. **The Power of Nutrition**: A diet rich in fiber, probiotics, and nutrients supports a healthy gut microbiome and mental health.

5. **Holistic Approach**: A holistic approach to mental health includes managing stress, physical activity, and emotional well-being, with mindfulness and meditation being key.

These insights highlight how gut health directly influences mental well-being, emphasizing the importance of a balanced gut microbiome.

Why Gut Health Matters for Mental Well-Being

Research shows that improving gut health through diet, probiotics, and stress management can positively impact mental health. Practices like mindfulness, a healthy diet rich in fibre and probiotics, and reducing stress can improve the gut microbiome and, consequently, mental well-being.

Gut health has a powerful impact on mental well-being because of the **gut-brain connection**, a communication network between the digestive system and the brain. The gut is sometimes called the **"second brain"** due to its extensive network of neurons and its ability to produce neurotransmitters like serotonin and dopamine, which influence mood and emotions. This connection means that an unhealthy gut—often caused by poor diet, stress, or inflammation—can disrupt neurotransmitter production and lead to mood swings, anxiety, or even depression.

In a balanced state, the gut microbiome helps reduce inflammation, support brain function, and promote feelings of well-being. Studies show that a healthy gut can boost resilience to stress and improve overall emotional stability. On the other hand, an imbalance in gut bacteria, known as dysbiosis, has been linked to mental health disorders. Thus, maintaining a healthy gut can play a crucial role in promoting both emotional stability and psychological resilience.

How the Gut Affects Mental Health

The gut has a surprisingly significant role in influencing mental health due to its deep connection to the brain, often called the "gut-brain axis."

1. **The Microbiome's Role in Emotions**

    - **Understanding the Microbiome**: The gut houses trillions of bacteria, collectively called the gut microbiome, which plays a central role in digestive health. However, these bacteria do more than aid in digestion—they impact emotions and mood. A balanced microbiome contributes to a stable mental state, while an imbalance (often from diet, antibiotics, or stress) can disrupt mental well-being.

    - **Gut Imbalance and Mental Health**: When the microbiome is out of balance (a state known as dysbiosis), it can contribute to anxiety, depression, and mood swings. Dysbiosis can increase inflammation in the body and brain, potentially leading to emotional disturbances. Studies suggest that certain types of gut bacteria may produce metabolites that have a calming effect, while others may exacerbate stress and anxiety.

2. **The Role of Neurotransmitters**

- **Serotonin and Neurotransmitter Production**: The gut produces around 90% of the body's serotonin—a key neurotransmitter that regulates mood, sleep, and appetite. Other neurotransmitters, like dopamine and gamma-aminobutyric acid (GABA), are also produced in the gut, and these chemicals play vital roles in reducing stress and enhancing mood.

- **Impact on Mood and Mental Health**: The neurotransmit-ters produced in the gut travel to the brain through the bloodstream and the vagus nerve, directly affecting emotional well-being. A healthy gut helps maintain balanced neurotransmitter levels, while an unhealthy gut can lead to lower production of these mood-regulating chemicals, potentially causing mood disorders and impacting overall mental health.

Understanding the gut's impact on mental health highlights the importance of maintaining a balanced microbiome through a nutritious diet, stress management, and healthy lifestyle choices.

The Impact of Stress on Gut Health

Stress significantly impacts both gut health and mental well-being, primarily due to its effect on the gut-brain axis, which is the communication network between the brain and gut. Here's a breakdown of how stress influences gut health.

1. **Stress and the Gut-Brain Axis**

- **How Stress Impacts Gut Function**: Stress triggers the release of hormones like cortisol, which can affect the gut in various ways. Under stress, the digestive system may slow down, speed up, or experience spasms, leading to symptoms like indigestion, bloating, and changes in bowel habits. Prolonged stress can even damage the lining of the gut, making it more permeable—a condition often called "leaky gut." This allows toxins and harmful bacteria to enter the bloodstream, which can further exacerbate stress and anxiety.

- **Chronic Stress, Mental Clarity, and Emotional Stability**: When stress becomes chronic, it can lead to persistent inflammation in the gut, affecting not just digestion but also mental clarity and mood. Chronic inflammation may interfere with the production of essential neurotransmitters in the gut, like serotonin and dopamine, which play a key role in emotional stability. This often results in increased anxiety, mood swings, and even depression, as the gut struggles to maintain balance.

2. **Insights on Stress and the Gut**

- **Stress and Microbiome Disruption**: Many doctors emphasize how stress can disrupt the balance of gut bacteria, leading to a negative cycle between mental and digestive health. Stress-induced changes in the microbiome can reduce the population of beneficial bacteria, which are essential for gut health and emotional well-being. An imbalance in the microbiome often translates to heightened stress and reduced resilience against daily challenges, creating a feedback loop that exacerbates mental health struggles.

- **Linking Gut Disruptions to Mental Health Challenges**: Doctors explain that stress affects not only the body but also mental clarity and emotional regulation. By impacting the gut microbiome, stress diminishes the gut's ability to produce mood-stabilizing neurotransmitters. Understanding and managing stress can improve gut health, helping individuals maintain mental clarity and a stable emotional state.

In summary, stress has a profound impact on gut health by disrupting gut function and altering the microbiome balance, which can lead to mental health issues. Doctor's approach underlines the importance of managing stress to support both physical and emotional health, as the state of the gut strongly influences our overall well-being.

The Importance of Diet for Mental Health

Diet plays a crucial role in supporting both gut health and mental well-being. Here's a breakdown of how specific foods influence the gut microbiome, mood, and cognitive function.

1. **Foods that Support Gut Health**

- **Gut-Balancing Foods:**
    - **Fiber-Rich Foods**: Fiber is essential for maintaining a healthy gut microbiome, as it feeds beneficial bacteria. Vegetables, fruits, legumes, and whole grains are excellent sources of fibre, which promotes digestion and supports gut health.
    - **Probiotics**: These are live beneficial bacteria that help balance gut flora. Foods like yogurt, kefir, sauerkraut, kimchi,

and miso are rich in probiotics, which can enhance gut health and potentially reduce anxiety and stress by stabilizing the gut-brain axis.

- **Prebiotics**: Prebiotics serve as food for probiotics, helping them thrive. Common sources include garlic, onions, bananas, and asparagus. These foods contribute to a balanced gut, indirectly promoting better mood regulation.
- **How a Healthy Gut Enhances Mood and Cognitive Function**:
  - A healthy gut produces essential neurotransmitters like serotonin and dopamine, which are responsible for stabilizing mood and improving mental clarity. By nurturing gut health through diet, you can potentially improve emotional stability, reduce anxiety, and support cognitive health.

2. **Nutritional Recommendations**
   - **Foods for Physical and Mental Well-Being**: Many doctors emphasize the importance of a balanced diet for mental and physical health. He recommends foods rich in omega-3 fatty acids, such as fatty fish, flaxseeds, and walnuts, as they support brain health and reduce inflammation. He also advises on incorporating leafy greens, which are packed with vitamins and antioxidants that support both physical and mental well-being.
   - **Mindful Eating for Mental Clarity**: Doctors suggest that mindful eating practices—such as focusing on whole, minimally processed foods—can help enhance both mental clarity and emotional stability. By avoiding processed foods high in sugars and unhealthy fats, you reduce the risk of inflammation and mood swings, supporting a more balanced mental state.

In summary, a diet that includes fiber, probiotics, and nutrient-dense foods can support gut health, improve mood, and enhance cognitive function. Following doctor's recommendations, incorporating omega-3s, leafy greens, and whole foods can further boost both mental and physical well-being, making diet a key aspect of maintaining a healthy mind-gut connection.

The Vagus Nerve and Emotional Health

The vagus nerve plays a central role in connecting the gut and the brain, profoundly influencing emotional health and mental well-being.

1. The Vagus Nerve's Role in the Gut-Brain Connection
   - **Link Between Gut and Brain**: The vagus nerve is the primary communication pathway that connects the gut and the brain. It sends signals from the gut directly to the brain and vice versa,

allowing them to influence each other. This bidirectional link means that when the gut experiences issues (like inflammation or bacterial imbalance), it can affect mood, stress levels, and emotional health. Similarly, the brain can impact gut health, especially under stress.

- **Influence on Emotional and Physical Reactions**: Through the vagus nerve, signals can trigger the release of neurotransmitters and hormones like serotonin and dopamine, which regulate mood and emotions. A healthy, well-functioning vagus nerve helps maintain a balance of these chemicals, supporting mental clarity and emotional resilience.

2. **How Stimulating the Vagus Nerve Can Improve Emotional and Mental Health**

- **Vagus Nerve Stimulation (VNS)**: Stimulating the vagus nerve has been found to enhance mood and reduce symptoms of depression and anxiety. Techniques to stimulate the vagus nerve include deep breathing exercises, meditation, and cold exposure (such as splashing cold water on the face).

- **Benefits of VNS for Mental Health**: VNS helps activate the parasympathetic nervous system, which counters the effects of stress by calming the body and mind. By enhancing this connection, VNS promotes a more relaxed state, reducing stress, improving mood stability, and even boosting cognitive function.

The vagus nerve is a vital bridge between the gut and brain, and actively supporting it can lead to improved emotional health, better stress management, and greater overall well-being.

Techniques to Support the Vagus Nerve

Supporting the vagus nerve can have significant benefits for mental and emotional health, and simple practices can help activate and strengthen this vital nerve.

Techniques to Activate the Vagus Nerve:

- **Deep Breathing**: Slow, deep breathing—especially diaphragmatic breathing (breathing deeply into the belly)—stimulates the vagus nerve and activates the parasympathetic nervous system. Try inhaling slowly through your nose, holding the breath for a few seconds, and exhaling slowly. This can promote calmness and reduce stress.

- **Mindfulness and Meditation**: Practicing mindfulness or meditation encourages a relaxed state, which supports vagus nerve function. Techniques such as body scan meditation, where you focus on each part of your body, or mindfulness breathing exercises can help.

- **Cold Exposure**: Exposing the body to cold, like splashing cold water on the face or taking a cold shower, can stimulate the vagus nerve. Cold exposure activates the nerve, which can help improve resilience to stress.

- **Gentle Exercise**: Activities such as yoga, tai chi, and moderate aerobic exercise are shown to increase vagal tone, which helps the body manage stress and improves emotional balance.

- **Humming or Singing**: The vagus nerve passes through the vocal cords, so activities like humming, chanting, or singing can stimulate it. This simple technique can help reduce stress and promote a sense of relaxation.

Each of these practices supports vagus nerve activity, contributing to improved mood regulation, reduced anxiety, and better stress response over time.

Holistic Approaches to Gut and Mental Health

Holistic approaches consider the body and mind as interconnected, aiming to improve both physical and emotional well-being simultaneously. Focusing on gut health alongside mental health practices supports overall wellness and resilience to stress.

Combining Gut Health with Mental Health Practices

- **Importance of a Holistic Approach**: Addressing both gut and mental health together can enhance overall well-being. For example, a balanced diet promotes gut health, which, in turn, supports mental clarity and emotional stability. Combining nutritional habits with mental health practices like mindfulness and stress management yields more comprehensive results.

- **Exercise, Stress Management, and Sleep**: Regular physical activity, quality sleep, and effective stress management practices are foundational for both gut and mental health. Exercise promotes a healthy microbiome, while restful sleep allows the gut and brain to restore. Managing stress reduces inflammation in the gut and enhances mood, forming a supportive cycle.

Holistic Recommendations

- **Mindfulness and Meditation**: Doctors emphasize practices like mindfulness and meditation, which benefit both the mind and the gut. These practices calm the nervous system, reducing stress and helping maintain a balanced microbiome.

- **Other Practices for Gut and Brain Health**: Additional techniques recommended include breathing exercises, yoga, and incorporating whole foods with probiotics, which foster a supportive environment for both gut health and mental resilience.

Practical Tips for Improving Gut and Mental Health

Lifestyle Changes for Better Gut and Brain Health

- **Diet Adjustments**: Prioritize foods that are rich in fiber, prebiotics, and probiotics, such as leafy greens, fruits, whole grains, and yogurt. These support a healthy microbiome, which in turn positively impacts mood and cognitive functions.
- **Regular Exercise**: Engaging in physical activity, like walking, running, or yoga, is beneficial for gut health by promoting good digestion and reducing stress, which affects mental well-being.
- **Stress Reduction**: Managing stress through activities like deep breathing, mindfulness, and adequate rest helps maintain gut health. Chronic stress can lead to inflammation and gut imbalance, which may impact emotional health.
- **Quality Sleep**: Getting sufficient, uninterrupted sleep allows the gut and brain to repair and process information, supporting overall emotional resilience.

Personal Recommendations

- **Stress Management**: Doctors recommend regular practices like meditation, breathing exercises, and spending time in nature as effective ways to reduce stress and support both gut and brain health.
- **Mindful Eating**: Focusing on food quality, eating slowly, and avoiding overly processed foods are among his suggestions to improve digestion, reduce gut-related issues, and promote mental clarity.
- **Holistic Living**: Emphasizing the integration of balanced nutrition, exercise, and relaxation routines for a lifestyle that nurtures both physical and mental wellness, fostering a healthy gut-brain connection.

These practices create a strong foundation for better mental clarity, emotional stability, and improved gut function, promoting a cycle of wellness across body and mind.

Real-Life Examples from Lectures and Podcasts
Case Studies and Examples from Many Doctors & Nutritionists

- **Stories of Transformation**: Doctors often share real-life cases of individuals who experienced significant mental well-being improvements by addressing their gut health. For instance, one common case he discusses involves a person who struggled with chronic stress and anxiety. Through dietary adjustments, mindfulness practices, and focusing on gut health, they noticed a remarkable decrease in anxiety levels and an increase in daily energy.

- **Enhanced Emotional Resilience**: Another example highlights someone who had been facing severe mood swings. By incorporating probiotic-rich foods and reducing processed foods, they were able to stabilize their emotions, which in turn helped them handle personal and professional challenges more effectively.

Impact of Gut Health on Personal Growth and Success

- **Improved Focus and Productivity**: Doctor's talks often emphasize how improved gut health can boost productivity. One example features an entrepreneur who, after focusing on gut-friendly habits like better nutrition and regular exercise, found greater mental clarity and decision-making abilities, directly benefiting their career.

- **Increased Motivation and Optimism**: Stories of individuals who, after managing gut health through a balanced diet and relaxation techniques, found a renewed sense of motivation and optimism in their personal lives. This often led to increased confidence, willingness to take on new projects, and overall growth, both mentally and professionally.

These real-life examples illustrate the powerful influence of gut health on mental and emotional well-being, demonstrating how small changes can lead to significant personal and professional gains.

Keynotes on Real-Life Examples from Lectures and Podcasts of Nutritionists

- **Transformation through Gut Health:**
  - Individuals experienced reduced anxiety and stress after improving gut health through dietary changes and mindfulness.

- **Enhanced Emotional Stability:**
  - Stories of people overcoming mood swings and achieving emotional balance with gut-focused strategies.

- **Improved Focus and Productivity:**
  - Entrepreneurs saw increased clarity and decision-making after adopting gut-friendly habits.

- **Boosted Motivation and Personal Growth:**
  - Individuals found greater motivation and confidence, improving personal and professional life.

- **Practical Case Studies:**
  - Doctors share how focusing on gut health led to tangible improvements in mental well-being, personal growth, and success.

Additional Resources

Here are some recommended books on the "Gut and Mind" connection that explore how gut health impacts mental well-being:

1. **"The Mind-Gut Connection"** by Emeran Mayer - This book provides insights into how the brain and gut communicate and the role of the gut microbiome in mental health, with practical advice for optimizing brain-gut health.

2. **"The Second Brain"** by Michael D. Gershon - A detailed exploration of the enteric nervous system, often called the "second brain," and its profound influence on mood, behaviour, and mental health.

3. **"Brain Maker"** by David Perlmutter - Discusses the connection between gut health and mental clarity, memory, and mood, emphasizing the importance of gut microbiota in maintaining brain health.

In conclusion, the gut-brain connection is a powerful and essential link that influences mental health, affecting our emotions, stress levels, mood, and cognitive functions. The gut, often referred to as our **"second brain,"** is slowly gaining recognition as a primary center for mental well-being, with scientists acknowledging its vital role in brain health. Prioritizing gut health through diet, stress management, and mindfulness can have a significant impact on mental well-being, leading to improved emotional balance and overall health. A holistic approach that includes nurturing both the gut and the mind is key to long-term well-being. For further exploration and practical tips, his podcasts and lectures offer valuable resources to deepen our understanding of how gut health shapes our mental state and personal growth.

Chapter 7

Positive Affirmations
Building a Positive Mindset
(Law of attraction & Subliminal)

What are Positive Affirmations?

Positive affirmations are short, powerful statements or phrases that you repeat to yourself with the intention of promoting positive thinking and changing negative thought patterns. They help to encourage a mindset shift by focusing on positive beliefs and goals, rather than doubts or fears. The idea is to use these affirmations to program your mind for success, happiness, and confidence.

For example, a positive affirmation might be:

- "I am confident and capable."
- "I attract success and positivity into my life."
- "Every day, I grow stronger and more resilient."

These affirmations can be repeated daily, helping to replace negative thoughts with empowering beliefs. The goal is to rewire your subconscious mind, making it easier for you to stay focused, motivated, and optimistic in various aspects of life.

Why they are important for developing a positive mindset

Positive affirmations are important for developing a positive mindset because they help rewire your brain to focus on empowering thoughts and beliefs rather than on negativity, fear, or self-doubt. Here's why they are so effective:

1. **Reprogramming Negative Thought Patterns**: Many of us grow up with negative self-talk or limiting beliefs that hold us back. Positive affirmations act like a tool to counter those negative patterns. Repeating affirmations helps break down self-doubt and encourages a shift towards a healthier, more optimistic outlook on life.

   Example: If someone has always believed they aren't good enough, they could use an affirmation like, "I am worthy and capable of achieving my goals." Over time, this repetition can help replace the negative belief with one that supports self-esteem and confidence.

2. **Focusing on What You Want**: Instead of focusing on what you don't want, positive affirmations encourage you to focus on what you do want in your life. This helps align your thoughts and actions towards your desired outcomes.

   Example: Rather than saying "I don't want to be stressed," an affirmation like "I am calm and in control" helps to focus the mind on the desired state of peace and balance.

3. **Building Self-Belief**: Regular use of affirmations helps you believe in your own potential and capabilities. When you believe in yourself, you're more likely to take action towards your goals and stay motivated.

   Example: An affirmation like "I am confident in my abilities" encourages someone to take on challenges with more assurance, rather than holding back due to self-doubt.

4. **Increased Resilience**: Positive affirmations help increase mental resilience by reminding you of your strengths and capacity to handle difficulties. This mindset makes it easier to navigate challenges without getting discouraged.

   Example: If you're facing a difficult task, an affirmation like "I am strong and capable of overcoming any obstacle" can help keep you grounded and focused on finding solutions.

5. **Positive Impact on Mental Health**: Using affirmations daily can help reduce stress and anxiety by promoting feelings of control and peace. They help to calm the mind and reduce the impact of negative thoughts on mental health.

   Example: Saying "I choose happiness and peace" daily can help reduce feelings of anxiety, allowing you to handle life's challenges more calmly.

By integrating positive affirmations into your daily routine, you create a habit of focusing on what you can control and what you want to manifest in your life. Over time, this leads to a more positive, optimistic mindset.

How Positive Affirmations Work

Positive affirmations work by influencing our thoughts, beliefs, and actions through the repeated use of empowering, positive statements. Here's how they work:

1. **The Power of Words in Shaping Thoughts and Beliefs**

   Words have a profound effect on our thoughts and beliefs. When we repeat words or phrases to ourselves, they shape our perception of the world and influence our emotions and actions. This is because our mind responds to what we tell it, consciously and unconsciously.

- **Words Affect Emotions**: When we say something positive, it triggers positive emotions. For example, telling yourself "I am confident and capable" can make you feel more self-assured and ready to take on challenges.

- **Words Influence Behaviour**: Repeating positive affirmations can gradually change your behaviour. When you affirm "I am successful," it motivates you to take the actions needed to achieve success, reinforcing the belief that you can succeed.

Example: Imagine someone saying, "I am worthy of love and happiness" each morning. Over time, this affirmation will influence how they perceive their self-worth, which can improve their relationships and overall mental health.

2. **The Science Behind Affirmations and the Subconscious Mind**

The effectiveness of positive affirmations can be explained through the science of the **subconscious mind**. The subconscious mind is responsible for many of our automatic thoughts, habits, and behaviours. It is constantly recording experiences, memories, and beliefs, and often operates below our conscious awareness.

- **Reprogramming the Subconscious Mind**: Affirmations are a tool to reprogram the subconscious mind. By repeatedly stating positive affirmations, we replace negative or limiting beliefs that may have been ingrained over time with new, positive beliefs.

- **Neuroplasticity**: Neuroplasticity is the brain's ability to reorganize itself by forming new neural connections. When you repeat affirmations, you're essentially training your brain to create new pathways that support your positive beliefs. This makes it easier to think and act in ways that align with your new mindset.

- **Cognitive Behavioural Theory (CBT)**: Affirmations align with the principles of CBT, which focus on changing negative thought patterns. By using positive statements, we challenge and replace the negative self-talk that holds us back, leading to improved mental well-being and increased motivation.

Example: If someone constantly thinks, "I'm not good enough," their subconscious mind may reinforce these feelings of inadequacy. However, by repeating the affirmation "I am enough as I am," they can start to replace the negative thought with a belief of self-worth, changing how they feel and act.

3.   **The Law of Attraction and Affirmations**

The **Law of Attraction** suggests that by focusing on positive thoughts and desires, we can attract similar positive experiences into our lives. Affirmations are a tool that aligns with this law, as they help us focus on what we want, rather than what we don't want.

- **Vibration and Energy**: According to the Law of Attraction, everything in the universe is energy, including our thoughts. Positive affirmations raise our energy or vibrational frequency, aligning us with the things we want to manifest in our lives.

- **Visualization and Belief**: When you say an affirmation, especially with strong belief and emotion, it helps visualize your goals. The more you believe in the affirmation, the more you start acting in ways that align with that belief, bringing you closer to your desired outcome.

Example: A person who repeatedly affirms "I am attracting wealth and success" is subconsciously aligning themselves with opportunities and actions that lead to prosperity.

In summary, affirmations work by influencing our conscious and subconscious mind, changing the way we think, feel, and behave. They help us shift from negative to positive thought patterns, ultimately fostering a mindset that attracts positivity and success into our lives.

The Role of the Law of Attraction

The **Law of Attraction (LoA)** is a powerful concept that suggests we attract into our lives whatever we focus on, whether positive or negative. It operates on the idea that our thoughts, emotions, and beliefs send out vibrations into the universe, and in turn, the universe sends back experiences that match those vibrations.

Understanding the Law of Attraction

At its core, the Law of Attraction is based on the principle that like attracts like. When you focus your thoughts and energy on something, you are drawing that thing towards you. The universe, according to this philosophy, will respond to the vibrations you emit.

- **Positive Thinking**: When you think positively, you emit positive energy. The universe, in turn, will send you experiences that are in harmony with your positive thoughts.

- **Focus and Belief**: What you focus on with belief, intention, and emotion will manifest in your life. If you focus on your desires and believe they are possible, the Law of Attraction brings those desires into reality.

Example: If you focus on feelings of abundance and gratitude, you are more likely to notice and attract opportunities that bring financial or personal wealth into your life.

How Positive Affirmations Align with the Law of Attraction

Positive affirmations are a direct tool to harness the Law of Attraction. By repeating positive affirmations, you are actively sending out vibrations that align with your desires. These affirmations help to reprogram the mind, replacing negative or limiting beliefs with empowering ones that attract what you want.

- **Affirmations Create Positive Focus:** Repeating affirmations daily directs your attention to your goals, dreams, and desires. This positive focus enhances the energy you emit, helping you attract similar positive experiences.

- **Belief and Visualization:** When you say an affirmation, especially with belief and emotion, you also visualize the outcome you want. This enhances the power of your thoughts and sends out stronger vibrations to the universe, aligning your actions with your desires.

For example, someone who wants to improve their career might affirm: "I am attracting opportunities that align with my skills and passion." This statement not only creates positive focus but also aligns their energy with the specific career opportunities they wish to attract.

Real-life Examples of the Law of Attraction in Action

1. **Example 1: Oprah Winfrey** Oprah Winfrey has often spoken about how she uses the Law of Attraction in her life. Early in her career, she visualized being on the cover of magazines and achieving great success. By focusing on her goals and believing in herself, she attracted the opportunities and resources that helped her become one of the most successful women in television history. Her positive affirmations and visualization techniques played a key role in manifesting her dreams into reality.

2. **Example 2: Jim Carrey** Jim Carrey is another well-known example of the Law of Attraction in action. In the early 1990s, he wrote himself a check for $10 million for "acting services rendered." He kept the check in his wallet and visualized himself receiving such an amount for a movie. In 1994, he received a movie deal for *Dumb and Dumber*, which paid him exactly $10 million, fulfilling his vision. Carrey's

belief and affirmation helped him manifest his success using the Law of Attraction.

3. **Example 3: A Business Owner's Growth** A small business owner, struggling to attract customers, decided to apply the Law of Attraction by regularly affirming, "I am attracting loyal customers who appreciate the value of my products." Along with this affirmation, she worked on her business, provided excellent customer service, and trusted that the universe would bring the right people to her. Slowly but surely, her customer base grew, and she saw more sales and greater satisfaction in her work. By focusing on the positive outcome and aligning her actions with her goals, she manifested success.

The Law of Attraction is a powerful force that helps you manifest your desires by focusing on positivity and aligning your thoughts with your goals. Positive affirmations are a practical tool for activating the Law of Attraction, as they focus your thoughts, create belief, and send out powerful energy into the universe. When used consistently, affirmations can attract the outcomes you desire, just as seen in the stories of successful individuals who have applied this principle to their lives.

I recommend the following movies:

1. **The Secret** – This movie introduces the concept of the Law of Attraction, showcasing how positive thinking can bring about real change and success in life.

2. **Jab We Met** – A heartwarming Bollywood movie that illustrates how embracing positivity and living in the present can transform one's life, emphasizing self-discovery and resilience.

Both movies reinforce the power of mindset and affirmations in shaping reality.

Subliminal Messages and Positive Affirmations

What Are Subliminal Messages and How Do They Work?

Subliminal messages are messages that are sent to your subconscious mind without you being fully aware of them. These messages can be in the form of sounds, images, or words that are hidden or played very quietly, so your conscious mind doesn't notice them. But your subconscious mind, which is always alert, can pick them up.

For example, if you're listening to music with affirmations quietly embedded in the background, your conscious mind is only hearing the music, but your subconscious is absorbing the positive messages, like "You are strong" or "You are worthy."

How Do Subliminal Affirmations Influence the Subconscious Mind?

Our **subconscious mind** is a powerful part of our brain. It is where we store beliefs, memories, and habits that we aren't always aware of. When you listen to subliminal affirmations, your subconscious absorbs these messages. Over time, these messages can help change the way you think and feel.

- **Reprogramming Negative Thoughts**: If you have negative beliefs about yourself, like "I'm not good enough" or "I can't succeed," these beliefs are stored in your subconscious. Subliminal affirmations can help replace these negative thoughts with positive ones. For example, listening to affirmations like "I am good enough" and "I am capable" can help reprogram your subconscious mind and change your beliefs.

- **Boosting Confidence and Self-Esteem**: If you often feel unsure of yourself or have low self-esteem, subliminal affirmations can help. By listening to affirmations like "I believe in myself" or "I am confident," your subconscious mind starts to believe these things, even if you're not consciously aware of it. Over time, this can make you feel more confident and positive about yourself.

- **Changing Habits**: Our subconscious mind controls many of our daily habits. If you want to change a habit, such as being more positive or more productive, subliminal affirmations can help. For example, if you listen to "I am productive" or "I focus easily," your subconscious mind starts to believe it, and you might find yourself becoming more focused and productive.

How Subliminal Messages Complement Affirmations in Fostering Positivity

When **subliminal messages** and **positive affirmations** are combined, they become even more powerful. The affirmations are repeated at a level that the conscious mind doesn't hear, but the subconscious mind picks them up easily. Over time, these messages can help improve your thoughts, feelings, and even your behaviour.

Here are some examples of how subliminal messages complement affirmations:

1. **Example 1: Overcoming Self-Doubt** Imagine a person who often feels insecure and doubts their abilities. They decide to use subliminal affirmations like "I am confident," "I trust myself," and "I am capable of achieving my goals." They listen to these affirmations through a subliminal audio track while they sleep or relax. Even though they may not consciously hear the affirmations, their subconscious mind starts to believe them. Over time, the person feels more confident, takes more action, and believes in their abilities.

2. **Example 2: Attracting Abundance** A person who wants to attract more wealth or opportunities into their life may use subliminal affirmations like "Money comes easily to me," "I am financially abundant," or "I attract success." Listening to these affirmations repeatedly can help shift their mindset about money and success. As their subconscious mind starts to accept these beliefs, they may begin to notice more opportunities for financial growth and success in their life.

3. **Example 3: Improving Relationships** Someone who wants to improve their relationships may use subliminal affirmations like "I am loving and kind," "I attract positive relationships," or "I communicate effectively." These messages can slowly replace negative thoughts or fears about relationships with more positive, loving beliefs. Over time, the person may notice they feel more confident in their relationships and experience more harmony with others.

4. **Example 4: Boosting Motivation** A student preparing for exams might feel stressed or lack motivation. They listen to subliminal affirmations like "I am focused," "I study with ease," and "I am motivated to succeed." Even though they don't consciously hear the affirmations, their subconscious mind absorbs them and helps them feel more driven and confident while studying.

Subliminal messages work by sending positive affirmations to the subconscious mind without your conscious awareness. Over time, these messages can help change your beliefs, improve your confidence, and boost your overall mindset. By using subliminal affirmations alongside traditional affirmations, you can create a powerful combination that helps bring about positive changes in your life. Whether you're looking to overcome self-doubt, attract abundance, or improve relationships, subliminal affirmations can help you foster positivity and create lasting change.

How to Listen to Subliminal Affirmations Effectively

1. **Search for Subliminal Audio**
   Start by searching for subliminal affirmation audios on YouTube. You can use keywords like:
   - "Subliminal Confidence Boost"
   - "Subliminal Affirmations for Success"
   - "Subliminal Love and Relationships"
   - "Subliminal Stress Relief and Relaxation"

These searches will lead you to a variety of videos that cater to different goals like building self-esteem, attracting wealth, or enhancing mental clarity.

2. **Read the Video Description Carefully**

   Once you find a video that interests you, **read the description carefully**. This will help you understand what the audio focuses on, the kind of affirmations it contains, and whether it aligns with your personal goals.

   Make sure the affirmations are relevant to your needs and are positive in nature. Check for details like:

   - **Duration of the audio** – Is it long enough to be effective?
   - **Audio quality** – Is it clear and pleasant to listen to?
   - **Affirmations mentioned** – Are they in line with your desired changes?

3. **Check for Authenticity and Quality**

   Be cautious of fraudulent or low-quality subliminal audios. Look for videos that have a **positive reputation**, lots of views, and good feedback from listeners.

   Avoid audios with poor sound quality, vague descriptions, or videos that promise unrealistic results. Stick to well-reviewed content from reliable sources.

4. **Start Listening to the Audio**

   Once you've found an audio that meets your requirements, **press play and listen attentively**. For maximum benefit, I recommend using **headphones**, as they will help you experience the audio more clearly and effectively. Headphones also block out external distractions, allowing you to fully focus on the affirmations.

5. **Listen on a Loop**

   Let the audio play on a loop for an extended period. This continuous exposure to the affirmations will help your subconscious mind absorb them more deeply. You can listen while:

   - Doing your daily activities, like working, cleaning, or even relaxing.
   - During meditation or yoga to enhance your mindfulness practice.

6. **Consistency is Key**

   For the best results, make listening to subliminal audios a **regular habit**. Set aside time each day to immerse yourself in these positive affirmations. Over time, you'll notice a shift in your mindset and the way you perceive challenges.

Be Aware of Fraudulent Subliminal Audios

While subliminal audios can be powerful tools for change, it's important to be cautious about where you get them from. Here are a few things to keep in mind:

- **Don't fall for promises of instant results**. Personal growth takes time, so if something seems too good to be true, it likely is.
- **Avoid low-quality videos** that don't provide clear descriptions or have poor audio quality.
- Stick with channels and creators who have **positive reviews** and a **track record** of producing effective subliminal content.

Feel Free to Listen While Doing Other Tasks

One of the best things about subliminal audio is that it can work in the background while you do other tasks. You don't need to sit in complete silence or focus all your attention on it. You can:

- Listen while working, exercising, or even just relaxing.
- Make it a part of your daily routine, so you're constantly feeding your mind with positive thoughts, even if you're multitasking.

By following these simple steps, you can harness the power of subliminal affirmations to transform your mindset and bring positive changes into your life. Just remember to be consistent, stay mindful of authenticity, and trust the process. With time, you'll start seeing real benefits in your thoughts, emotions, and actions.

How to Create Effective Affirmations

Creating affirmations is a powerful tool for personal growth, but to make them truly effective, it's important to follow some key guidelines. Below are some tips to help you craft affirmations that can bring positive change into your life:

Key Guidelines for Creating Powerful, Personal Affirmations

- **Use the Present Tense** Affirmations should always be in the **present tense** because the subconscious mind only responds to what it believes is happening right now.
  - **Example**: Here are some positive affirmations:
    a) I don't chase, I attract
    b) I am a magnet for positive energy.
    c) I attract abundance effortlessly.
    d) I don't compete, I create.
    e) I am worthy of all the good things coming my way.

f) I trust the process and allow success to come to me.

g) I am open to receiving limitless opportunities.

h) I attract only what is meant for me.

i) I am aligned with my purpose and success follows me.

j) I am a magnet for love, light, and positivity.

k) I welcome what is meant for me with open arms.

l) These affirmations encourage the mindset of attracting, rather than chasing, and focus on the power of abundance and self-worth.

- **Example**: Instead of saying "I will be confident," say "I am confident." This helps your mind believe that the change is already happening.

1. **Keep Them Positive** Focus on the **positive** outcome you want, rather than the negative. This allows you to attract positive energy and thoughts.

   - **Example**: Instead of saying "I am not afraid of failure," say "I embrace success and growth."

2. **Be Specific** A good affirmation is **clear and specific** about what you want to achieve. The more specific you are, the better your mind can focus on your goal.

   - **Example**: "I am calm and peaceful during stressful situations," is more specific than "I am calm."

3. **Make Them Personal** Affirmations should reflect your own needs and desires. They should be **personal** and relevant to your life.

   - **Example**: "I attract positive people into my life" is personal because it reflects your desire for positive connections.

4. **Keep Them Short and Simple** A simple, **short affirmation** is easier to remember and repeat regularly.

   - **Example**: "I am strong," or "I am capable."

Common Mistakes to Avoid When Using Affirmations

1. **Using Negative Words** Avoid using negative words like "not" or "don't." Your subconscious mind focuses on the positive words, so a statement like "I am not afraid" focuses on fear, rather than the opposite of fear.

   - **Mistake**: "I am not scared of failure."
   - **Correction**: "I am confident and successful."

2. **Being Too Vague:** Vague affirmations like "I am happy" may not have the same impact as affirmations that are more specific about what you're trying to achieve.
   - **Mistake:** "I am happy."
   - **Correction:** "I am happy and content with my career and relationships."

3. **Overloading with Too Many Affirmations** Focusing on too many affirmations at once can overwhelm your mind. It's better to start with 1-3 powerful affirmations that resonate deeply with you, rather than trying to change everything all at once.
   - **Mistake:** Saying 10 affirmations at once.
   - **Correction:** Focus on 2-3 affirmations that align with your most important goals.

4. **Expecting Instant Results** Affirmations work over time. Be patient and trust the process. **Consistency** is key. If you don't see immediate changes, it doesn't mean they aren't working.
   - **Mistake:** Expecting instant transformation.
   - **Correction:** Be patient and continue practicing your affirmations daily.

The Importance of Affirmations Being in the Present Tense, Positive, and Personal

1. **Present Tense:** When you say an affirmation in the present tense, your subconscious mind begins to accept it as true in the here and now. This leads to quicker transformation.
   - **Example:** "I am confident" versus "I will be confident."

2. **Positive:** Focusing on positive words creates a mindset of abundance and possibility. If your affirmation focuses on something negative, it will only bring more of that negativity into your life.
   - **Example:** "I am healthy and full of energy" versus "I don't feel tired anymore."

1. **Personal:** When you make affirmations personal, they connect more deeply with your inner desires. You're speaking directly to yourself, which reinforces your sense of worth and personal power.
   - **Example:** "I am worthy of love and happiness" versus "People love me."

Example of a Strong Affirmation
- **Weak affirmation:** "I don't want to be poor."
- **Powerful affirmation:** "I am abundant and attract wealth easily."

By following these guidelines and avoiding common mistakes, you can create affirmations that work effectively and help bring your dreams and desires into reality. Remember, the key is **clarity, positivity, and consistency**. Affirmations aren't a quick fix; they're a tool for long-term growth, so make them a regular part of your daily routine.

Practical Applications of Positive Affirmations

Incorporating positive affirmations into your daily routine can help reprogram your subconscious mind and create lasting changes in various areas of your life. Here's how you can practically use affirmations:

1. 1. How to Incorporate Affirmations into Your Daily Routine:

    - **Morning Routine:** Start your day by repeating affirmations as soon as you wake up. This helps set a positive tone for the day and aligns your mind with your goals.
        - **Example:** Stand in front of the mirror and say, "Today is going to be a successful and productive day," or "I am confident and capable."

    - **During Meditation or Yoga:** Incorporating affirmations during meditation or yoga helps you focus and deepen your practice. Say your affirmations silently or aloud as you breathe.
        - **Example:** As you inhale, say "I am at peace." As you exhale, say "I release all negativity."

    - **Before Bed:** Repeating positive affirmations before sleep helps your subconscious mind absorb them while you're resting.
        - **Example:** "I am grateful for today and excited for tomorrow's opportunities."

    - **In Your Work or Study Time:** Throughout your day, take moments to pause and repeat affirmations, especially if you're facing a challenge.
        - **Example:** Before a presentation or meeting, say, "I am confident and clear in my communication."

2. Tools and Methods to Keep Your Affirmations Consistent:

    - **Vision Boards:** A vision board is a visual tool that helps you focus on your goals. You can add words or phrases from your affirmations to remind you of your intentions daily.
        - **How to Use:** Collect images and words that align with your affirmations (e.g., success, health, love) and place them on a board you can view regularly.

- **Example:** If your affirmation is "I am healthy and full of energy," you might add pictures of healthy food, people exercising, or nature to your vision board.

- **Affirmation Cards:** You can create affirmation cards that contain your positive statements and keep them with you. Pull out a card whenever you need a mental boost.
  - **How to Use:** Write your affirmations on index cards and keep them in your wallet, bag, or desk drawer.
  - **Example:** Write "I am attracting abundance into my life" on one card and pull it out when you feel uncertain about money or opportunities.

- **Phone Reminders:** Set reminders or alarms on your phone with your affirmations. This will prompt you throughout the day to pause and repeat your affirmations.
  - **How to Use:** Use the reminder feature on your phone to send you an affirmation at a set time each day (e.g., 3 PM) to reinforce positivity.

3. Using Affirmations to Change Specific Areas of Life:
- **Self-Esteem:** If you want to improve your self-worth, use affirmations that affirm your value, confidence, and ability to succeed.
  - Example Affirmations:
  - "I am worthy of love and respect."
  - "I am proud of who I am becoming."
  - "I embrace my uniqueness with confidence."

- **Career Success:** Use affirmations that focus on your skills, opportunities, and success in your professional life.
  - Example Affirmations:
  - "I am a valuable asset to my company."
  - "I attract exciting career opportunities every day."
  - "I am constantly growing and advancing in my career."

- **Health and Well-being:** To improve your health, use affirmations that promote healing, vitality, and overall well-being.
  - Example Affirmations:
  - "My body is strong, healthy, and full of energy."

- "Every cell in my body is healing and thriving."

- "I choose healthy habits that support my well-being."

- **Relationships:** Affirmations can also help you improve relationships by fostering love, respect, and understanding.

  - Example Affirmations:

  - "I am surrounded by loving and supportive people."

  - "I give and receive love freely."

  - "I attract positive, loving relationships into my life."

Incorporating positive affirmations into your daily routine doesn't have to be complicated. With consistency and dedication, you can create lasting change in any area of your life. The key is to make affirmations a regular part of your life and to use tools that will keep you motivated, such as vision boards, affirmation cards, and reminders. Whether you're working on your self-esteem, career, health, or relationships, affirmations help align your thoughts with your desired outcomes, empowering you to achieve your goals.

Overcoming Challenges in Using Affirmations

Using affirmations is a powerful tool for transforming your mindset, but it can come with some challenges. Here's how you can overcome them:

1. Common Obstacles People Face When Practicing Affirmations:

- **Self-Doubt:** When starting affirmations, it's common to feel suspicious or doubt their effectiveness. You might feel that repeating positive statements doesn't match your current reality.

  - **Solution:** It's important to start small. Don't jump into big affirmations like "I am a millionaire" if you don't believe it. Instead, begin with affirmations that feel more believable, like "I am on the path to financial growth," or "I am worthy of success."

- **Inconsistent Practice:** Many people start using affirmations with great enthusiasm but then lose consistency. Life gets busy, and affirmations get forgotten.

  - **Solution:** Make affirmations a part of your routine. Set a specific time each day to repeat them, like first thing in the morning or before bed. Consistency is key, and even five minutes a day can make a difference.

- **Resistance to Change:** Affirmations work by changing old patterns of thinking. However, if you have deeply ingrained negative thoughts, it can be difficult to break free from them.

- **Solution:** Be patient with yourself. Change takes time. Start by focusing on one area of your life where you want to see improvement, and use affirmations to gently replace negative thoughts in that area.

2. How to Stay Consistent and Positive During Challenging Times:

- **Set Realistic Goals:** It can be hard to stay motivated if your goals are too big or too vague. Break them down into smaller, achievable steps.
  - **Example:** Instead of saying, "I will be rich," you can say, "I am taking steps every day to improve my financial situation." This gives you a clearer, more attainable target to work toward.

- **Use Affirmations to Focus on the Present:** During tough times, it's easy to focus on what's wrong, but affirmations are about shifting your focus to what's going right.
  - **Example:** When facing stress, affirm "I am calm and in control," rather than focusing on the stress itself. This helps you stay grounded and optimistic, even in challenging situations.

- **Visual Reminders:** Keep your affirmations visible. Write them down and place them where you can see them daily. Having a visual reminder can keep you on track, especially during tough times when you might forget to repeat them.
  - **Example:** Put a post it notes with an affirmation like "I am capable of overcoming challenges" on your computer, mirror, or desk.

- **Celebrate Small Wins:** Every small victory, no matter how minor it seems, is worth celebrating. Recognizing progress, no matter how small, keeps you motivated.
  - **Example:** If you've been affirming that you're a confident speaker and you speak up in a meeting, celebrate that win! It's evidence that your affirmations are working.

3. Techniques for Overcoming Self-Doubt and Negative Thinking:

- **Replace Negative Thoughts Immediately:** Whenever you catch yourself thinking something negative, replace it with a positive affirmation. The more you do this, the more automatic it will become.
  - **Example:** If you think, "I'm not good enough," replace it with "I am worthy of all the good things coming to me."

- **Use the "Cancel, Cancel" Technique:** If you have a negative thought, say "Cancel, cancel!" out loud or in your mind, and immediately follow it with a positive affirmation.
  - **Example:** If you think, "I'll never be able to do this," say "Cancel, cancel," then repeat an affirmation like "I have the ability to succeed, and I'm learning every day."
- **Start with Gratitude:** One of the most effective ways to push through self-doubt is by practicing gratitude. When you focus on the good in your life, it shifts your mindset away from negative thoughts.
  - **Example:** Before you start your affirmations, take a moment to reflect on what you are grateful for. Then, follow it with affirmations like "I am grateful for the opportunities I have," or "I am grateful for my health and happiness."
- **Affirmations with Visualization:** Combine your affirmations with visualizing the success you want. Picture yourself already living the life you desire as you repeat your affirmations.
  - **Example:** If your affirmation is "I am a confident speaker," close your eyes and imagine yourself speaking confidently in front of a group, feeling calm and in control.

While challenges in practicing affirmations are common, they are not insurmountable. With patience, consistency, and the right techniques, you can overcome self-doubt, stay positive during tough times, and create lasting change. The key is to make affirmations a part of your daily routine, stay focused on the present moment, and replace negative thoughts with empowering ones. Over time, this will help rewire your brain for success, leading to a more positive and fulfilling life.

Here Are Examples of Few Successful People Who Use Positive Affirmations

Many successful individuals and famous celebrities have openly shared how they have used positive affirmations to transform their lives and careers. Here are a few examples of well-known people who credit their success to the power of affirmations:

1. **Oprah Winfrey**

   Oprah Winfrey, one of the most influential women in the world, has been very open about her use of positive affirmations. She believes that affirmations helped her build confidence and achieve success, both in her career and personal life.

Affirmation Used: "I am worthy of everything good."

Oprah has often shared how she used this affirmation to help overcome self-doubt and build the mindset that she deserved success. She attributes her ability to manifest opportunities and create a positive life to her consistent practice of affirmations.

2.   **Jim Carrey**

Jim Carrey, the famous actor known for his roles in movies like *Ace Ventura* and *The Truman Show*, is another celebrity who has used affirmations to manifest his dreams. He is known for his story about writing himself a check for $10 million for "acting services rendered," which he used as an affirmation.

Affirmation Used: "I am the highest-paid actor in Hollywood."

Jim Carrey wrote himself this check in 1987 and kept it in his wallet. He believed that this affirmation would come true one day. In 1994, he received a $10 million pay check for his role in the movie **Dumb and Dumber**. Carrey is a strong believer in the Law of Attraction and uses affirmations to focus on his goals and dreams.

3.   **Tony Robbins**

Tony Robbins, the world-renowned motivational speaker and author, has spent decades teaching the power of positive thinking and affirmations. He believes that the use of affirmations helps rewire the brain and create the mindset needed for success.

Affirmation Used: "I am in control of my destiny, and I am capable of achieving all my goals."

Robbins frequently uses affirmations in his seminars, encouraging people to speak empowering words to themselves. He credits much of his success to his daily practices, which include positive affirmations and visualization techniques.

4.   **Lady Gaga**

Lady Gaga, one of the most iconic pop stars of our time, has shared how positive affirmations have played a role in her rise to fame. She believes that affirmations helped her overcome her insecurities and transform her mindset to become a global superstar.

Affirmation Used: "I am beautiful, I am worthy, I am enough."

Lady Gaga has talked about using these affirmations during tough times when she was feeling insecure about her career and appearance. By focusing on affirmations, she learned to embrace her uniqueness and achieve her dreams.

5. Will Smith

Will Smith, the famous actor and producer, has openly discussed how he uses positive affirmations to maintain a mindset of success. He believes that affirmations help him stay focused and determined, whether in his career or personal life.

Affirmation Used: "I am the best at what I do."

Smith uses this affirmation to remind himself of his abilities and to keep his self-confidence high. He has said that believing in his own potential has been a key part of his success, and affirmations help him stay motivated and inspired.

6. Sarah Jessica Parker

Sarah Jessica Parker, best known for her role as Carrie Bradshaw on *Sex and the City*, has spoken about how affirmations helped her to stay grounded and motivated throughout her career.

Affirmation Used: "I am deserving of success and happiness."

Parker uses affirmations to remind herself that she is worthy of the opportunities that come her way. Her belief in her own worth has helped her navigate the challenges of a competitive industry, and she uses affirmations to stay focused on her goals.

7. Ellen DeGeneres

Ellen DeGeneres, the beloved talk show host, has been a strong advocate for the power of positive thinking and affirmations. She has shared that using affirmations has helped her through tough moments in her career, especially when she faced rejection early on.

Affirmation Used: "I am at peace with who I am, and I attract love and positivity."

DeGeneres believes that affirmations help keep her grounded and focused on what truly matters, both professionally and personally. By using positive words to shape her thoughts, she has been able to maintain a successful career and live a fulfilling life.

8. Jessica Alba

Actress and businesswoman Jessica Alba, the founder of The Honest Company, is another celebrity who practices affirmations regularly. She believes that affirmations have helped her build confidence and trust in her own abilities, especially in her transition from acting to entrepreneurship.

Affirmation Used: "I am strong, I am capable, I am a leader."

Alba credits affirmations with helping her balance her acting career and her business endeavours, and they have been a key part of her success as an entrepreneur.

9. **Sharon Stone**

Actress Sharon Stone has openly discussed how she uses positive affirmations to maintain a positive attitude and keep her mind focused on success. She believes that her ability to stay grounded in the face of challenges is due to her use of affirmations and visualization.

Affirmation Used: "I am a magnet for success and good fortune."

Stone believes that positive thinking, including affirmations, helps her keep a positive outlook on life, which is key to her career and personal growth.

Many successful celebrities and influencers credit their use of positive affirmations for their achievements. From Oprah Winfrey to Jim Carrey, these individuals have harnessed the power of affirmations to reshape their beliefs, build self-confidence, and manifest their dreams. By incorporating affirmations into your daily routine, you too can transform your mindset and attract success in your life.

Tips for Enhancing Your Affirmation Practice

Positive affirmations are a powerful tool for building a positive mindset and manifesting your desires. However, to truly enhance their effectiveness, you can combine them with other practices like visualization, meditation, and gratitude. Here are some practical tips to help you get the most out of your affirmation practice.

1. **Use Visualization Alongside Affirmations**

Visualization is a powerful technique that can amplify the effectiveness of your affirmations. It involves creating a vivid mental image of the desired outcome as if it has already happened. When you visualize while saying your affirmations, you align your mind and emotions with your goals, making them more likely to manifest.

How to Do It:

- **Close your eyes and relax.**
- **Think about your affirmation.** For example, if your affirmation is "I am confident and capable," visualize yourself confidently achieving your goals, speaking in front of a crowd, or succeeding in your career.
- **Engage your senses.** Imagine what it looks like, sounds like, and feels like to achieve your goal.

- **Feel the emotion.** The more emotional you get about your visualization, the more powerful it becomes.

Example:

If you're affirming, "I am healthy and strong," close your eyes and imagine yourself enjoying physical activities like hiking or running, feeling energized and vibrant.

2. **Practice Meditation to Strengthen Your Mindset**

Meditation helps calm the mind and allows you to focus fully on the positive thoughts you're trying to affirm. It clears away distractions, making it easier to internalize your affirmations.

How to Do It:

- **Find a quiet space** where you can sit comfortably without interruption.
- **Take a few deep breaths** to relax and center yourself.
- **Repeat your affirmation silently or aloud.** Focus on the words and let them resonate with your inner self.
- **Allow yourself to feel the affirmation deeply.** Experience the peace and positivity it brings.

Example:

You can combine affirmations like "I am worthy of love and success" with a short meditation. As you sit quietly, breathe deeply, and repeat the affirmation while visualizing yourself surrounded by love and success.

3. **Incorporate Gratitude for Extra Power**

Gratitude is a powerful tool that helps to reinforce the positive mindset you're cultivating with your affirmations. By expressing gratitude for what you already have, you open yourself to receiving even more of what you desire.

How to Do It:

- **Write down things you're grateful for** before or after saying your affirmations. This sets a positive tone and shifts your energy.
- **Say thank you** to the universe for all the good things in your life, whether big or small.
- **Express gratitude** for the things you are affirming, even before they come into your life.

Example:

If you're affirming, "I am financially abundant," take a moment to express gratitude for the money you already have, no matter how small. This can help you attract more abundance by focusing on what's already in your life.

4. **Believe in Your Affirmations**

Belief is one of the most important aspects of making affirmations work. If you don't truly believe in the affirmation, it can be difficult for it to have a real impact. You must trust that the affirmation is possible and that it is already true for you.

How to Do It:

- **Start with smaller, believable affirmations.** If you're struggling to believe in a larger affirmation, begin with something simpler, like "I am becoming more confident every day."
- **Repeat your affirmations with conviction.** The more you say them with belief, the stronger the effect will be.
- **Challenge limiting beliefs.** If negative thoughts arise, counter them with your affirmations to strengthen your belief.

Example:

If you're affirming, "I am a successful entrepreneur," but you're not sure if that's true for you, try breaking it down: "I am learning new skills every day," or "I am confident in my business abilities."

5. **Track Your Progress and Celebrate Wins**

One of the best ways to stay motivated with your affirmation practice is to track your progress and celebrate the small wins along the way. This helps you see how far you've come and reinforces your belief in the power of affirmations.

How to Do It:

- **Keep a journal** where you can write down your affirmations and note any progress or changes you notice.
- **Record your emotions and thoughts** after doing your affirmations to understand how they affect your mood and mindset.
- **Celebrate small victories.** Whether it's landing a new client, feeling more confident, or achieving a goal, take a moment to acknowledge and celebrate these wins.

Example:

If you're using the affirmation, "I am attracting positive opportunities," and you receive a great work opportunity, write it down in your journal and acknowledge it as a sign that your affirmation is working.

6. **Be Patient and Consistent**

The key to success with affirmations is consistency. You may not see immediate results, but with regular practice, you will start to notice subtle shifts in your mindset and life. Don't get discouraged by temporary setbacks.

How to Do It:

- **Make affirmations a daily practice.** Set aside time each day to repeat your affirmations, ideally in the morning or before bed when your mind is most receptive.
- **Be kind to yourself.** It's normal for self-doubt to creep in, but keep going. Trust the process.

Example:

If you're working on affirming, "I am at peace with myself," practice it daily. Over time, you'll notice that you feel calmer and more centered, and the positive shifts in your mindset will become more evident.

Incorporating visualization, meditation, gratitude, and belief into your affirmation practice can significantly enhance their power. Tracking your progress and celebrating small wins will also help you stay motivated and consistent. Remember, affirmations are a journey, and with patience, consistency, and positivity, they can lead you to the life you desire.

Key Notes of the Chapter: *Enhancing Your Affirmation Practice*

1. **Visualization with Affirmations:**
   - Combine affirmations with visualization to make them more effective.
   - Visualize your goals as already achieved to create a deeper emotional connection.
   - Example: If your affirmation is "I am confident," imagine yourself confidently speaking or succeeding.

2. **Meditation to Strengthen Affirmations:**
   - Practice meditation to calm the mind and focus on your affirmations.
   - Repeating affirmations during meditation allows you to internalize them more deeply.
   - Example: Meditate with the affirmation "I am worthy of love," and feel the emotions it brings.

3. **Incorporating Gratitude:**

- Gratitude enhances the power of affirmations by focusing on what you already have.
- Express gratitude for the present moment and what you're affirming, even before it manifests.
- Example: Be thankful for your current health as you affirm, "I am healthy and strong."

4. **Belief and Emotion:**

- For affirmations to work, you must believe in them and feel the emotion behind them.
- Start with small affirmations that are easier to believe and gradually build up.
- Example: "I am becoming more confident every day" can be a starting affirmation before "I am confident."

5. **Track Progress and Celebrate Wins:**

- Keep a journal to track your progress with affirmations and celebrate small victories.
- Recognize the positive shifts in your mindset and life as they occur.
- Example: If you affirm "I am attracting success," and you receive a compliment or recognition, note it as a sign of progress.

6. **Patience and Consistency:**

- Consistency is key to successful affirmations. Results may take time, but with regular practice, you will start to see positive changes.
- Be patient with the process and trust that the shifts will happen.
- Example: Repeat your affirmations daily, even if you don't see immediate results, and trust that progress is being made.

By following these tips and combining them with your affirmations, you can enhance their effectiveness and bring about lasting change in your life.

Final Words on Positive Affirmations – Building a Positive Mindset

Positive affirmations are much more than just words; they are tools that can transform the way we think, feel, and ultimately, the way we live. Throughout this chapter, we've explored how affirmations can reshape our mindset, improve our lives, and bring about lasting change. By understanding and using affirmations effectively, we can cultivate a more positive outlook on life and align ourselves with our goals and dreams.

Affirmations help us by reinforcing positive beliefs, which support a strong, optimistic mindset. Words have the power to shape our thoughts, and our thoughts shape our reality. When we choose words that encourage growth, self-belief, and resilience, we naturally begin to see and experience life in a more positive way. This impact becomes even more powerful when we link affirmations with practices like the Law of Attraction and subliminal messaging, which tap into our subconscious, guiding us toward what we truly desire.

Creating and using affirmations correctly—keeping them positive, personal, and in the present tense—makes them much more powerful. When we say affirmations as though they're already true, our subconscious mind begins to accept them as reality. Over time, these positive statements help shift our mindset, build confidence, and attract more of what we desire into our lives. By practicing daily and using tools like vision boards and affirmation cards, we can make affirmations an easy, uplifting part of our everyday lives.

The path to using affirmations effectively isn't always smooth; it's normal to encounter doubts and obstacles along the way. But with patience, consistency, and belief, anyone can overcome these challenges. It's also helpful to remember that affirmations are deeply personal, so they should resonate with you and feel true to who you are and what you aspire to be. Listening to success stories of those who have benefited from affirmations can give you that extra push to keep going, knowing that positive changes are possible.

To make the most out of your affirmation journey, try combining affirmations with practices like visualization, meditation, and gratitude. These additions not only deepen the impact but also make your affirmation practice more engaging. Track your progress and celebrate the small wins, as these will encourage you to keep going and reinforce your belief in the power of affirmations.

In the end, using positive affirmations is a powerful yet simple way to guide ourselves toward a life filled with positivity, growth, and peace. By consistently applying affirmations with intention and belief, we build a strong foundation for a positive mindset that can benefit us throughout our lives. So, make affirmations a part of your day, stay consistent, and watch as they help transform your inner world and bring about the positive changes you seek. Remember, each small step counts, and over time, the changes add up to create a happier, more fulfilling life.

Chapter 8

Mindfulness and Prayer

Connecting with Your Inner Self

Mindfulness and Prayer

In today's fast-paced world, where distractions are everywhere, the need to connect with our inner selves has never been more important. Two powerful practices that can help us achieve this connection are mindfulness and prayer.

Mindfulness is the practice of being fully present in the moment, aware of our thoughts, feelings, and surroundings without judgment. It means paying attention to what is happening right now, rather than getting lost in worries about the past or future. This practice helps us slow down and appreciate life as it unfolds.

The significance of mindfulness lies in its ability to reduce stress, improve focus, and enhance overall well-being. By cultivating mindfulness, we learn to manage our emotions better, respond thoughtfully to challenges, and develop a greater sense of clarity and peace in our daily lives. For young people, practicing mindfulness can lead to improved mental health, better relationships, and a deeper understanding of themselves and their surroundings.

Prayer is a spiritual practice that has been used across cultures and religions for centuries. It is a way to communicate with a higher power, seek guidance, and reflect on our lives. Prayer can take many forms, such as speaking aloud, meditating in silence, or writing down our thoughts and feelings.

Using prayer as a tool for connection allows individuals to feel a sense of belonging and purpose. It can provide comfort during difficult times and foster gratitude during moments of joy. Prayer encourages reflection, helping us to contemplate our actions, values, and the world around us. It also strengthens our connection to our beliefs, whether they are religious or spiritual, guiding us on our personal journey.

Together, mindfulness and prayer offer a powerful combination for personal growth and self-discovery. By being present and reflecting on our thoughts and feelings through prayer, we can create a deeper connection with ourselves and the world. In this chapter, we will explore how to incorporate both practices into our lives, helping us to live more consciously and purposefully.

Understanding Mindfulness

Mindfulness is the practice of focusing your attention on the present moment in a non-judgmental way. It means paying attention to your thoughts, feelings, and sensations without trying to change them. Instead of worrying about what happened yesterday or stressing about tomorrow, mindfulness encourages you to experience life as it is right now. This practice can be as simple as noticing your breath, observing the sounds around you, or severing the taste of your food.

The Importance of Being Present in the Moment

Being present in the moment is essential for several reasons. First, it helps us appreciate life more fully. When we are mindful, we can enjoy simple pleasures, like a beautiful sunset or a warm cup of tea, instead of rushing through our day. Second, mindfulness helps us reduce stress and anxiety. When our minds are focused on the present, we are less likely to get caught up in negative thoughts about the past or future. Finally, being present allows us to connect more deeply with others. When we are truly listening and engaged in conversations, we can build stronger relationships and understand each other better.

Benefits of Practicing Mindfulness in Daily Life

Practicing mindfulness can lead to numerous benefits in our daily lives, including:

1. **Reduced Stress**: Mindfulness helps calm the mind and body, leading to lower levels of stress and anxiety. By focusing on the present, we can let go of worries that often weigh us down.

2. **Improved Focus and Concentration**: Regular mindfulness practice can enhance our ability to concentrate and focus on tasks, making us more productive in school or work.

3. **Better Emotional Regulation**: Mindfulness helps us become more aware of our emotions, allowing us to respond thoughtfully rather than react impulsively. This can lead to healthier relationships and better decision-making.

4. **Enhanced Self-Awareness**: By being mindful, we learn more about ourselves, our thoughts, and our habits. This self-awareness can guide us in making positive changes in our lives.

5. **Greater Sense of Peace and Contentment**: Mindfulness fosters a sense of peace by encouraging us to accept life as it is. This acceptance can lead to greater happiness and fulfilment.

Incorporating mindfulness into our daily routines can transform our lives, helping us to feel more connected, balanced, and at ease. As we continue this chapter, we will explore practical ways to cultivate mindfulness and integrate it into our everyday activities.

The Role of Prayer

Prayer is a way of communicating with a higher power or the universe. It is a practice found in many religions and cultures around the world, and it can take various forms. Prayer can be spoken aloud, written down, or said silently in our minds. It can also include meditative practices, where one focuses on the divine, the universe, or their own inner thoughts and feelings. The purpose of prayer is often to seek guidance, express gratitude, find comfort, or connect with something greater than ourselves.

1. **Different Forms of Prayer**:

   - **Spoken Prayer**: This is when you vocalize your thoughts or feelings. It can be done individually or in groups, such as in a religious service. Spoken prayers often follow traditional scripts, but they can also be spontaneous, coming from the heart.

     - **Silent Prayer**: Silent prayer is when you pray quietly in your mind. This form allows for personal reflection and can be done anywhere and anytime, making it accessible for everyone.

     - **Meditative Prayer**: This involves a deep focus on the divine or on certain concepts, often using techniques such as visualization or repetition of sacred words (mantras). Meditative prayer helps calm the mind and deepen the connection with oneself and the universe.

How Prayer Helps in Connecting with Oneself and the Universe

Prayer serves as a bridge between our inner selves and the world around us. When we pray, we open ourselves to introspection, allowing us to explore our thoughts and feelings. This practice encourages self-reflection and can lead to greater self-awareness. Through prayer, we can seek answers to our questions, clarify our values, and find a sense of purpose.

On a larger scale, prayer connects us to the universe and the larger community of life. It reminds us that we are part of something greater than ourselves, which can be comforting during challenging times. Many people find solace in the belief that their prayers can have an impact, whether it is through seeking support for themselves or for others.

The Psychological and Emotional Benefits of Prayer

Engaging in prayer can offer numerous psychological and emotional benefits:

1. **Stress Relief**: Prayer can be a source of comfort during stressful times. It provides a moment of pause and reflection, helping to calm racing thoughts and anxieties.

2. **Sense of Purpose**: Regular prayer can foster a sense of purpose and direction in life. By connecting with our beliefs and values, we can gain clarity about our goals and aspirations.

3. **Emotional Support**: Prayer often brings feelings of hope and peace. It can create a sense of community when shared with others, providing emotional support and encouragement.

4. **Improved Mental Health**: Studies have shown that individuals who engage in regular prayer tend to have better mental health outcomes, including lower levels of depression and anxiety. The act of prayer can also promote a positive outlook on life.

5. **Increased Resilience**: Prayer can enhance our ability to cope with difficulties and setbacks. By fostering a sense of connection to a higher power or the universe, we can draw strength and resilience during challenging times.

In summary, prayer plays a vital role in connecting with ourselves and the universe. It offers various forms of expression that can provide comfort, insight, and emotional support. As we continue exploring this chapter, we will discuss how to incorporate prayer into our daily lives to enhance mindfulness and foster a deeper connection with ourselves and the world around us.

The Connection Between Mindfulness and Prayer

How Mindfulness Enhances the Practice of Prayer

Mindfulness is the practice of being fully present in the moment, paying attention to our thoughts, feelings, and surroundings without judgment. When we incorporate mindfulness into our prayer practice, we can deepen our connection with ourselves and the divine. Here's how mindfulness enhances prayer:

1. **Heightened Awareness**: Mindfulness encourages us to be aware of our thoughts and emotions as we pray. This awareness helps us to recognize any distractions or wandering thoughts, allowing us to gently refocus on our prayer. By being present, we can engage more fully with our spiritual practice.

2. **Deeper Connection**: When we practice mindfulness during prayer, we create space for deeper reflection and connection. We can listen

more attentively to our inner voice and the feelings that arise during prayer, fostering a more meaningful spiritual experience.

3. **Cultivation of Peace**: Mindfulness helps calm the mind, reducing anxiety and stress. When we approach prayer with a calm and focused mindset, we are more likely to experience a sense of peace and connection. This serenity can enhance our prayer experience, making it more profound and impactful.

4. **Gratitude and Appreciation**: Mindfulness helps us appreciate the present moment and recognize the blessings in our lives. This awareness of gratitude can transform our prayers into expressions of thankfulness, allowing us to acknowledge the positive aspects of our lives and deepen our spiritual connection.

The Synergy Between Being Present and Spiritual Reflection

The combination of mindfulness and prayer creates a powerful synergy that enhances our spiritual practice. Being present allows us to fully engage with our prayers, while spiritual reflection enriches our mindfulness practice. Here are some key points about their synergy:

- **Intentionality**: When we practice mindfulness, we become more intentional in our prayers. Instead of reciting words mindlessly, we can focus on the meaning behind our prayers, making each word resonate with our hearts.

- **Clarity of Purpose**: Mindfulness encourages us to reflect on our intentions and desires during prayer. This clarity helps us articulate our thoughts more effectively, creating a stronger connection with our spiritual beliefs.

- **Integration of Experiences**: Mindfulness allows us to integrate our daily experiences into our prayers. When we are present, we can bring our joys, struggles, and questions into our prayer practice, creating a holistic and authentic spiritual experience.

Personal Anecdotes or Stories That Illustrate This Connection

To illustrate the connection between mindfulness and prayer, consider the following personal anecdotes:

1. **A Calm Morning Routine**: A young woman named Priya begins her day with a mindful prayer. Instead of rushing through her morning routine, she takes a few minutes to sit quietly, breathe deeply, and focus on her surroundings. As she prays, she feels more connected to her intentions for the day. This practice helps her remain calm

and centered, allowing her to navigate challenges with a positive mindset.

2. **Finding Peace During Turmoil**: During a difficult time in his life, a man named Raj turned to prayer for comfort. He decided to incorporate mindfulness by focusing on each word as he prayed. He closed his eyes and breathed deeply, allowing himself to feel his emotions fully. This practice of being present helped him process his feelings, ultimately leading to a sense of peace and clarity about his situation.

3. **Reflective Gratitude**: A mother named Anjali found that incorporating mindfulness into her evening prayer helped her reflect on her day. Instead of simply reciting a list of thanks, she took a moment to think about specific moments of joy and connection with her family. This reflection deepened her appreciation for her loved ones and allowed her to end the day with a heart full of gratitude.

In these examples, the connection between mindfulness and prayer is evident. By being present and intentional in their spiritual practices, individuals can cultivate deeper connections with themselves, their emotions, and the divine. This synergy allows for a more meaningful and fulfilling prayer experience, enriching both mindfulness and spiritual reflection.

Practicing Mindfulness

Practicing mindfulness is a simple yet powerful way to enhance your daily life. It helps you stay present and aware of your thoughts, feelings, and surroundings. Here are some easy exercises for beginners and tips for incorporating mindfulness into your everyday routine.

Simple Mindfulness Exercises for Beginners

1. **Breathing Techniques**:
   Focusing on your breath is one of the simplest ways to practice mindfulness. Here's a basic technique:

   - **Find a Comfortable Position**: Sit or lie down in a quiet space where you won't be disturbed.

   - **Close Your Eyes**: Gently close your eyes or soften your gaze.

   - **Take a Deep Breath**: Inhale deeply through your nose, filling your lungs with air. Hold it for a moment.

   - **Exhale Slowly**: Breathe out through your mouth, releasing all the air. Notice how your body feels as you breathe out.

   - **Repeat**: Continue this process for several minutes, focusing solely on your breath. If your mind starts to wander, gently bring your attention back to your breathing.

2. **Body Scan:**
A body scan helps you connect with different parts of your body and release tension.
- **Lie Down Comfortably**: Find a quiet space to lie flat on your back.
- **Start at Your Toes**: Bring your attention to your toes. Notice any sensations, such as warmth or tension.
- **Move Up Your Body**: Gradually shift your focus to your feet, legs, hips, abdomen, chest, arms, neck, and finally your head. Spend a few moments on each area, observing how it feels without judgment.
- **Release Tension**: As you focus on each body part, consciously relax any tension you notice. Imagine it melting away with each breath.

3. **Mindful Walking:**
This exercise allows you to practice mindfulness while moving.
- **Choose a Quiet Space**: Find a place where you can walk slowly, like a garden or a quiet room.
- **Walk Slowly**: Start walking at a slower pace than usual. Focus on the sensation of your feet touching the ground.
- **Notice Your Surroundings**: As you walk, pay attention to the sights, sounds, and smells around you. Notice how your body feels as you move.
- **Stay Present**: If your mind drifts to other thoughts, gently guide it back to the experience of walking.

4. **Mindful Eating:**
This exercise helps you appreciate the food you eat and promotes awareness.
- **Choose a Small Snack**: Take a piece of fruit, a nut, or a small piece of chocolate.
- **Look at Your Food**: Observe its colour, shape, and texture. Appreciate its appearance before eating.
- **Take Small Bites**: As you eat, take small bites and chew slowly. Focus on the Flavors and textures in your mouth.
- **Reflect**: Consider where the food came from and the effort that went into producing it. Notice how it makes you feel.

Tips for Incorporating Mindfulness into Daily Routines

1. **Set Reminders:**
   Use phone alarms or sticky notes in visible places to remind yourself to practice mindfulness throughout the day. These reminders can prompt you to take a few deep breaths or pause for a moment.

2. **Start with Small Moments:**
   You don't need long periods to practice mindfulness. Start by taking just a few minutes each day. Gradually increase the time as you become more comfortable.

3. **Practice Gratitude:**
   Incorporate gratitude into your mindfulness practice. At the end of the day, take a moment to reflect on three things you are grateful for. This can enhance your overall sense of well-being.

4. **Be Present During Routine Activities:**
   Whether you're brushing your teeth, washing dishes, or commuting, practice being fully present in those moments. Notice the sensations and thoughts associated with each activity.

5. **Create a Mindful Space:**
   Designate a corner of your home as a mindful space. Decorate it with calming items like plants, candles, or comfortable seating. Use this space for your mindfulness practices to help you establish a routine.

6. **Mindfulness Apps and Resources:**
   Consider using mindfulness apps or online resources for guided meditation and exercises. Many apps offer free sessions that can help you get started.

By incorporating these simple exercises and tips into your daily life, you can develop a mindfulness practice that enhances your connection to yourself and enriches your spiritual journey through prayer and reflection. Mindfulness is a skill that improves with practice, so be patient and compassionate with yourself as you begin this journey.

Incorporating Prayer into Daily Life

Integrating prayer into your everyday life can help you connect more deeply with yourself, others, and the world around you. Here are some simple suggestions for how to make prayer a regular part of your daily routine, along with examples to guide you.

Suggestions for How to Integrate Prayer into Everyday Practices

1. **Set a Specific Time for Prayer:**
   Choose a specific time each day to dedicate to prayer. This could be

in the morning when you wake up, during a break at work, or before you go to bed. Setting a routine helps make prayer a regular habit.

- **Example**: If you decide to pray every morning after you wake up, set your alarm 10 minutes earlier. Use this time to sit quietly, reflect, and pray. You can express gratitude for the day ahead or ask for guidance.

2. **Use Prayer During Daily Activities**:
You can incorporate prayer into activities you already do. For instance, you might say a short prayer while cooking, commuting, or exercising. This helps you stay mindful and present throughout your day.

- **Example**: While cooking dinner, you can take a moment to pray for your family's well-being or for those in need. As you stir the pot, reflect on the blessings in your life and ask for strength to face challenges.

3. **Incorporate Prayer into Family Time**:
If you have a family, consider making prayer a part of your family gatherings or meals. This strengthens bonds and creates a shared space for spiritual reflection.

- **Example**: Before dinner, have everyone gather around the table and say a short prayer together. You can thank the universe for the food you have and share any hopes or intentions for the family.

4. **Use Prayer as a Form of Journaling**:
Writing can be a powerful way to pray. You can keep a prayer journal where you write down your thoughts, prayers, and feelings. This not only helps you organize your thoughts but also allows you to look back and see how your prayers have evolved.

- **Example**: Each evening, take a few minutes to write in your journal. Start with a gratitude list, then write your prayers or intentions for yourself and others. This helps you reflect on what is important in your life.

Creating a Personal Prayer Space or Ritual

Creating a special place for prayer or developing a prayer ritual can enhance your experience and help you feel more connected during your prayer time.

1. **Designate a Prayer Space**:
Find a quiet corner in your home where you can create a prayer space. It doesn't have to be large—just a place where you feel peaceful and can focus on your thoughts.

- **Example**: You might choose a corner of your bedroom. Place a small table with a candle, a picture that inspires you, or some meaningful objects like stones or crystals. This space can be your sanctuary for prayer and reflection.

2. **Establish a Prayer Ritual**:
   A ritual can make your prayer time more meaningful. This could include lighting a candle, using incense, or playing soft music before you start praying. Rituals create a sense of sacredness and help you transition into a focused mindset.

   - **Example**: Before you pray each evening, light a candle in your designated prayer space. Take a few deep breaths, and then begin your prayer. You might say a few words of gratitude and set an intention for your prayer time.

3. **Incorporate Symbols and Reminders**:
   Adding symbols that remind you of your spiritual journey can enrich your prayer practice. This could be a quote, a religious symbol, or even photos of loved ones you want to pray for.

   - **Example**: Hang a beautiful quote about peace and love on the wall near your prayer space. Every time you see it, it will remind you to take a moment for prayer and reflection.

By incorporating prayer into your daily life and creating a dedicated space for it, you can deepen your spiritual connection and find peace and clarity amidst life's challenges. Remember, there is no right or wrong way to pray—what matters most is that you approach it with an open heart and mind.

The Benefits of Mindfulness and Prayer Together

Combining mindfulness and prayer creates a powerful synergy that can lead to greater inner peace and emotional well-being.

How Combining Mindfulness and Prayer Can Lead to Greater Inner Peace

When mindfulness and prayer are practiced together, they encourage individuals to be fully present in the moment, fostering a deeper connection with both their inner selves and the universe. Mindfulness helps to focus the mind, reducing distractions and allowing for a more meaningful engagement in prayer. This state of presence enhances spiritual reflection and encourages individuals to express their thoughts and feelings authentically. As a result, this practice can lead to a profound sense of peace as one connects with something greater than oneself.

Enhancing Emotional Well-Being Through These Practices

Mindfulness fosters awareness of emotions, enabling individuals to acknowledge and accept their feelings without judgment. When this awareness is combined with prayer, it creates a supportive space for emotional healing and growth. Individuals can express their emotions during prayer, whether they feel joy, sadness, or fear, facilitating a release of pent-up feelings. Additionally, both mindfulness and prayer promote a focus on gratitude, shifting mindsets from negativity to positivity. This combined approach enhances overall emotional well-being by cultivating resilience, allowing individuals to respond to life's challenges with calmness and determination.

In summary, the integration of mindfulness and prayer not only leads to greater inner peace but also enriches emotional health, creating a holistic approach to personal growth and spiritual fulfilment.

Example: For instance, someone might practice mindfulness to center themselves before engaging in prayer, enhancing the sincerity and depth of their spiritual experience.

Overcoming Challenges in Practicing Mindfulness and Prayer

Practicing mindfulness and prayer can offer significant benefits, but many people encounter challenges along the way. Recognizing and addressing these barriers is essential for developing a consistent practice.

Common Barriers

1. **Distractions**: In today's fast-paced world, distractions are everywhere. It can be difficult to find a quiet moment to practice mindfulness or prayer, especially with constant notifications from phones, social media, and other demands of daily life.

2. **Doubts**: Many individuals experience self-doubt when starting mindfulness or prayer practices. They might wonder if they are doing it "correctly" or if it will make a difference in their lives, leading to frustration and discouragement.

3. **Time Constraints**: With busy schedules, finding time for mindfulness and prayer can feel challenging. People often prioritize other responsibilities over these practices, thinking they don't have enough time to commit.

Example: A working parent might feel too busy to meditate or pray. They decide to wake up just 10 minutes earlier each day to fit in a short mindfulness session, making it a priority in their morning routine.

Tips for Staying Committed and Overcoming Obstacles

1. **Create a Dedicated Space**: Designate a specific area in your home for mindfulness and prayer. This space should be free of distractions and comfortable, making it easier to engage in your practice regularly.

2. **Start Small**: Begin with short sessions, even just a few minutes each day. Gradually increase the duration as you become more comfortable with the practices. This approach makes it easier to fit mindfulness and prayer into your daily routine without feeling overwhelmed.

3. **Set a Routine**: Incorporate mindfulness and prayer into your daily routine, such as practicing in the morning or before bed. Having a set time helps build consistency and makes it a natural part of your day.

4. **Limit Distractions**: Turn off notifications on your devices or find a quiet space where you won't be interrupted. This allows you to focus fully on your mindfulness or prayer practice without external interruptions.

5. **Be Patient with Yourself**: Understand that it's normal to face challenges when starting new practices. Be kind to yourself and recognize that growth takes time. If you miss a day or struggle to focus, don't give up. Just return to your practice when you can.

6. **Seek Support**: Join a group or find a buddy to practice mindfulness and prayer with. Sharing your experiences with others can motivate you to stay committed and overcome challenges together.

Example: A person joins a local meditation group, where they can share their experiences and learn from others, helping them stay motivated in their practice.

By identifying these barriers and implementing strategies to overcome them, individuals can create a more fulfilling and consistent practice of mindfulness and prayer. This commitment can lead to deeper inner peace and enhanced emotional well-being, enriching their lives in meaningful ways.

Activities to Deepen Your Practice

Engaging in activities that promote mindfulness and prayer can significantly enhance your understanding and application of these practices. Here are some effective ways to incorporate both mindfulness and prayer into your daily life, including examples relevant to the Indian context.

Group Activities for Practicing Mindfulness and Prayer Together

1. **Mindfulness Meditation Sessions**: Organizing regular group meditation sessions can create a supportive environment for practicing mindfulness. Participants can gather to practice guided meditations led by a facilitator. These sessions often focus on breath

awareness, body scans, or loving-kindness meditation, fostering a sense of connection and shared experience.

Example: In a local wellness centre in Punjab, a group meets every Saturday morning for a mindfulness meditation session. Each week, a different member leads the session, sharing their favourite meditation practice. This communal effort not only helps everyone deepen their meditation skills but also strengthens friendships and support among participants.

2. **Prayer Circles at Temples or Gurudwaras**: Gathering at a temple or gurudwara allows individuals to come together to share their prayers, intentions, and reflections. Participants can take turns expressing what they want to pray for, creating a nurturing atmosphere that promotes spiritual growth and connection.

   Example: At a nearby gurudwara, members of the community organize a monthly prayer circle where they gather to share personal prayers and support each other. One member might pray for family health, while another expresses gratitude for recent blessings. This practice helps everyone feel more connected and reassured that they are not alone in their challenges.

3. **Mindful Nature Walks**: Group walks in nature provide a beautiful opportunity to practice mindfulness collectively. Participants can focus on their surroundings, noticing the details of the environment while practicing gratitude through prayer.

   Example: A community group in Punjab organizes a mindful nature walk in a local park or near the river. Participants are encouraged to engage their senses—listening to the birds, observing the trees, and feeling the breeze. At the end of the walk, they gather to share a moment of gratitude, where each person expresses appreciation for something they experienced during the walk.

Journaling (Pen down) Prompts to Reflect on Personal Experiences with These Practices

Incorporating journaling into your mindfulness and prayer routine can help clarify your thoughts, feelings, and experiences. Here are some prompts to get you started:

1. **Daily Gratitude Entries**: Write about three things you are grateful for each day. This practice can enhance your sense of appreciation and mindfulness.

Example: At the end of each day, Aradhya writes in her dairy or journal about the small joys she experienced, such as a delicious meal, a kind word from a friend, or the beauty of the sunset. This daily ritual helps her maintain a positive outlook, even during challenging times.

2. **Reflection on Mindfulness Moments**: Reflect on a specific moment when you practiced mindfulness. Describe how it felt and what insights you gained from the experience.

    Example: Pratham takes a moment to write about a time he practiced mindfulness while waiting in line at a local market. Instead of feeling frustrated, he focused on his breath and the sensations in his body. In his journal, he notes that this practice helped him feel calmer and more present.

3. **Prayer Reflections**: After a prayer session at a temple or gurudwara, write about the intentions you set and any feelings that arose during the prayer. Consider how these reflections may guide your actions.

    Example: After a quiet evening of prayer at the gurudwara, Mehak writes about her intentions for peace and clarity in her life. She reflects on the calmness she felt during her prayer and sets a goal to carry that feeling throughout her week.

By participating in these group activities and utilizing journaling prompts, you can deepen your practice of mindfulness and prayer, creating a more meaningful connection with yourself and your community.

Key Notes on Mindfulness and Prayer

1. **Definition of Mindfulness**: Mindfulness is the practice of being fully present in the moment, aware of your thoughts, feelings, and surroundings without judgment. It encourages individuals to engage with their experiences actively rather than passively observing them.

2. **Importance of Prayer**: Prayer serves as a spiritual practice that connects individuals with their inner selves, providing a sense of purpose and reflection. It can take various forms, including spoken, silent, or meditative prayer, helping people express their hopes, gratitude, and desires.

3. **Connection Between Mindfulness and Prayer**: Combining mindfulness with prayer enhances both practices. Mindfulness allows individuals to approach prayer with a clearer mind and heart, while prayer deepens the mindfulness experience by fostering a sense of connection with something greater than oneself.

4. **Benefits of Practicing Together**: Engaging in mindfulness and prayer with others fosters community, strengthens relationships, and creates a supportive environment for spiritual growth. Group activities enhance motivation and commitment to practice.

5. **Overcoming Challenges**: Practicing mindfulness and prayer can come with challenges, such as distractions, self-doubt, and time constraints. Recognizing these barriers and implementing strategies to overcome them can help maintain a consistent practice.

6. **Activities to Deepen Practice**: Incorporating specific activities, such as group sessions, nature walks, and journaling prompts, can significantly enhance the mindfulness and prayer experience, leading to greater self-awareness and emotional well-being.

Actionable Insights for Readers

1. **Start a Daily Mindfulness Practice**: Dedicate a few minutes each day to practice mindfulness. Try simple techniques like focusing on your breath or conducting a body scan to become more aware of your physical sensations and thoughts.

2. **Establish a Personal Prayer Routine**: Set aside time each day for prayer, whether in the morning, evening, or during a break. Create a quiet space where you can connect with your thoughts and express gratitude or intentions.

3. **Engage in Group Activities**: Join or form a group that practices mindfulness and prayer together. Regular meetings can provide encouragement, inspiration, and a sense of belonging.

4. **Journaling**: Keep a journal to document your experiences with mindfulness and prayer. Use prompts to reflect on your feelings, challenges, and insights. This practice can help clarify your thoughts and track your progress.

5. **Practice Gratitude**: Incorporate gratitude into your mindfulness and prayer practices. Spend a moment each day acknowledging what you are thankful for, whether through journaling or during prayer.

6. **Be Patient and Kind to Yourself**: Remember that developing a consistent mindfulness and prayer practice takes time. Be gentle with yourself as you navigate distractions and challenges, and celebrate small victories along the way.

By integrating these insights into your daily life, you can cultivate a deeper connection with your inner self, enhance your emotional well-being, and foster a sense of peace and fulfilment.

Mindfulness and prayer are powerful tools that can significantly enhance our lives by fostering a deeper connection with our inner selves. In today's fast-paced world, it is easy to become overwhelmed by distractions and lose sight of what truly matters. By practicing mindfulness, we can cultivate awareness of the present moment, allowing us to appreciate the beauty of life and navigate challenges with greater ease. Similarly, prayer offers us a space for reflection, connection, and intention-setting, guiding us toward a more purposeful existence.

The combination of mindfulness and prayer provides a unique pathway to inner peace and emotional well-being. Together, they encourage us to slow down, reflect on our thoughts and feelings, and nurture our spiritual growth. As we incorporate these practices into our daily routines, we become more resilient, empathetic, and fulfilled individuals.

I encourage you to embrace mindfulness and prayer as essential components of your life. Take the time to connect with your inner self, explore your beliefs, and reflect on your experiences. This journey will not only deepen your understanding of yourself but also lead to a more meaningful and enriched life. By fostering these practices, you will cultivate a sense of calmness and purpose that can guide you through life's ups and downs, ultimately leading to a greater sense of accomplishment.

Chapter 9

Wabi-Sabi

Embracing Imperfection and Finding
Beauty in the Impermanent

What is Wabi-Sabi?

Wabi-sabi is a Japanese philosophy and aesthetic that embraces the beauty of imperfection, impermanence, and incompleteness. Rooted in Zen Buddhism, wabi-sabi encourages us to find grace and elegance in simplicity, naturalness, and authenticity, rather than seeking flawlessness. It reminds us that life is constantly changing, and that beauty often lies in things that are humble and weathered with age.

The word *wabi* originally referred to a sense of quietness and solitude, appreciating the peacefulness of being alone in nature. *Sabi*, on the other hand, conveys the beauty that comes with age, like the patina on old silver or the cracks in antique pottery. Together, wabi-sabi suggests a mindset that finds beauty in things that are imperfect and that appreciates the fleeting nature of life.

In Japanese culture, wabi-sabi is not just a concept but also a way of life that influences art, architecture, and personal philosophy. Examples include tea ceremonies, where simple, handmade pottery is used, often with visible imperfections that add character and uniqueness. The core of wabi-sabi is to embrace a deeper appreciation for life's natural cycles and to see value in things that might seem incomplete or unpolished by conventional standards.

Wabi-sabi offers a unique perspective on beauty that contrasts sharply with conventional, often Western, ideas of perfection and flawlessness. Conventional beauty standards often prioritize symmetry, smoothness, and a sense of "newness" or refinement. This traditional view tends to focus on achieving an ideal or polished appearance—often equated with what is flawless, durable, and unchanging.

In contrast, **wabi-sabi** values the irregular, the worn, and the naturally aging. Here's how it differs:

1. **Imperfection over Perfection:**
   Conventional beauty often emphasizes "flawlessness" and strives to eliminate imperfections, such as wrinkles or cracks. Wabi-sabi,

136

however, finds beauty in these very imperfections. For instance, a crack in a ceramic bowl or a faded colour in fabric is not seen as a defect but as an expression of the object's history and resilience.

2. **Transience over Permanence:**
   Conventional beauty celebrates permanence and unchanging quality. Wabi-sabi, on the other hand, appreciates the beauty that comes with age, weathering, and even decay. It recognizes that everything is in a process of change and that beauty can be found in each stage of an objects or person's life.

3. **Natural Simplicity over Elaborate Perfection:**
   Mainstream ideas of beauty often celebrate extravagance or luxury, aiming for refined and polished presentations. Wabi-sabi appreciates simplicity and rustic charm, favouring the raw, the unrefined, and the humble. It might find beauty in a plain, hand-carved wooden spoon or an asymmetrical stone, valuing its connection to nature and the hands that created it.

4. **Acceptance vs. Control:**
   Conventional beauty often requires manipulation and control to achieve a certain look—whether in objects, spaces, or even personal appearance. Wabi-sabi, however, embraces things as they naturally are, valuing authenticity and uniqueness. It encourages an attitude of acceptance, where one finds peace in the imperfect rather than constantly seeking to "correct" or "perfect."

Overall, wabi-sabi celebrates the art of being content with what is real, authentic, and transient, rather than what is perfectly idealized or eternal. This approach not only broadens the concept of beauty but also offers a peaceful, reflective way of living.

Wabi-sabi is deeply rooted in simplicity and authenticity, offering a perspective that values the beauty of things in their natural, unadorned state. Unlike styles that rely on excess or perfection, wabi-sabi encourages embracing minimalism—focusing on what is essential and letting go of anything superficial or overly polished. This simplicity is reflected in wabi-sabi design, where rustic, unrefined materials like natural wood, stone, and aged fabrics are often favoured, each telling its own story of time and use.

Authenticity in wabi-sabi means valuing things as they are, without the need to alter or mask their imperfections. Cracks, uneven surfaces, and signs of wear are celebrated rather than hidden, as they reveal an item's journey and character. For example, a handcrafted clay pot with small irregularities or a weathered, old photograph carries a unique charm because they're honest expressions of their history and origins.

Together, simplicity and authenticity make wabi-sabi a philosophy that encourages a deeper connection to the natural world and to ourselves, allowing us to appreciate beauty without striving for perfection and to find comfort in what is real.

A simple real-life example of wabi-sabi could be an old wooden table in your home. Over time, it may have scratches, dents, and fading from years of use. Instead of throwing it away or trying to cover up these marks, you embrace its imperfections. You might even feel a sense of warmth or nostalgia when you look at it, remembering family gatherings or how it has served you over the years.

In this way, the table becomes more beautiful and valuable because of its history, wear, and authenticity—exactly what wabi-sabi teaches: finding beauty in imperfection and appreciating the passage of time.

How Wabi-Sabi is different from Anicca (Chapter No 10)

Wabi-sabi and Anicca both revolve around the idea of impermanence, but they differ in focus and cultural perspective. Here's how they stand apart:

1. Cultural Background:
   - Wabi-Sabi is a Japanese concept deeply rooted in Zen Buddhism and Japanese aesthetics. It reflects a way of seeing beauty in imperfection, simplicity, and the natural aging of things.
   - Anicca is a Buddhist concept from India that focuses on the idea that all things are temporary. It is one of the core principles of Buddhism and encourages awareness of life's transient nature, which is meant to lead to spiritual growth and less attachment.
2. Focus on Imperfection vs. Transience:
   - Wabi-Sabi emphasizes the beauty found in natural imperfections, like a crack in a piece of pottery or the weathering of an old building. It's about appreciating things as they are, with all their flaws, and valuing the authenticity that comes with age.
   - Anicca, in contrast, is not about celebrating imperfections but rather understanding that all things, including life itself, are in a state of constant change and decay. It serves as a reminder to accept change and reduce attachment.
3. Application in Daily Life:
   - Wabi-Sabi often translates into aesthetics and lifestyle, encouraging people to adopt a simpler, more intentional life that appreciates the imperfect and incomplete.

- Anicca serves more as a spiritual and philosophical guide, helping people reduce suffering by understanding that attachment to things, people, or ideas can lead to pain, as all things are fleeting.

4. Emotional Impact:
   - Wabi-Sabi encourages a sense of peace and acceptance by appreciating the beauty in life's flaws and natural cycles.
   - Anicca encourages detachment, helping people embrace life's ups and downs by understanding that everything is temporary, and thus reducing suffering through acceptance of this truth.

In essence, wabi-sabi embraces the imperfect beauty of the world, while Anicca emphasizes the transient nature of all existence, guiding people towards inner peace by reducing attachment.

The Philosophy of Wabi-Sabi

Understanding the Principles of Imperfection, Impermanence, and Incompleteness

Wabi-sabi, a Japanese philosophy, revolves around three important principles: **imperfection**, **impermanence**, and **incompleteness**. These principles teach us to find beauty in the natural, unpolished aspects of life. Let's break them down:

1. Imperfection

   The principle of imperfection reminds us that nothing in life is perfect. Whether it's a cracked teacup, a weathered building, or a person's smile with a small imperfection, wabi-sabi teaches us to appreciate these flaws. In the traditional sense of beauty, perfection is often sought after, but wabi-sabi invites us to find value in things that may not meet conventional standards of flawlessness. It celebrates the unique marks of time, use, and experience. For example, a handmade pottery cup with small irregularities in shape is considered more beautiful in wabi-sabi than one that is perfectly symmetrical. These imperfections show the object's story and character, making it special.

2. Impermanence

   Impermanence highlights the temporary nature of everything in life. Nothing lasts forever, and wabi-sabi teaches us to accept this truth. The changing seasons, the fading of flowers, the aging of a person—all of these are reminders that time is constantly moving forward. Instead of fearing change or loss, wabi-sabi encourages us to appreciate the fleeting moments. For example, a flower that wilts and loses its petals still has beauty in the moment of transition, showing us that beauty exists even in decline. The idea of impermanence can help us live more fully, as we learn to value each moment because we know it won't last forever.

3. Incompleteness

Incompleteness refers to the idea that things do not need to be finished or perfect to have meaning. Life is a continuous process of growth and change, and nothing is ever truly "complete." In wabi-sabi, beauty lies in the potential of what is unfinished or in the space between beginning and end. This principle is often represented in art or design, such as a painting that is left with parts unfinished or a building that is never fully completed. It encourages us to see value in the process rather than the final product. For example, a garden that is still being tended to or a piece of music that is being composed can be just as beautiful as something that's "finished," reminding us that the journey is as valuable as the destination.

Together, these three principles of **imperfection**, **impermanence**, and **incompleteness** invite us to embrace the reality of life as it is, without trying to force it into a Mold of perfection. They help us find deeper meaning in the present moment and appreciate the beauty that comes from what is natural and real, rather than idealized.

The Spiritual Side of Wabi-Sabi: Appreciating the Natural Flow of Life

The spiritual side of **wabi-sabi** encourages us to connect deeply with the natural flow of life, embracing the impermanence, simplicity, and beauty of the world around us. It is not just a design aesthetic or philosophical concept; it also reflects a profound way of seeing and living. Here's how wabi-sabi helps us appreciate the natural flow of life:

1. Embracing the Flow of Change

At its core, wabi-sabi recognizes that everything in life is in a constant state of change. This includes nature, relationships, and even ourselves. From the way the seasons shift to how we grow older, wabi-sabi teaches us to accept change with grace. The spiritual practice of embracing change aligns with the Buddhist concept of **impermanence** (Anicca), which encourages us to let go of attachment to things that are fleeting.

For instance, when we look at a tree, we might notice how it blossoms in spring, bears fruit in summer, loses its leaves in fall, and becomes bare in winter. Each phase is part of its natural cycle. Instead of wishing for the tree to remain forever in full bloom, wabi-sabi encourages us to appreciate each season's beauty, understanding that each phase is just as valuable as the next.

2. Finding Peace in Simplicity

Wabi-sabi invites us to live simply and peacefully by minimizing distractions and focusing on what truly matters. In a world full of noise, rush, and endless desire for more, wabi-sabi teaches us to slow down, reduce clutter, and appreciate the beauty in the simplest moments.

Spiritually, this aligns with mindfulness practices, where the focus is on being present and aware of our surroundings, emotions, and actions without judgment. A quiet moment of tea drinking, watching the rain, or listening to the sound of birds can bring us peace. The simplicity of these moments connects us with the rhythm of life and invites us to live in harmony with it.

For example, sitting in a **Gurudwara** (a Sikh temple), listening to the soothing sounds of **kirtan** (devotional singing), and reflecting on the simplicity of the space can bring a sense of calm and connection to the present moment. There is no rush, no need for external distractions; just the pure act of being present with the energy of the space.

3. Appreciating the Imperfect Self

Wabi-sabi also teaches us to embrace our own imperfections. Spiritually, this means accepting ourselves as we are, without striving for an unattainable ideal. This practice encourages self-compassion and helps us realize that we are worthy of love and acceptance, just as we are. By releasing the need for perfection, we allow ourselves to flow naturally with the ups and downs of life.

For instance, a person may look at the lines on their face and see them as signs of aging. Instead of seeing these lines as flaws, wabi-sabi encourages the individual to appreciate them as a reflection of their life's journey. The wrinkles represent wisdom, experience, and the passage of time, not something to be feared or hidden.

4. Spiritual Awakening Through Nature

Wabi-sabi finds beauty in nature's simplicity and impermanence, and it encourages us to feel a spiritual connection with the natural world. Whether it's a mountain, a river, or a quiet garden, nature offers us constant reminders of the flow of life. By spending time in nature, we can reconnect with the spiritual essence of life and gain insight into our own existence.

A walk through a **Sikh Gurudwara garden** (often known as a **Sarovar**), where you can sit by the calm water, take in the sights and sounds, and contemplate, helps foster a sense of peace and belonging to something greater. This experience reinforces the idea that everything in nature is interconnected and constantly changing, just like ourselves.

In summary, the spiritual side of wabi-sabi is about accepting the natural flow of life, finding peace in simplicity, and appreciating the beauty of imperfection and transience. By embracing these principles, we can achieve a deeper connection with ourselves, others, and the world around us, leading to a more peaceful, contented, and spiritually enriched life.

How Wabi-Sabi Can Teach Us to Let Go of Perfectionism and Embrace Authenticity

Wabi-sabi, with its emphasis on imperfection, impermanence, and incompleteness, offers a powerful approach to help us let go of perfectionism and embrace authenticity. In a world that often promotes flawless standards and idealized images, wabi-sabi invites us to appreciate the beauty in life's natural flaws, imperfections, and the passage of time. Here's how it helps us shift from striving for perfection to embracing who we truly are:

1. Recognizing the Beauty of Imperfection

   Perfectionism often leads us to focus on what is "wrong" with us, our work, or our lives, striving for an unattainable ideal. Wabi-sabi challenges this by teaching us that imperfection itself holds beauty. In the same way that a cracked ceramic tea cup may be valued for its history and uniqueness, wabi-sabi teaches us to view our own flaws as a part of what makes us authentic and special.

   For example, in many traditional **Indian art forms**, like **Warli** or **Madhubani** painting, artists intentionally leave small imperfections or elements that are not "perfect." These imperfections are not seen as mistakes but as part of the soul of the artwork, adding character and authenticity. By adopting this mindset, we begin to appreciate the "imperfect" parts of ourselves—the small flaws that make us human and real.

2. Letting Go of Unrealistic Expectations

   In a world constantly bombarded by social media images of perfect lives and flawless appearances, we often set unrealistic expectations for ourselves. Wabi-sabi teaches us to let go of these standards, emphasizing that true beauty lies in the natural flow of life, where nothing is permanent and everything is evolving. By accepting this, we free ourselves from the weight of perfectionism.

For example, when we look at the natural world—like a **temple garden** in India where the flowers bloom and fade, or the weathered stones of a historic **Gurudwara**—we understand that things are not meant to last forever in the same way. This teaches us that change is beautiful and inevitable, and perfection is not the ultimate goal. Instead, we should focus on being authentic in every moment, accepting ourselves as we are.

3. Appreciating the Process Over the Outcome

    Wabi-sabi encourages us to focus more on the journey and process than on achieving a flawless result. In our fast-paced world, we often place value on results, outcomes, and accomplishments. Wabi-sabi asks us to slow down and appreciate the process itself—the little moments, the small imperfections, and the progress that comes naturally with time.

    In an everyday example, think about preparing a simple **Indian meal** with love and care. The process of chopping vegetables, cooking, and seasoning is what makes the meal authentic. If we focus too much on achieving a perfect presentation or following every step flawlessly, we might miss out on the joy of cooking and the authenticity of the experience. The meal, no matter its perfection, is an expression of the cook's soul and effort.

4. Living Authentically and True to Yourself

    Wabi-sabi invites us to live authentically, embracing who we truly are, imperfections and all. It encourages us to let go of societal pressures to conform to idealized standards and to instead live in alignment with our true nature. In doing so, we find peace in knowing that authenticity is far more valuable than perfection.

    Take, for example, **Indian classical dance** (such as **Bharatanatyam**). Dancers, over time, might develop small quirks in their style—perhaps a hand gesture that's uniquely theirs or a slight variation in movement. While these differences may not be "perfect" by traditional standards, they add to the dancer's authenticity and expression. In wabi-sabi terms, this individuality is valued because it reflects the true essence of the dancer, rather than a robotic adherence to perfection.

5. Appreciating the Present Moment

    Wabi-sabi teaches us to be present in the moment, appreciating what we have now, rather than constantly seeking something better or more "perfect." This encourages us to let go of the need to control everything and simply experience life as it unfolds, with all its imperfections.

An example could be a visit to a **Gurudwara** to meditate or reflect. The space is not perfect—there may be noise, people walking by, or the sound of the **Dhol** drums in the distance. But rather than focusing on the discomfort or imperfections, wabi-sabi invites you to embrace the entire experience, finding peace in the imperfect moment. You begin to appreciate the raw authenticity of being there, present and aware.

By embracing the philosophy of wabi-sabi, we learn to appreciate the imperfections that make us who we are and to let go of the relentless pursuit of perfection. This shift allows us to experience life more fully, accept ourselves with compassion, and live authentically, without the pressure to conform to unattainable ideals. Just as a cracked pot holds water or a faded flower brings its own form of beauty, our imperfections create a life that is uniquely ours, and that, in itself, is perfectly authentic.

Wabi-Sabi in Daily Life

Bringing wabi-sabi into our daily lives is about learning to see beauty in things as they are, even if they aren't perfect. It helps us enjoy simple, everyday moments and lets us relax, knowing that things don't have to be flawless to be valuable or meaningful.

1. Adding Wabi-Sabi to Our Surroundings

    One way to use wabi-sabi is to create cozy spaces by choosing natural, simple items. Instead of only new and perfect decorations, try things that have a bit of history or are handmade, like wooden tables or clay pots. These items add warmth because they look unique and have small imperfections that make them special.

    For example, in many Indian homes, families treasure older furniture that has been passed down through generations. It may have scratches, but it's loved because it reminds us of family memories. Wabi-sabi is about seeing the beauty in these well-used items.

2. Enjoying Small Moments in Daily Life

    Wabi-sabi teaches us to slow down and find happiness in simple, everyday activities. This could mean enjoying a cup of tea quietly, noticing the beauty of sunlight through a window, or appreciating morning rituals. By being fully present in these moments, we feel calm and connected to life.

    For instance, taking a moment to watch the sunrise or hearing birds in the morning lets us appreciate nature and brings a sense of peace. In India, lighting a diya (lamp) or saying a prayer each morning connects us to something greater, helping us start the day with gratitude and calm.

3. Using Natural or Handmade Items in Daily Life

Choosing natural or handmade items in our daily routines reflects wabi-sabi because these things often have small flaws that make them unique. Choosing a handwoven cotton cloth or a simple clay diya over something factory-made feels more personal and meaningful.

For example, using a handmade wooden spoon or clay pot adds a warm touch to the kitchen. These items are not just tools; they have a unique look that grows more special with time and use.

4. Accepting Imperfection in Ourselves and Others

Wabi-sabi can also help us accept imperfections in ourselves and in our relationships. Instead of aiming for perfection, we can allow ourselves and others to be human. This means understanding that it's okay to make mistakes, that we don't have to look perfect all the time, and that our loved ones don't need to be perfect either.

For instance, in family gatherings, wabi-sabi would mean enjoying the time together without worrying about making everything perfect. Even if the meal isn't fancy or everything goes as planned, the love and connection make it meaningful.

Living with wabi-sabi is about focusing on what's real and present, appreciating things as they are. It helps us feel more peaceful, grateful, and connected by teaching us to embrace simplicity and find joy in the everyday moments and imperfections that make life special.

Embracing Imperfection

Embracing imperfection is a core part of wabi-sabi. It's about letting go of the need to always look or act perfectly and learning to value our flaws and the flaws of others. In wabi-sabi, imperfections make things unique and special, whether in objects, nature, or people. This perspective encourages self-acceptance and helps us build more authentic relationships.

1. Letting Go of Perfection

Wabi-sabi teaches that we don't have to be flawless to be valuable. Life is naturally imperfect, and aiming for perfection can create stress, frustration, and self-doubt. By learning to accept our mistakes, we can feel happier and more at peace.

For example, if you make a small error at work, rather than feeling bad about it, you can see it as a chance to learn and grow. Wabi-sabi helps us remember that mistakes are part of the journey, and they don't define our worth.

2. Wabi-Sabi and Self-Acceptance

    The concept of wabi-sabi connects deeply with self-acceptance. When we appreciate natural imperfections, we begin to accept our own limitations and quirks. This can mean being kinder to ourselves, even when things don't go as planned. Instead of trying to meet unrealistic standards, we can focus on being our true selves.

    For example, instead of always striving to look picture-perfect, embracing wabi-sabi allows us to feel confident with simple, natural beauty. We don't need to hide signs of aging or flaws in our appearance; they are part of who we are.

3. Embracing Imperfections in Relationships

    In relationships, accepting imperfections means allowing people to be themselves without unrealistic expectations. This approach builds trust and closeness, as both sides feel accepted for who they are. Instead of trying to "fix" others, we can appreciate their unique qualities and differences.

For instance, a family member may have habits that sometimes annoy us, but wabi-sabi reminds us to see past these small flaws and value the bigger picture of love and connection. Embracing imperfections leads to relationships that are honest and deeply rooted in acceptance.

Embracing imperfection through wabi-sabi encourages us to let go of rigid standards and focus on what truly matters: self-acceptance and genuine relationships. When we accept ourselves and others as we are, we find a deeper, more meaningful connection to life and the people around us. This approach brings freedom from the pressure of perfection, allowing us to live with greater peace and joy.

The Art of Finding Beauty in the Unfinished

Wabi-sabi teaches us to see beauty in things that are not perfect, polished, or completely finished. It helps us appreciate things that are incomplete, old, or worn. This mindset reminds us that life is a journey, and we don't always need to focus only on the final result. Instead, there is beauty in the process itself and in the changes that happen along the way.

Seeing Value in the Incomplete

In wabi-sabi, things don't need to be perfect to be beautiful. Something unfinished or aged can have a special charm. For example, a plant that's just beginning to grow or a painting that isn't yet complete still holds value. We can find joy in watching things develop, change, and grow.

An example of seeing value in the incomplete could be a handwritten letter from a loved one that was never quite finished. Even though the letter might lack a proper ending or final signature, it's still meaningful because it captures the writer's thoughts and feelings in a way that's raw and genuine. The incomplete nature of the letter makes it unique—it's a snapshot of a moment in time, with its imperfections adding depth and emotional value.

Another example could be a home garden that you've just started planting. While the garden may look a bit patchy with bare spots and sprouting seeds, it holds potential and beauty even in its early stages. Each tiny leaf represents growth and care, reminding you of the effort and patience it takes to nurture something. Embracing the incomplete garden helps you appreciate each small step toward what it will become.

Wabi-Sabi in Art and Everyday Objects

The idea of wabi-sabi can be seen in both art and everyday items. For example, in Japanese pottery, artists often leave visible cracks or rough textures in the clay, celebrating the imperfections rather than trying to hide them. This style, known as *kintsugi*, uses gold to fill cracks in pottery, turning what others might see as flaws into a beautiful and unique feature. Each piece tells a story of resilience and adds character.

In everyday life, you might notice wabi-sabi in the items you use daily, like a favourite coffee mug with a small chip. Although it's not perfect, its worn appearance and familiar feel make it special. Rather than discarding it, you continue to use and value it, finding beauty in its imperfections and history.

Appreciating the Process of Growth

Wabi-sabi also encourages us to enjoy the process, not just the result. Life is constantly changing, and things are always growing or developing. We can learn to appreciate these steps, even if they are messy or imperfect. For instance, instead of focusing only on reaching a goal, we can value each small step that takes us there, seeing each part of the journey as meaningful.

Wabi-sabi teaches us to find beauty in the journey rather than just focusing on the end result. For instance, imagine you're growing a plant from a seed. Each stage—watching the tiny sprout emerge, seeing the first leaf unfurl, and waiting patiently as it slowly grows taller—is valuable. The plant isn't fully grown yet, but each small step brings joy and a sense of accomplishment.

Similarly, in our own lives, we might be learning a new skill or working toward a goal. We might make mistakes along the way or take longer than expected, but every effort and every improvement matters. Wabi-sabi reminds us that these "in-progress" moments are just as beautiful as reaching the final goal.

Wabi-sabi helps us find beauty in things that are unfinished, aged, or imperfect. It teaches us to value the journey, embrace change, and see charm in things that are not complete or polished. By focusing on these ideas, we can find more joy and peace in everyday life.

Cultivating a Wabi-Sabi Mindset

1. **Shift Your Perspective on Perfection**

   In today's world, we're often pressured to achieve "perfection" in everything we do—from our work to our appearance. To adopt a wabi-sabi mindset, try to let go of the need for everything to be flawless. Instead, look for beauty in imperfections. For example, if you've made a mistake at work or home, rather than feeling disappointed, consider how that mistake can be a valuable lesson or even add a unique quality to what you're creating.

2. **Mindfulness Practices for Recognizing Impermanence**

   Practicing mindfulness can help you stay aware of the natural flow of life, where things are always changing. Spend a few minutes each day in silence, focusing on your breath, and noticing the small, ordinary changes around you—like the way sunlight shifts through your window or the subtle sounds of your environment. Mindfulness helps you see these everyday changes, helping you appreciate the beauty of each passing moment, rather than focusing on what's missing.

3. **Exercises for Self-Reflection on Embracing Flaws and Impermanence**

   Take some time to reflect on aspects of yourself or your life that you feel aren't "perfect." For example, you might write in a journal about a personal trait or a part of your daily routine that you're trying to improve. Instead of focusing on what you don't like, write down ways this trait or part of your life contributes positively or gives you room to grow. This self-reflection exercise helps cultivate a mindset of acceptance, seeing value in the way things are now, even as you work toward growth.

By following these steps, you can begin to embrace the wabi-sabi mindset and find a deeper sense of peace and appreciation for life as it is.

Wabi-Sabi in Your Environment

1. **Create a Wabi-Sabi-Inspired Living Space**

   A wabi-sabi-inspired space values simplicity, natural materials, and subtle imperfections. Instead of focusing on pristine or high-gloss items, try using elements that feel grounded and warm. For example, a wooden table with natural grain and slight imperfections brings a sense of history and character, connecting us to the beauty of nature's irregularities. Incorporating earthy tones and using materials like stone, wood, or clay can help create an environment that feels both simple and authentic.

2. **Bringing Wabi-Sabi into Your Home without Major Changes**
    You don't need to make big changes to introduce wabi-sabi into your home. Start with small touches, like swapping out highly polished decor for pieces that have a natural, handcrafted feel. Consider adding a few items that have personal significance or history, such as a well-worn rug from a family member or an old vase with chipped edges that adds charm. These touches can make your space feel more personal and meaningful without the need for a full renovation.

3. **Examples of Interior Elements that Reflect Wabi-Sabi**
    Handmade decor, like ceramic bowls with slight irregularities or a piece of driftwood used as wall art, exemplifies wabi-sabi by embracing the beauty of the handmade and imperfect. Similarly, rustic items such as exposed brick walls, linen cushions, or a simple clay pot show an appreciation for natural textures and colours. These pieces add warmth and character to a space, reminding us that beauty can often be found in the humble and unrefined.

By choosing items that tell a story and opting for natural, unfinished materials, you can create a living environment that feels both calming and uniquely yours, rooted in the peaceful simplicity of wabi-sabi.

Real-Life Examples of Wabi-Sabi in Action

1. **People Finding Beauty in Imperfections**
    Imagine a woman who owns an old, slightly chipped tea cup that belonged to her grandmother. Though the cup is not perfect, it holds special memories and brings her joy each time she uses it. Instead of buying a new cup, she treasures this one because it connects her to the past and reminds her of her grandmother. This is wabi-sabi— seeing beauty in the imperfect and valuing the story behind objects.

    *   **The Artist Who Embraces Imperfection**
        There's an artist named Tvisha, who creates pottery. She used to stress over making each piece perfect—every curve, every detail had to be flawless. However, after learning about wabi-sabi, she began to appreciate the beauty in imperfection. Now, when she makes pottery, she purposefully leaves some cracks or uneven shapes, embracing them as part of the art's unique character. She finds peace in knowing that the imperfections make each piece

special. Tvisha has learned to stop worrying about perfection and instead focuses on the joy of creating, which has brought her more satisfaction and fulfilment in her work.

- **A Family Who Found Peace Through Simplicity**
  The Singh family, who live in a small village in Punjab, embraced wabi-sabi by focusing on the beauty of simplicity. They stopped trying to keep up with the latest trends in home decor and instead chose to decorate their home with simple, handmade items. Their kitchen table, made from reclaimed wood, has visible scratches and marks. These imperfections remind them of the hard work and love that went into making the table. By letting go of their obsession with having a "perfect" home, the Singhs found more contentment and joy in their everyday life. They now appreciate the little moments, the cozy evenings, and the memories made around their imperfect table.

- **The Traveler Who Found Beauty in the Journey**
  Ashwani, a traveller, always dreamed of seeing the world in the perfect way—checking off a list of top destinations, taking perfect photos, and living the "ideal" travel life. However, after he learned about wabi-sabi, he realized that the journey itself, with all its unpredictability, was just as beautiful as any destination. He started to embrace the unplanned moments, like getting lost in a new city or having an unplanned conversation with a stranger. These imperfections, which he once saw as frustrating, became the most memorable parts of his travels. Ashwani now feels more content, appreciating the imperfections in his experiences rather than chasing an ideal version of life.

These stories show how embracing wabi-sabi—accepting imperfections and the fleeting nature of things—can bring a sense of contentment and peace. It teaches people to enjoy life as it is, without the pressure of perfection.

1. **How People Worldwide Embrace Wabi-Sabi**
   In many parts of Japan, people practice kintsugi, the art of mending broken pottery with gold. Instead of hiding cracks, they fill them with gold to make them beautiful. This approach teaches us that broken things can become even more valuable when they're repaired. By celebrating flaws, people find peace in knowing that imperfections add character rather than taking away from beauty.

2. **Personal Stories of Letting Go of Perfectionism**
   Aditya was a man who always stressed about keeping his home perfectly organized. He would spend hours cleaning, rearranging furniture, and ensuring every item was in its exact place. Every little

scratch on the furniture or misplaced object would upset him, and he constantly felt the need to fix things. One day, Aditya learned about the concept of wabi-sabi, which teaches embracing imperfection and finding beauty in the simple and incomplete. Slowly, he decided to stop worrying about the small flaws in his home. Instead of stressing over every detail, he began to focus on simply enjoying his space as it was.

Over time, Aditya noticed that he felt much more relaxed and happier in his home. He realized that a little mess or imperfection didn't take away from the beauty of his surroundings. His home still felt warm and inviting, even with the occasional clutter or minor imperfections. By letting go of the need for perfection, Aditya found peace in his daily life and started to appreciate the little things that made his home truly his own.

These stories show how wabi-sabi encourages us to accept things as they are, find beauty in flaws, and enjoy life without chasing perfection.

Overcoming Challenges in Embracing Wabi-Sabi

Embracing wabi-sabi can be difficult for some people, especially when we live in a world that values perfection. Many face challenges like the fear of imperfection or the pressure to always look flawless, which can make it hard to embrace the beauty of imperfection. Here's how you can overcome these challenges:

1. **Fear of Imperfection**
   - **Challenge:** We often fear that imperfections will make us or our surroundings look unappealing.
   - **Tip:** Start by reminding yourself that imperfections are part of what makes something unique and beautiful. Instead of seeing flaws as negative, try seeing them as part of the natural process of life. For example, instead of hiding cracks in a wall, appreciate them as a part of your home's history.

2. Pressure for Perfection
   - **Challenge:** Social pressure, whether from family, friends, or media, can make it feel like we always need to be perfect.
   - **Tip:** Practice self-compassion. Acknowledge that no one is perfect, and trying to achieve perfection all the time is exhausting. Instead, aim to find beauty in the small things and let go of the need for everything to be "just right." Focus on progress, not perfection.

3. Cultural or Personal Habits of Perfectionism
   - **Challenge**: Many cultures place high value on perfection, making it difficult to embrace wabi-sabi, which values simplicity and imperfection.
   - **Tip**: Gradually challenge these habits by changing small daily practices. For instance, allow yourself to leave the dishes for a few hours rather than cleaning them immediately, or wear clothes with small imperfections proudly. Over time, these small steps can help shift your mindset away from perfectionism.
4. Staying Consistent in Applying Wabi-Sabi
   - **Challenge**: It can be hard to maintain a wabi-sabi mindset consistently, especially when faced with the pressures of daily life.
   - **Tip**: To stay consistent, remind yourself every day of the value of simplicity and imperfection. One simple technique is to take a moment each day to reflect on one thing in your life or environment that you appreciate for its imperfection. Whether it's a handmade piece of art or a weathered item in your home, focusing on these will help you stay connected to the spirit of wabi-sabi.

By addressing these challenges step by step, you can begin to embrace the imperfections in life and find more peace and happiness in the process.

Activities for Practicing Wabi-Sabi

1. **Exercises to Appreciate Imperfection**
   - **Finding Beauty in Natural Objects:**
     One simple exercise is to take a walk in nature and find something that reflects imperfection. This could be an old, weathered tree, a cracked stone, or a leaf with holes in it. Rather than focusing on the damage, try to appreciate the story behind the imperfection. For instance, an old, cracked tree in your neighbourhood might symbolize endurance, resilience, and the passage of time. By appreciating these imperfections, you start to shift your mindset from looking for perfection to valuing what's naturally flawed.
     - **Example**: Imagine you go to a local park and find a worn-out bench with peeling paint. Instead of seeing it as something that needs fixing, you sit on it and admire the beauty in its age, the memories it holds, and how it blends with the surroundings. This can help you appreciate imperfection in a more profound way.

- **Creating Imperfect Art**:
  A great way to practice wabi-sabi is by creating art that embraces flaws rather than trying to make everything perfect. You can try your hand at pottery, where imperfections like cracks or unevenness in the glaze add to its beauty. Alternatively, you can make a handmade craft like a painted pot or a stitched piece of fabric, allowing each imperfection to tell its own story.

  - **Example**: If you try making a simple clay pot at home, you might notice a small crack forms while shaping it. Instead of fixing it, leave it as is. The crack adds character to the pot, making it unique. Displaying this imperfect piece of art can remind you that beauty often lies in what is unfinished or flawed.

2. **Journaling Prompts to Explore Personal Experiences with Imperfections** Writing about your own experiences with imperfection is a great way to embrace wabi-sabi. Here are some journaling prompts to get started:

   - **Prompt 1**: Write about a time when you felt self-conscious about a flaw or imperfection in yourself. How did it impact you at the time, and how do you view it now? Did the flaw teach you something valuable?

   - **Prompt 2**: Think of an object in your home that is not perfect—maybe it's an old book, a scratched plate, or a worn-out sweater. Reflect on why this object has value to you, even though it's imperfect. How does it make you feel when you see it every day?

   - **Prompt 3**: How can you apply wabi-sabi to your life today? Is there an area where you could embrace imperfection rather than striving for perfection? Write about what that would look like.

     - **Example**: Aditya, a person who once struggled with perfectionism, might journal about his favourite old pair of shoes, which are now a little worn out and faded. Instead of seeing them as "ugly," he might reflect on how these shoes have served him well and bring comfort and memories. By writing this down, he acknowledges the beauty in the imperfections.

3. **Group Activities Encouraging the Sharing of Imperfections** Group activities can create a supportive environment to explore and appreciate flaws together. Here are some ideas for group exercises:

- **Wabi-Sabi Storytelling:** Gather a group of friends or family and share stories about imperfections. Each person can tell a story about something in their life that they once considered a flaw but now see as beautiful. It could be a scar, an old piece of furniture, or a moment when they embraced failure and grew from it.

  - **Example:** In a family gathering, a mother might share the story of a vase that was accidentally broken by her child but was later glued together. Instead of throwing it away, they use it as a decoration. The crack in the vase has become a symbol of resilience and love in their family, and everyone appreciates it differently.

  - **Imperfect Art Session:** Host a group activity where everyone creates something without focusing on making it perfect. This could be drawing, painting, or even making simple crafts like origami. Encourage everyone to leave mistakes visible and to share their work without any shame.

  - **Example:** In a community centre, a group of people from all walks of life come together to create small sculptures out of clay. Each person is encouraged to embrace their imperfections and share the process rather than focusing on the final product. At the end of the session, everyone admires how each sculpture is unique, with its own flaws and story.

- **Mindful Sharing Circle:** Create a space where group members can talk about how they've been dealing with perfectionism in their lives. Sharing experiences allows everyone to feel supported and reminds them that imperfection is part of the human experience.

  - **Example:** In a group of friends, one person might share how they used to be bothered by every little mistake at work. By embracing the philosophy of wabi-sabi, they learned to let go of the need to be perfect. The others in the group might also share their own challenges and how they're learning to appreciate their imperfections.

Through these activities, you can develop a deeper understanding of wabi-sabi, learn to embrace imperfections, and find beauty in everyday moments and objects.

Key Notes on Wabi-Sabi

1. **Definition of Wabi-Sabi:**
   Wabi-sabi is a Japanese philosophy that finds beauty in imperfection, impermanence, and incompleteness. It teaches us to embrace flaws and appreciate the transient nature of life, objects, and experiences. Instead of chasing after perfection, wabi-sabi encourages us to find beauty in the things that are aging, cracked, or unfinished.

2. **The Principles of Wabi-Sabi:**
   - **Imperfection:** Wabi-sabi celebrates flaws and asymmetry, focusing on the unique beauty that comes from being imperfect.
   - **Impermanence:** It acknowledges that all things change over time, and that decay or aging adds character and beauty.
   - **Incompleteness:** Embracing things that are unfinished or evolving, rather than looking for the final perfect result.

3. **The Connection with Authenticity:**
   Wabi-sabi emphasizes authenticity over superficial perfection. It invites us to let go of societal expectations of flawlessness and to embrace our true, natural selves. By doing so, we form deeper, more genuine relationships with others and ourselves.

4. **Wabi-Sabi in Art and Everyday Life:**
   Wabi-sabi can be seen in art, home decor, and nature. Items like cracked pottery, weathered wood, and hand-crafted goods embody wabi-sabi principles. This mindset helps us appreciate the beauty of ordinary, everyday moments and objects, focusing on their history and uniqueness rather than their flaws.

5. **The Spiritual Aspect of Wabi-Sabi:**
   It encourages mindfulness and presence, guiding us to appreciate the current moment, the natural flow of life, and the inevitable changes that come with time.

6. **Overcoming Perfectionism:**
   Wabi-sabi offers a way out of the constant struggle for perfection, teaching us that imperfection is what makes life rich and meaningful. By letting go of the need to be perfect, we open ourselves to a deeper sense of peace and contentment.

Actionable Insights to Incorporate Wabi-Sabi into Everyday Life:

1. **Embrace Imperfections**:
    Instead of striving for perfection, start seeing value in the small flaws around you. Whether it's a chipped mug or a dented door, appreciate it for its uniqueness and story. In relationships, accept the flaws in yourself and others.

2. **Simplify Your Surroundings**:
    Create spaces that reflect simplicity and nature. Use natural materials like wood, stone, and clay, which often carry imperfections. These can make your environment feel calming and authentic, reflecting the wabi-sabi philosophy.

3. **Mindful Practices**:
    Begin practicing mindfulness by appreciating the present moment. Focus on the beauty of ordinary things—a rainy day, the sound of wind, or the texture of a handmade scarf. Let go of any desire to perfect these moments and enjoy them as they are.

4. **Let Go of Perfectionism**:
    Challenge yourself to do things imperfectly. Whether it's cooking, painting, or organizing your space, allow yourself to make mistakes without judgment. Notice how this shift in mindset helps you feel more relaxed and freer.

5. **Engage in Simple, Creative Activities**:
    Explore activities like pottery, gardening, or crafting where you can embrace imperfection. Make something with your hands and let go of expectations for how it should turn out. You might discover that the beauty lies in the process, not the outcome.

6. **Appreciate the Aging Process**:
    Rather than discarding things that show wear or age, find beauty in their history. Whether it's an old piece of furniture, an aging book, or a timeworn garden, take the time to appreciate the way these things evolve and tell a story.

7. **Share the Wabi-Sabi Mindset**:
    Share the concept of wabi-sabi with your friends and family. Discuss imperfections and how they contribute to the beauty of life. Through conversations and shared experiences, you can help others appreciate the natural flow of life and its beauty.

By incorporating these small, mindful changes into your life, you can start embracing wabi-sabi and live with more authenticity, peace, and contentment.

Final Words

In today's fast-paced world, where perfection is often celebrated and flaws are hidden, wabi-sabi offers a refreshing perspective. It reminds us that beauty is not about flawless appearances or the constant pursuit of perfection. Instead, it teaches us to find value in imperfection, appreciate the passing of time, and embrace the natural cycles of life.

Wabi-sabi invites us to slow down and savour the moments we often overlook—the cracks in a cherished object, the rust on an old fence, or the imperfect smile of a loved one. These are the things that tell a story, that carry history, and that make life rich and meaningful. By embracing wabi-sabi, we learn to let go of the pressure to be perfect and open ourselves to the beauty that exists in everything around us, just as it is.

In a world where we are constantly striving for more, wabi-sabi encourages us to pause and appreciate the fleeting, imperfect, and unfinished aspects of life. It reminds us that true contentment comes not from achieving perfection, but from accepting life as it is, with all its flaws and uncertainties.

So, let us embrace the impermanent, the imperfect, and the incomplete. Let us find beauty in the cracks, the wrinkles, and the moments that pass by too quickly. In doing so, we can live a life that is not only authentic but also peaceful, content, and filled with a deeper appreciation for the world around us.

Chapter 10
Anicca (Impermanence)
Understanding and accepting that everything changes

What is Anicca?

Anicca, pronounced as "uh-nee-chah," is a Pali word that translates to impermanence. It is a fundamental concept in Buddhist philosophy, emphasizing that all things—whether they are material objects, emotions, relationships, or experiences—are in a constant state of change. According to the teaching of Anicca, nothing remains the same forever; everything is subject to the natural processes of birth, growth, decay, and ultimately, dissolution.

Anicca is part of the Three Marks of Existence in Buddhism, which also includes Dukkha (suffering) and Anatta (non-self). Together, these teachings provide a framework for understanding the human condition and the nature of reality. Recognizing Anicca is about acknowledging the transient nature of life and the world around us.

Here are a few real-life examples that illustrate the concept of Anicca (impermanence):

1. **Seasons Changing**

   Consider the change of seasons. Each year, we experience winter, spring, summer, and fall, each bringing its own unique beauty and challenges. As winter ends and spring begins, the cold and bleakness of winter fade away, making way for blooming flowers and warmer weather. This natural cycle shows how everything is temporary; just as winter will eventually pass, so will the difficulties we face in life.

2. **Relationships**

   Think about a close friendship that has changed over time. Perhaps you were best friends with someone during school, but as life progressed, you both went your separate ways due to differing interests, jobs, or locations. While this change may bring sadness, it also opens up opportunities to form new friendships and experiences. Understanding that relationships can come and go helps us cherish the moments we have with others and remain open to new connections.

3. **Personal Growth**

Consider a student named Riya who struggles with self-confidence. At the beginning of her high school journey, she feels overwhelmed and unsure of herself. However, as the years pass, she takes on new challenges—joining clubs, participating in activities, and seeking help from teachers and friends. Gradually, she begins to grow more confident and capable. Riya's transformation exemplifies Anicca; her feelings of inadequacy were temporary, and through effort and change, she discovered her strengths.

4. **Career Changes**

Think about a professional like Amit, who started his career in a corporate job. Over time, he realized that he was not passionate about his work and felt unfulfilled. After some reflection, he decided to pursue his love for photography. Although the transition was difficult and filled with uncertainty, Amit embraced the change. Eventually, he found success and joy in his new career. This example shows that career paths are not fixed; they can evolve as we discover more about ourselves.

5. **Physical Changes**

Consider the physical changes that occur throughout life. A child grows into a teenager, then an adult, and eventually ages into an elderly person. Each stage brings new experiences, challenges, and perspectives. Understanding that our bodies and appearances will change can help us appreciate our health and youth while also embracing the wisdom that comes with age.

6. **Technology**

In the realm of technology, think about how rapidly things evolve. A smartphone model might be the latest and greatest one year, but within a few months, a newer version is released, making the previous one seem outdated. This constant advancement shows that technological tools we rely on today will eventually be replaced, urging us to adapt and stay current in an ever-changing world.

These examples highlight that Anicca is a universal concept that permeates all aspects of life, from nature and relationships to personal growth and technology. Embracing the idea of impermanence allows us to navigate change with greater ease and openness, fostering a mindset that values the present while remaining adaptable to whatever comes next.

Importance of Understanding Impermanence

Understanding impermanence, or Anicca, is essential for several reasons:

1. **Acceptance of Change**: Recognizing that everything is temporary helps us accept changes in life, reducing resistance and anxiety about the unknown.

2. **Emotional Resilience**: When we understand that difficult times are not permanent, we can develop resilience. This mindset allows us to cope better with challenges and setbacks.

3. **Appreciation of the Present**: Awareness of impermanence encourages us to cherish the present moment and enjoy experiences as they happen, rather than taking them for granted.

4. **Letting Go**: Understanding that all things, including relationships and possessions, are transient can help us let go of attachments that may cause suffering.

5. **Motivation for Growth**: Accepting impermanence can inspire us to pursue our goals and passions, knowing that life is constantly changing and there is always room for personal growth.

6. **Empathy and Connection**: Realizing that everyone experiences change fosters empathy towards others, as we recognize that they, too, navigate the ups and downs of life.

Understanding impermanence is crucial for fostering emotional well-being, appreciating life, and embracing the journey of change. Anicca is a powerful concept that reminds us of the transient nature of life. By understanding and accepting impermanence, we can cultivate resilience, reduce attachment, appreciate the present, and foster personal and spiritual growth. Embracing Anicca empowers us to navigate life's changes with grace and awareness, enhancing our overall well-being and sense of fulfilment.

The teachings of Guru Nanak, Buddha, and Krishna all reflect the concept of impermanence in their philosophies. Here are examples from each figure that illustrate this idea:

Guru Nanak

1. **Maya (Illusion)**:
   - Guru Nanak emphasized the idea of **Maya**, or illusion, which represents the deceptive nature of the material world. He taught that worldly possessions and status are temporary and ultimately unimportant compared to spiritual enlightenment. He famously said:

   "Maya is the cause of all suffering; it leads to attachment and forgetfulness of God."

   This saying emphasizes that clinging to material things can lead to pain and distract us from our spiritual purpose.

2. **Transience of Life:**

   - In the Guru Granth Sahib, Guru Nanak reflects on the fleeting nature of human life:

   "Life is like a dew drop; it is here for a moment and gone the next."

   - This metaphor conveys the idea that life is temporary and should be cherished while encouraging a focus on spiritual growth.

Buddha

1. **Four Noble Truths:**

   - Central to Buddhism is the **First Noble Truth**, which states that suffering (Dukkha) is an inherent part of life. Buddha taught that everything is impermanent (Anicca), and attachment to things that change is a source of suffering.

   - He explained this in his teachings, saying:

   "All things are impermanent; all things are subject to change. When one sees this with wisdom, one turns away from suffering."

   - This teaching encourages individuals to recognize the transient nature of all experiences and to seek liberation from attachments.

2. **Example of the Rose:**

   - Buddha often used natural examples to illustrate impermanence. He compared life to a blooming rose:

   "Just as a flower blooms and wilts, so does life. We must appreciate its beauty in the moment, for it will not last."

   - This imagery highlights the beauty and temporariness of life, encouraging mindfulness and appreciation of the present.

Krishna

1. **Bhagavad Gita Teachings:**

   - In the **Bhagavad Gita**, Krishna imparts wisdom about the impermanence of the physical body and the eternal nature of the soul (Atman). He says:

   "The soul is eternal; it is never born and never dies. It only changes bodies, just as person changes clothes."

   - This teaching emphasizes that while the physical form is temporary, the essence of who we are—the soul—remains unchanged.

2. **Metaphor of the Seasons**:
   - Krishna often used the changing seasons as a metaphor for life's impermanence:

   "Just as the seasons change, so do our circumstances and experiences. Embrace each phase without attachment."

   - This analogy reminds us that life is cyclical, and just as seasons come and go, so too do the moments in our lives.

Through these teachings and examples, Guru Nanak, Buddha, and Krishna convey the important lesson of impermanence, urging individuals to recognize the fleeting nature of life, cultivate detachment from material possessions, and focus on spiritual growth and understanding. Their philosophies encourage us to live mindfully, appreciate the present moment, and seek deeper truths beyond the transient experiences of life.

The Nature of Change

Change is an inevitable part of life. It can occur in various forms, ranging from small, everyday adjustments to significant life-altering events. Understanding the nature of change helps us navigate our experiences and emotions more effectively. Here, we will explore examples of change in everyday life and how these changes can affect our emotions and experiences.

Examples of Change in Everyday Life

1. **Seasons**:
   - The shift from one season to another is a natural and recurring change. Each season brings different weather patterns, activities, and moods. For instance, winter may bring cold, snow, and indoor activities, while spring ushers in warmer temperatures, blooming flowers, and outdoor events. The changing seasons remind us that time passes, and life evolves.

2. **Personal Relationships**:
   - Relationships often undergo transformations. Friendships may fade, romantic relationships may blossom or dissolve, and family dynamics can shift due to life events such as marriage, divorce, or the birth of a child. Each of these changes brings new experiences and emotional responses.

3. **Education and Career**:
   - Students experience change throughout their educational journey. Transitioning from elementary school to high school, graduating from college, or changing careers are significant life changes. Each step involves learning new skills, adapting to different environments, and interacting with new people.

4. **Health and Aging:**
   - Our physical and mental health can change over time. For instance, a young person may enjoy good health, but as they age, they might face health challenges that require lifestyle adjustments. This reality teaches resilience and adaptability as we learn to cope with the changes that come with aging.

5. **Technology:**
   - In today's digital age, technology is constantly evolving. New devices, software, and platforms emerge regularly, altering how we communicate, work, and interact with the world. Staying current with technology requires flexibility and a willingness to adapt to new tools and methods.

6. **Personal Goals and Aspirations:**
   - Individuals often change their goals and aspirations as they gain new insights about themselves and the world. For example, someone might start their career focused on a specific job, only to realize that they have a passion for something entirely different, leading them to change their career path.

How Change Affects Emotions and Experiences

1. **Emotional Responses:**
   - Change can elicit a wide range of emotions. For some, change may bring excitement and anticipation, such as starting a new job or moving to a new city. For others, it can create feelings of anxiety or sadness, especially when dealing with loss, like the end of a relationship or the death of a loved one. Understanding that these emotional responses are normal can help individuals process their feelings.

2. **Fear and Resistance:**
   - Many people experience fear or resistance when facing change. This can stem from the uncertainty that accompanies the unknown. Fear of failure, fear of loss, or fear of leaving one's comfort zone can hinder personal growth. Acknowledging these fears allows individuals to address them and build resilience.

3. **Opportunities for Growth:**
   - Change often presents opportunities for personal growth and development. When individuals step outside their comfort zones and embrace new experiences, they may discover hidden talents, develop new skills, or cultivate deeper relationships.

Each challenge can become a stepping stone toward greater self-awareness and confidence.

4. **Reflection and Perspective:**

    - Changes in life often prompt reflection. Individuals may find themselves evaluating their priorities, values, and goals. This reflection can lead to a clearer understanding of what is truly important, allowing people to align their actions with their values and make more intentional choices.

5. **Adaptation and Resilience:**

    - The ability to adapt to change is a vital life skill. Those who cultivate resilience can bounce back from setbacks and navigate new circumstances more effectively. Adapting to change may involve developing new coping strategies, seeking support from others, or practicing mindfulness to stay present during transitions.

6. **Mindfulness and Acceptance:**

    - Embracing the concept of Anicca, or impermanence, can foster a sense of mindfulness. By accepting that change is a natural part of life, individuals can learn to appreciate each moment as it comes. This acceptance reduces anxiety about the future and promotes a sense of peace and contentment in the present.

In conclusion, change is a fundamental aspect of human existence. By recognizing and understanding the nature of change in our lives, we can better navigate our emotions and experiences. Embracing change as a natural process can lead to personal growth, deeper connections, and a greater appreciation for the journey of life.

Acceptance of Impermanence

Acceptance of impermanence is the recognition that all things in life—whether joyful or sorrowful—are temporary. Embracing this concept can bring numerous benefits, leading to a more fulfilling and peaceful existence. Here, we explore the benefits of accepting that everything is temporary and how this acceptance can cultivate peace of mind.

The Benefits of Accepting That Everything is Temporary

1. **Reduced Fear of Loss:**

    - When we accept that nothing lasts forever, we become less fearful of losing things, whether they be relationships, material possessions, or even our youth. This understanding allows us to engage more fully in our experiences without the constant worry of what might be lost.

2. **Increased Gratitude:**
    - Acceptance of impermanence encourages a mindset of gratitude. When we recognize that our moments, experiences, and relationships are fleeting, we are more likely to appreciate them fully. This gratitude enhances our enjoyment of life and helps us focus on the positives rather than dwelling on what we lack.

3. **Flexibility and Adaptability:**
    - Accepting change as a natural part of life fosters flexibility and adaptability. When we realize that situations can shift unexpectedly, we become more willing to adjust our plans and expectations. This adaptability helps us navigate life's challenges with greater ease.

4. **Encouragement of Mindfulness:**
    - Understanding that everything is temporary encourages mindfulness—being fully present in the moment. This practice allows us to savor life's experiences, whether they are simple daily activities or significant milestones. Mindfulness fosters a deeper connection to ourselves and our surroundings.

5. **Openness to New Experiences:**
    - Embracing impermanence allows us to be open to new opportunities and experiences. When we understand that life is constantly changing, we become more willing to step outside our comfort zones and try new things, whether it's traveling to a new place, meeting new people, or exploring new hobbies.

6. **Enhanced Emotional Resilience:**
    - Accepting that life is filled with ups and downs helps build emotional resilience. When we encounter difficult times, knowing that they are temporary can provide comfort and strength, allowing us to cope better with adversity. We learn to ride the waves of emotions rather than being overwhelmed by them.

7. **Prioritization of What Matters:**
    - Acceptance of impermanence encourages us to reflect on what is truly important in our lives. By understanding that time is limited, we may prioritize meaningful relationships, personal growth, and pursuits that bring us joy. This clarity helps us live more intentionally.

How Acceptance Can Lead to Peace of Mind

1. **Letting Go of Attachments:**

    - When we accept impermanence, we learn to let go of attachments that may cause suffering. Whether it's clinging to past relationships or worrying about the future, releasing these attachments allows us to experience peace. We can appreciate what we have without the burden of fear or longing.

2. **Reduced Anxiety and Stress:**

    - Acceptance of change can significantly reduce anxiety and stress. When we stop resisting the inevitable and embrace the flow of life, we free ourselves from the mental burden of trying to control everything. This sense of surrender promotes calmness and serenity.

3. **Cultivation of Inner Peace:**

    - By acknowledging that everything is temporary, we cultivate a deeper sense of inner peace. We become less reactive to external circumstances, realizing that our emotional well-being is not solely dependent on the stability of our environment. This inner peace enables us to navigate life's challenges with grace.

4. **Perspective on Life's Challenges:**

    - Acceptance of impermanence provides a broader perspective on life's challenges. Difficulties become part of the journey rather than insurmountable obstacles. This perspective shift allows us to approach problems with curiosity and a willingness to learn rather than despair.

5. **Focus on Growth and Change:**

    - Accepting that change is part of life encourages us to view experiences as opportunities for growth. Rather than fearing the unknown, we begin to embrace it, knowing that each change can lead to personal development and a deeper understanding of ourselves.

6. **Embracing Life's Transience:**

    - Finally, acceptance of impermanence teaches us to embrace life's transience. We learn to celebrate moments of joy, recognize the beauty in fleeting experiences, and find contentment in the present. This embrace of life's temporary nature enriches our experiences and fosters a sense of peace.

Accepting impermanence offers profound benefits that enhance our emotional resilience, foster gratitude, and promote peace of mind. By letting go of attachments and embracing change, we can navigate life with greater ease and appreciation, leading to a more fulfilling and serene existence.

The Role of Anicca in Personal Growth

Embracing Change as an Opportunity for Growth

Anicca, which means "impermanence" or "change," teaches us that everything in life is constantly changing. This can include our feelings, relationships, jobs, and even our physical surroundings. When we accept that change is a natural part of life, we can start to see it as an opportunity for personal growth.

1. **Understanding Change**: Change can be scary. We might worry about what will happen next or how we will cope. However, understanding that change is a part of life helps us become more open to new experiences. Instead of fearing change, we can view it as a chance to learn and grow.

2. **Adapting to New Situations**: When things change, we often have to adjust our plans and expectations. This adaptability is a valuable skill. By embracing change, we become more flexible and better at handling life's ups and downs. For example, if you move to a new city, you may feel lost at first, but over time, you will learn to navigate your new environment and meet new people.

3. **Finding New Opportunities**: Change can lead to new opportunities that we might not have considered before. For instance, if you lose a job, it might feel like a setback. But this change can also open the door to new career paths that you never thought about. By being open to these possibilities, you can discover new passions and strengths.

Learning to Let Go of Attachments

Another important aspect of Anicca is learning to let go of attachments. Attachments are strong emotional connections we have to people, things, or ideas. While attachments can provide comfort and security, they can also hold us back if we become too reliant on them.

1. **Understanding Attachments**: Attachments can make us feel safe, like when we have a favourite toy or a close friend. However, if we become too attached, we may struggle when things change. For example, if we cling to a friendship that is no longer healthy, we might miss out on new relationships that could bring us happiness.

2. **Accepting Change in Relationships**: People grow and change over time. Sometimes, friends or family members drift apart as their lives take different paths. Understanding Anicca helps us accept these

changes in our relationships. Instead of holding on to the past, we can cherish the good memories and be open to new connections.

3. **Letting Go of Material Possessions**: We often become attached to our belongings, whether it's our phone, clothes, or other possessions. When we learn to let go of these attachments, we free ourselves from the burden of materialism. This doesn't mean we have to give everything away, but we can learn to appreciate what we have without becoming overly dependent on it.

4. **Finding Inner Peace**: Letting go of attachments can lead to greater inner peace. When we stop clinging to things that are temporary, we can find contentment in the present moment. For example, instead of worrying about a future that we cannot control, we can focus on what makes us happy right now.

Understanding Anicca and embracing change as a part of life is crucial for personal growth. It teaches us to be flexible, to adapt, and to see new opportunities where we might have seen challenges before. Learning to let go of attachments helps us find freedom and peace, allowing us to appreciate the present moment without the weight of expectations or fears. By embracing both change and the process of letting go, we can grow into stronger, more resilient individuals who are ready to face whatever life brings our way.

Activities to Embrace Anicca

Reflection Exercises to Recognize Impermanence

1. **Daily Journaling**: Spend a few minutes each day writing about changes you observe in your life, such as the seasons, relationships, or personal feelings. Reflect on how these changes affect you and what you can learn from them.

2. **Change Inventory**: Create a list of significant changes you have experienced in the past year. Consider how each change has shaped your life, and think about the lessons you learned from those experiences.

3. **Nature Observation**: Spend time in nature and observe the changes around you. Notice how leaves change colour in autumn, flowers bloom in spring, and how landscapes evolve over time. Reflect on how this mirrors the changes in your own life.

Mindfulness Practices to Stay Present

1. **Mindful Breathing**: Take a few minutes each day to focus on your breath. Inhale deeply, hold for a moment, and exhale slowly. This

practice helps ground you in the present moment and reminds you of the impermanence of thoughts and feelings.

2. **Body Scan Meditation**: Lie down comfortably and slowly focus on different parts of your body, noticing any sensations without judgment. This practice encourages awareness of the present moment and helps you connect with the physical changes in your body.

3. **Gratitude Practice**: Each evening, write down three things you are grateful for that day. This activity helps you appreciate the present and recognize that these moments, like everything else, are temporary.

By engaging in these reflection exercises and mindfulness practices, you can embrace the concept of Anicca, fostering a deeper understanding of impermanence and enhancing your overall well-being.

Self-Reflection Exercise

Engaging in self-reflection is a powerful way to deepen your understanding of Anicca, or impermanence. By taking the time to consider how change affects your life, you can develop a healthier perspective on the ups and downs that come your way. Here are some guided questions and encouragement for journaling about your personal experiences with change.

Questions to Guide Thoughts on Impermanence

1. What changes have I experienced in the past year?
   - Reflect on significant events in your life, such as moving to a new place, starting a new job, ending a relationship, or experiencing a loss. Consider how these changes made you feel at the time and how they have influenced your current situation.

2. How did I respond to these changes?
   - Think about your emotional responses to the changes. Did you feel anxious, excited, sad, or relieved? Acknowledge your feelings without judgment, and consider how your reactions shaped your experience of change.

3. What lessons did I learn from these changes?
   - Every change offers an opportunity for growth. Reflect on what you learned about yourself or life in general from the changes you experienced. Did you discover new strengths or interests? Did you learn to adapt in ways you hadn't expected?

4. How do I cope with change?

    - Consider your coping mechanisms when faced with change. Do you seek support from friends and family? Do you turn to activities like exercise, art, or meditation? Understanding how you cope can help you identify strategies that work for you in the future.

5. What aspects of my life am I currently attached to?

    - Identify the people, possessions, or ideas you feel strongly attached to. Reflect on whether these attachments serve you positively or if they hold you back from embracing change. Are there attachments you might consider letting go of?

6. What positive changes would I like to invite into my life?

    - Think about the changes you desire. This could include personal growth, new experiences, or healthier relationships. Consider what steps you can take to make these changes a reality and how you can remain open to unexpected opportunities.

Encouragement to Journal About Personal Experiences with Change

Journaling Prompt: Find a quiet space where you can write freely. Set aside 10-15 minutes for this activity. Start by reflecting on the questions above, and allow your thoughts to flow onto the page. You don't need to worry about grammar or structure—just let your feelings and ideas pour out.

- **Describe a specific change you experienced**: Write about a moment in your life when you faced a significant change. What happened? How did you feel? What did you learn from this experience?

- **Explore your feelings**: Allow yourself to express the emotions tied to this change. Were you scared, relieved, confused, or hopeful? Writing about your feelings can help you process them and understand how they relate to the concept of impermanence.

- **Reflect on growth**: After describing the change, think about how it has shaped you as a person. What new perspectives or strengths have you gained? How has your understanding of impermanence deepened as a result?

- **Commit to embracing change**: As you conclude your journaling session, write down a commitment to embrace change in your life. This could be a simple statement, like "I will be open to the changes that come my way and see them as opportunities for growth."

By regularly engaging in self-reflection and journaling about your experiences with change, you can cultivate a deeper understanding of Anicca. This practice allows you to navigate the complexities of life with greater ease and acceptance, ultimately leading to personal growth and resilience.

Overcoming Fear of Change

Fear of change is a common experience that many young people face. It can hold us back from pursuing new opportunities, embracing growth, and living fully. Understanding these fears and learning strategies to manage them can empower us to navigate life's changes with confidence.

Common Fears Associated with Change

1. **Fear of the Unknown**: Many people fear what they cannot predict or control. The uncertainty that comes with change can be unsettling, leading to anxiety about the future.

2. **Fear of Failure**: The thought of failing in a new endeavour can be paralyzing. This fear may prevent individuals from taking risks or trying new things, as they worry about disappointing themselves or others.

3. **Fear of Loss**: Change often involves letting go of something familiar, whether it's a job, a relationship, or a comfortable routine. The fear of losing what we value can create resistance to change.

4. **Fear of Judgment**: Young people may worry about how others will perceive their decisions. Fear of judgment from friends, family, or peers can inhibit one's willingness to pursue change.

5. **Fear of Inadequacy**: Change can bring feelings of self-doubt, especially when facing new challenges. Young people might worry that they lack the skills or qualities needed to succeed in a new situation.

Strategies for Managing Fear and Uncertainty

1. **Acknowledge Your Feelings**: The first step in overcoming fear is to recognize and accept your feelings. Write down your fears and reflect on why they exist. Understanding that fear is a normal reaction can help lessen its power over you.

2. **Reframe Your Thoughts**: Instead of viewing change as a threat, try to see it as an opportunity for growth and learning. Remind yourself of past experiences where change led to positive outcomes.

3. **Break It Down**: When facing a big change, break it down into smaller, manageable steps. Focus on one step at a time rather than getting overwhelmed by the entire process.

4. **Set Realistic Goals**: Establish achievable goals related to the change you are facing. Setting small, attainable objectives can help build your confidence and reduce anxiety.

5. **Seek Support**: Talk to friends, family, or mentors about your fears. Sharing your concerns can provide relief and help you gain different perspectives on the situation.

6. **Practice Mindfulness**: Mindfulness techniques, such as deep breathing or meditation, can help calm your mind and reduce feelings of anxiety. Regular practice can foster a sense of peace and grounding in uncertain situations.

7. **Visualize Success**: Take a moment to visualize yourself successfully navigating the change. Imagine how you would feel and what steps you would take. This mental exercise can help build confidence and alleviate fears.

8. **Embrace a Growth Mindset**: Adopt the belief that abilities and intelligence can be developed through effort and learning. Viewing challenges as opportunities for personal development can shift your perspective and reduce fear.

9. **Reflect on Past Successes**: Recall previous changes you have navigated successfully. Remind yourself of the strengths and skills you used to overcome challenges, which can reassure you of your ability to handle new situations.

10. **Stay Open to Possibilities**: Embrace the idea that change can bring unexpected benefits. Stay curious about what might unfold as you take steps forward. This mindset can transform fear into excitement.

By recognizing and addressing the fears associated with change, young people can empower themselves to embrace new opportunities. Implementing these strategies can help manage anxiety, fostering a sense of resilience and adaptability in an ever-changing world.

The Journey Continues

As we navigate through life, it's essential to recognize that change is not just an event; it is a fundamental aspect of our existence. Everything around us is in a state of flux, from the seasons that shift outside our windows to the phases of our own lives. Change is natural and unavoidable, and embracing this truth can profoundly impact how we perceive and respond to the world.

Change as a Natural Part of Life

Change happens every day. It can be as small as a daily routine or as significant as moving to a new city or starting a new job. Life is like a river that keeps flowing, sometimes gently and sometimes with turbulence. When we accept that change is a normal part of life, we can approach it with curiosity rather than fear.

Think about the seasons. Winter brings a blanket of snow, spring bursts with new life, summer shines with warmth, and autumn presents a stunning array of colours. Each season has its beauty and challenges, reminding us that change can be enriching and transformative. Just like nature, we too experience different seasons in our lives. Understanding this can help us navigate our personal journeys with grace and resilience.

Growth Through Embracing Impermanence

When we embrace the idea of impermanence, we open ourselves to growth. Every change presents an opportunity to learn and evolve. It encourages us to step outside our comfort zones and discover new strengths we didn't know we had.

Consider a young artist who feels stuck in their creative process. By embracing the changes in their style, medium, or subject matter, they can unlock new avenues of expression. Each experiment, each moment of discomfort, contributes to their growth as an artist. The same applies to every individual—by allowing ourselves to explore the unfamiliar, we cultivate our potential and enrich our experiences.

Moreover, accepting that nothing is permanent can help us appreciate the present moment. When we realize that today's joys, struggles, and relationships are temporary, we learn to savor them fully. This mindset encourages gratitude and mindfulness, allowing us to live more fully in the here and now.

As you move forward, remember that your journey is ongoing. Embrace each change, whether big or small, as an essential part of your growth. Welcome the lessons that come with change, and allow them to shape you into the person you aspire to be.

In conclusion, the journey of understanding and embracing impermanence is a lifelong adventure. It is about finding strength in change, discovering beauty in uncertainty, and realizing that every moment holds the potential for growth. So, take a deep breath, open your heart to change, and embark on the journey ahead with courage and curiosity. The world is full of possibilities waiting for you to explore.

Key Notes on Anicca

1. Definition of Anicca: Anicca, or impermanence, is the understanding that everything in life is constantly changing. Nothing is permanent, and all experiences, emotions, and situations are temporary.

2. Examples of Change: Change is evident in everyday life, from the changing seasons to the evolution of relationships. Recognizing these changes can help us appreciate life's journey.

3. Importance of Understanding Impermanence: Understanding that everything is temporary can reduce suffering and help us manage our expectations. It encourages us to cherish the present moment.

4. Acceptance of Impermanence: Accepting that change is a natural part of life brings peace of mind. It allows us to let go of attachments and live more freely.

5. Wisdom from Spiritual Leaders: Teachings from figures like Guru Nanak, Buddha, and Krishna emphasize the significance of recognizing impermanence and the futility of attachment to the material world.

6. Growth Through Anicca: Embracing change can lead to personal growth. Each change is an opportunity to learn, adapt, and evolve.

7. Activities to Embrace Anicca: Reflection exercises and mindfulness practices can help individuals become more aware of impermanence and cultivate acceptance.

8. Overcoming Fear of Change: Understanding common fears associated with change and learning strategies to manage them can empower individuals to embrace life's uncertainties.

9. The Journey Continues: Life is a continuous journey of change. Embracing impermanence is essential for growth and discovering the beauty in every moment.

Actionable Insights

1. Practice Mindfulness: Spend a few minutes each day practicing mindfulness to stay present and appreciate the moment. Focus on your breath, surroundings, and feelings.

2. Reflect on Change: Keep a journal to reflect on changes in your life. Write about how these changes have affected you and what you have learned from them.

3. Let Go of Attachments: Identify areas in your life where you may be overly attached, whether to people, possessions, or routines. Practice letting go and see how it affects your sense of freedom.

4. Seek Growth Opportunities: Embrace new experiences and challenges. Whether it's trying a new hobby or meeting new people, stepping outside your comfort zone can lead to personal growth.

5. Accept Change: Remind yourself that change is a natural part of life. When faced with challenges, ask yourself how this change can help you grow.

6. Celebrate Small Changes: Acknowledge and celebrate small changes in your life, whether it's a new habit you've formed or a mindset shift. Recognizing these changes can build resilience.

7. Share Your Journey: Talk to friends or family about your experiences with change. Sharing can provide support and encourage others to embrace impermanence as well.

By understanding and implementing these key concepts and actionable insights about Anicca, readers can cultivate a healthier relationship with change, leading to personal growth and a more fulfilling life.

In conclusion, understanding Anicca, or impermanence, is crucial for navigating life's ever-changing landscape. It teaches us that nothing is permanent, prompting us to embrace change as a natural part of our journey. By accepting the transient nature of our experiences, we can let go of attachments that hold us back and cultivate a greater appreciation for the present moment. This mindset not only fosters resilience but also encourages us to live fully, cherish each experience, and grow from the inevitable changes we encounter. Embrace the beauty of impermanence, for it is through change that we discover our true selves and create a meaningful life.

Chapter 11

Digital Detox

Reclaiming Your Time and Focus

What is Digital Detox

A *digital detox* is a break from using electronic devices like smartphones, computers, and social media. It's about intentionally stepping away from screens and the internet to focus on other aspects of life. Just as our bodies benefit from a rest day after exercise, our minds benefit from taking breaks from digital devices.

In our fast-paced digital age, taking time to disconnect from technology has become more important than ever. With constant notifications, emails, and social media updates, it's easy to feel overwhelmed and overstimulated. This nonstop flow of information can make it difficult to focus, increase stress levels, and lead to digital burnout. By stepping away from screens, we allow our minds to rest, which helps reduce anxiety and improves our overall mental health.

Disconnecting from technology also gives us the chance to reconnect with ourselves and those around us. When we put down our devices, we're more present with our family, friends, and the world around us. This helps us build stronger relationships, enjoy real-life experiences, and truly appreciate the moment. Additionally, reducing screen time can improve sleep quality, as the blue light from screens disrupts our natural sleep cycles, making it harder to rest well.

Taking breaks from technology also helps increase productivity and creativity. Without the constant distractions of notifications and apps, we're able to focus better on tasks and think more clearly. This allows us to use our time more effectively and engage more deeply in activities that bring us fulfilment. Disconnecting from digital devices is a powerful way to reclaim our time, boost our well-being, and enjoy a more balanced, fulfilling life in a technology-driven world.

Understanding Digital Overload

Digital overload happens when we spend too much time on digital devices, leading to overstimulation and mental exhaustion. In our technology-driven lives, we're constantly bombarded by a flood of notifications, messages, and information. This can be overwhelming for our brains, which aren't designed to process so much input at once. Digital overload can make us feel anxious, distracted, and even disconnected from the world around us.

The impact of digital overload on mental health is significant. Studies show that excessive screen time, especially on social media, can lead to feelings of isolation, low self-esteem, and stress. Being constantly "plugged in" also affects our sleep, as exposure to screens disrupts our natural sleep cycle, leading to fatigue and reduced productivity during the day. This ongoing stress can harm our ability to focus, making it difficult to complete tasks or enjoy moments without reaching for a device.

Signs That Indicate the Need for a Digital Detox

There are some clear signs that may indicate you're experiencing digital overload and could benefit from a digital detox:

1. **Constant Checking**: Feeling the need to check your phone or other devices frequently, even when there are no new notifications.

2. **Difficulty Sleeping**: Trouble falling asleep or staying asleep, often after late-night screen use.

3. **Decreased Attention Span**: Difficulty focusing on tasks or conversations without the urge to check your phone.

4. **Stress and Anxiety**: Increased feelings of anxiety or stress that seem connected to online activity or social media.

5. **Reduced Social Interaction**: Avoiding face-to-face interactions or feeling distant from people around you due to digital distractions.

If these signs sound familiar, it may be time for a digital detox. Taking intentional breaks from screens can help you regain balance, improve mental clarity, and reduce stress.

Benefits of a Digital Detox

1. **Improved Mental Clarity and Focus**

   Being constantly connected can make our thoughts feel scattered and our attention fragmented. With every notification and message, our focus is disrupted, making it harder to think clearly. Taking time off from screens helps the mind recalibrate and find stillness, which allows us to concentrate better and prioritize tasks more effectively. For instance, imagine a student who temporarily disables their social media accounts while studying for exams. They may find they retain information better and complete tasks faster, ultimately improving both their learning and focus.

2. **Enhanced Relationships and Social Interactions**
   When we are too focused on our devices, we often miss out on meaningful interactions with the people around us. By stepping away from screens, we become more present with loved ones and more engaged in conversations. For example, families that designate "device-free" dinners or weekends often report a stronger sense of closeness and connection. By setting boundaries around digital usage, we can create space for genuine connections, allowing us to actively listen and communicate, which enriches relationships and nurtures trust.

3. **Better Sleep Quality and Overall Well-Being**
   Screen time, especially before bed, can disrupt sleep cycles due to the blue light emitted by devices, which interferes with melatonin production—the hormone that regulates sleep. Reducing or eliminating screen exposure before bedtime helps the body relax and promotes better sleep quality. For instance, someone who starts a "no screens one hour before bed" routine might soon notice they fall asleep faster and wake up feeling more refreshed. This improvement in sleep has a ripple effect on overall health, reducing stress and enhancing mood and energy levels.

In essence, a digital detox has profound benefits for mental clarity, relationships, and physical health. By disconnecting from technology at times, we allow ourselves to recharge, reconnect, and experience life more fully.

Identifying Your Digital Habits

1. **Self-Reflection Exercise to Assess Current Technology Use**
   Start by understanding your tech habits with a bit of self-reflection. This process involves observing your daily routines and noting how often, why, and for what purposes you reach for your devices. Consider keeping a simple log of your screen time over a few days. Record each time you pick up your phone or log onto social media, noting what you intended to do and how long you actually spent. You may find that while you originally picked up your phone to check a message, you end up scrolling through social media for an extra 30 minutes.

   Reflect on how these habits make you feel. For example, do you feel drained, stressed, or relaxed after certain activities? Are there specific times, like before bed or upon waking up, where tech usage affects your mood or productivity? Understanding the emotional impact of each digital activity helps you see where to adjust. This exercise reveals your unconscious habits, making it easier to choose where to focus your digital detox efforts.

2. **Identifying Time-Wasting Apps and Activities**

   Once you've tracked your tech use, take a closer look at which apps and online activities consume the most time without adding real value. These are often the "automatic" behaviours, such as aimlessly scrolling through social media, endlessly watching short videos, or repeatedly refreshing news feeds. Recognize the apps you instinctively reach for in idle moments, such as during a commute or a work break.

To help you identify these, consider asking yourself questions like:

- Are there apps or websites I tend to lose track of time on?
- Do certain apps leave me feeling unfulfilled or frustrated afterward?
- How often do I use specific apps simply out of habit?

For example, if you notice that TikTok, Facebook, WhatsApp or Instagram occupies hours of your day without much benefit, you might consider setting screen time limits for these apps or turning off their notifications to reduce the temptation to check them. Similarly, if checking your work emails frequently in the evening causes stress, you might decide to set a specific time limit for work-related activities outside of office hours.

Taking time to identify these patterns will empower you to make meaningful changes, allowing you to cut out distractions and make room for healthier, more fulfilling activities in your day-to-day life.

Strategies for a Successful Digital Detox

1. **Setting Boundaries Around Technology Use**

   Creating boundaries for tech use is a fundamental step in a digital detox. This can mean setting screen time limits on your phone or computer, especially for apps that tend to consume your time and attention. Most smartphones and computers have built-in tools to track usage and limit access to specific apps after a certain amount of time. You might, for example, decide to limit social media apps to 30 minutes per day or turn off notifications in the evenings to avoid distractions during relaxation time. Setting these limits allows you to control your tech use instead of letting it control you.

2. **Designating Tech-Free Zones and Times**

   Another effective strategy is to create "tech-free" zones or times where you consciously choose not to use digital devices. Tech-free zones can be specific areas in your home, like the dining table or the bedroom. Keeping devices out of the bedroom, for instance, helps improve sleep quality by reducing blue light exposure and allows you to start and end the day without screen distractions.

You can also designate tech-free times, such as an hour after waking up or during meals. Many people find it beneficial to avoid screens for an hour before bedtime, which can improve both the quality of sleep and relaxation. These tech-free spaces and times allow you to connect more deeply with yourself and others without digital distractions.

1. **Finding Alternative Activities to Engage In**
   A successful digital detox isn't just about limiting tech use but also about replacing screen time with meaningful offline activities. Consider exploring new or long-neglected hobbies, like reading, gardening, exercising, painting, or even learning to cook new dishes. Engaging in creative activities not only gives you something fulfilling to do in place of screen time but also provides a sense of accomplishment and joy.

Physical activities are especially beneficial, as they can improve mood and mental clarity. For instance, instead of watching videos after work, you might go for a walk, hit the gym, or take up a dance class. Replacing digital time with these kinds of enriching activities helps you recharge and makes the digital detox experience more enjoyable.

By setting clear boundaries, creating tech-free zones, and finding engaging alternatives, you can approach a digital detox as a positive lifestyle change, making it easier to stick with and enjoy the benefits.

Tips for Maintaining a Healthy Relationship with Technology

1. **Mindful Consumption of Digital Content**
   Mindful consumption means using technology with intentionality, paying attention to how it affects you, and choosing how much time to spend on it. For example, if you find yourself mindlessly scrolling through social media or checking your phone out of habit, it's a good practice to pause and ask: "Is this adding value to my day?"

   - **Example**: A person might realize that watching videos on YouTube for hours isn't bringing any joy, and instead, it is leaving them feeling drained or anxious. They decide to be more mindful by choosing to watch videos that are educational or uplifting, instead of mindlessly browsing. They might also set time limits for watching videos or reading online articles.

2. **Tools and Apps That Promote a Balanced Tech Lifestyle**
   Various apps and tools are designed to help people manage their

screen time and foster a more balanced relationship with technology. These tools can track your usage and give you insights into how you are spending your time, which helps you make more conscious decisions.

- **Example**: The "Screen Time" feature on iPhones allows users to track how much time they spend on individual apps. It can even block apps or set limits for certain apps, which helps reduce the time spent on distractions like social media. A person might use this tool to set a daily limit for Facebook or Instagram, helping them avoid unnecessary scrolling and promoting a healthier balance between offline and online life.
  - Another useful tool is the "Forest" app, which encourages users to stay focused by growing a virtual tree. The more you stay off your phone, the more your tree grows. It is a fun way to motivate yourself to avoid distractions and engage in more offline activities like reading, exercising, or spending time with family.

By being mindful of how we consume digital content and using tools that promote balance, we can create a healthier relationship with technology, helping us avoid digital burnout while benefiting from all the positive aspects it offers.

Real-Life Examples and Testimonials

A **Digital Detox** can have profound effects on a person's life, not only in terms of reducing stress and anxiety but also in improving mental clarity, relationships, and overall well-being. Let's explore a few real-life stories of individuals who embraced a digital detox and transformed their lives by reclaiming their time.

1. **Story of Pooja – Finding Balance Between Work and Personal Life**

   Pooja, a 34-year-old marketing executive, was constantly connected to her work through her smartphone and laptop. She would check emails late into the night and scroll through work-related messages on social media during weekends. This overexposure to work led to high stress levels, anxiety, and a feeling of being "always on." As a result, her personal life, including time with her family and friends, was suffering.

   The Digital Detox Process: Pooja decided to take a break from technology by establishing clear boundaries between work and personal time. She started by turning off work notifications after 6 p.m. and designating Sundays as her "tech-free day" – no emails, no social media, and no work-related calls. She also made it a rule not to check her phone immediately after waking up in the morning or right before going to bed.

Transformation: Over time, Pooja began to feel more present in her relationships. Her anxiety decreased, and she noticed that her focus during work hours improved. By reclaiming her time and disconnecting from digital distractions, she also found more time to engage in hobbies like reading and cooking, which she had neglected for years. Pooja was able to enjoy more fulfilling family time, reducing the negative impacts that constant digital engagement had on her well-being.

2.   **Story of Rupesh – Rediscovering Mindfulness**

Rupesh, a 42-year-old entrepreneur, had always been glued to his phone. He would check social media, news, and messages throughout the day, and it felt like he couldn't get away from his screen. His constant use of digital devices not only made him less productive but also impacted his emotional state. He felt drained, distracted, and disconnected from his own thoughts and feelings.

The Digital Detox Process: Rupesh decided to take a 7-day digital detox. He started by completely turning off all notifications, leaving his phone in another room for a couple of hours a day, and focusing on being present in the moment. He also practiced mindfulness meditation and spent more time in nature, disconnected from digital devices. He set time limits for checking emails and used his "phone-free" hours to read, exercise, and engage in activities that allowed him to recharge.

Transformation: After just a week, Rupesh felt calmer and more cantered. He began to experience greater emotional balance and found that he was able to be more productive at work. The time he spent off his devices allowed him to reconnect with his hobbies and deepen his relationships with loved ones. He became more mindful in his daily life, and this increased sense of awareness allowed him to be more present, improving his mental health and emotional well-being.

3.   **Story of Gehna – Reconnecting with Her Family**

Gehna, a 29-year-old software developer, was caught up in the fast-paced world of technology. She worked long hours on her computer and often found herself staring at her phone while having dinner with her family. This left her feeling disconnected from the people closest to her, and she realized that her relationship with her family was suffering.

The Digital Detox Process: Gehna decided to implement a digital detox routine by limiting her screen time in the evenings. She set a rule that no devices would be used during family dinners, and she dedicated her weekends to spending quality time with her family. She started going for evening walks without her phone, focusing on engaging in face-to-face conversations instead of getting lost in digital distractions.

Transformation: As a result, Gehna started to feel a stronger sense of connection with her family. They began to have meaningful conversations during dinner, and she realized how much she had been missing out on. Gehna also felt more relaxed, as taking a break from constant notifications and emails gave her time to focus on herself and the people who mattered most. Her newfound sense of balance and awareness made her work more enjoyable and gave her greater peace of mind.

4.   **Story of Pratham – Reclaiming Time for Self-Care**

Pratham, a 27-year-old university student, found that he was spending most of his free time online—watching videos, chatting with friends on social media, and browsing the internet. Although he was social and connected, he often felt exhausted and struggled to concentrate on his studies. He realized that his digital habits were taking up much-needed time for self-care and personal development.

The Digital Detox Process: Pratham decided to try a 30-day digital detox challenge. During this time, he set limits on social media use, only allowing himself 30 minutes per day to scroll through his feeds. He removed unnecessary apps from his phone and scheduled specific times to check his email. Pratham also replaced screen time with activities that benefited his mental and physical health, such as yoga, reading, and spending time outdoors.

Transformation: After a month of detoxing, Pratham felt more energetic and focused. He was able to dedicate more time to his studies, improving his academic performance. Additionally, he noticed improvements in his mental clarity and self-discipline. Taking time away from screens allowed him to prioritize his health and well-being, and he felt a greater sense of accomplishment and balance in his life.

These stories highlight how disconnecting from technology can lead to transformative changes in one's life. Whether it's regaining mental clarity, improving relationships, fostering emotional well-being, or making more time for self-care, the benefits of a digital detox are profound. For Sarah,

Ramesh, Priya, and Arjun, it wasn't just about reducing screen time—it was about reclaiming their time, focusing on what truly mattered, and taking steps towards a more balanced, fulfilled life. By taking a break from digital overload, these individuals were able to reconnect with themselves, their loved ones, and the world around them, finding deeper meaning and contentment in their lives.

Activities for Implementing a Digital Detox

Implementing a digital detox involves more than just disconnecting from your devices. It's about creating intentional moments of reflection and connection in the real world. Here are some activities that can help you stay committed to a digital detox, along with examples of how to carry them out in real life.

1. **Group Activities for Encouraging a Digital Detox**

   Engaging in group activities can create a supportive environment for everyone to disconnect and engage in a tech-free experience together. This can help motivate individuals to stay committed and reap the benefits of the detox as a group. Here are a few group activity ideas:

   Tech-Free Challenge Weekend

   A simple yet effective group activity is to organize a **tech-free weekend** with friends, family, or coworkers. The goal is for everyone to stay away from screens for the entire weekend, using the time instead for face-to-face conversations, outdoor activities, or creative hobbies.

   - **Example**: A group of friends decides to take a **"Tech-Free Saturday"** challenge, where they plan to spend the entire day without their phones or computers. They plan to visit a park, have a picnic, and enjoy an afternoon of board games, ensuring no one is distracted by their devices. By focusing on shared experiences and quality time, the challenge helps them reconnect with each other without the interference of technology.

   Digital Detox Book Club

   Another fun group activity is starting a **digital detox book club**, where participants agree to read books (instead of scrolling through their phones) and meet regularly to discuss them. The key element of this activity is to encourage participants to disconnect from digital distractions and focus on a meaningful activity like reading.

   - **Example**: A local community group forms a book club where members agree to leave their phones in another room while they read their selected book. After a week of reading, they meet at a local coffee shop to discuss the book and share their reflections, all while staying present and enjoying the conversation without the distractions of screens.

Outdoor Retreats

Organizing an **outdoor retreat** or weekend getaway is an excellent way to encourage digital detox. When everyone is immersed in nature, surrounded by the beauty of the natural world, there's less temptation to check phones or devices.

- **Example**: A family plans a weekend camping trip to a national park where the rule is no phones, tablets, or laptops. Instead, they spend time hiking, cooking meals together, playing games, and having conversations under the stars. The disconnection from technology helps everyone feel more relaxed, and they return from the retreat with a renewed sense of connection to each other.

2. **Journaling Prompts for Reflecting on Experiences During the Detox**

Journaling can be a powerful tool to reflect on your experiences during a digital detox. Writing about the process can help you track progress, notice patterns in your behaviour, and gain deeper insights into how your relationship with technology is affecting your life. Here are some journaling prompts you can use to reflect on your detox:

Before the Detox

Before beginning your digital detox, write about your current habits and mindset surrounding technology. This will give you a clear picture of your relationship with digital devices and where you want to improve.

- **Example**: "What role does technology currently play in my daily routine? How do I feel when I am constantly connected to_my phone or laptop? What do I hope to achieve from this digital detox?"

During the Detox

As you go through the detox process, write about how you feel each day. Pay attention to any physical, emotional, or mental changes that you notice. These reflections can help you stay motivated and understand the impact of a digital detox.

- **Example**: "Today is Day 3 of my digital detox. I felt uneasy in the morning, like I was missing out on something by not checking my phone. But by mid-day, I noticed I was more present with my family during lunch. I feel less stressed and more in tune with my surroundings. How does this experience feel compared to my usual routine?"

After the Detox

Once you complete your digital detox, reflect on how the experience has impacted you and what lessons you've learned. This will help solidify the benefits and guide you in creating a healthier relationship with technology moving forward.

- **Example**: "The digital detox is over, and I've learned so much about myself. I realized I don't need to check my phone every five minutes to feel connected. I now feel more confident setting boundaries around my technology use, and I'm excited to continue using the lessons I learned. How do I want my relationship with technology to change moving forward?"

Reflection on Connections and Relationships

Use journaling to reflect on how your relationships and social interactions have changed since your digital detox. Writing down your thoughts on reconnecting with loved ones can help you see the positive effects of the detox on your life.

- **Example**: "During the digital detox, I spent more time talking to my family face-to-face. I realized how much more meaningful our conversations were when we weren't distracted by phones. It felt so good to truly connect with them. How can I continue to make space for these kinds of conversations in my daily life?"

These group activities and journaling prompts work because they encourage intentional breaks from technology, promoting mindfulness and self-awareness. Whether you're participating in a tech-free challenge or reflecting in your journal, both practices help you reconnect with the present moment and real-life connections. These activities are practical steps that can help you establish a healthier relationship with technology, and they provide a roadmap for maintaining a balanced and focused life.

Overcoming Challenges in Digital Detox

Embarking on a digital detox is not always easy, as it involves breaking free from habits that have become deeply ingrained in our daily lives. During the detox, you may face several challenges that can make it difficult to stay committed. Here are some common barriers to a digital detox and tips for overcoming them.

1. **Common Barriers to a Digital Detox**
   FOMO (Fear of Missing Out)

One of the biggest challenges when doing a digital detox is the fear of missing out on social events, news, or updates. Social media often creates a sense of urgency to stay connected and updated, and stepping away from it can make you feel disconnected or isolated.

1. **Example**: You may feel like you're missing important social interactions or updates about your friends, work, or the world. This can be especially challenging if you rely on your phone for social validation or to keep in touch with others.

Work Requirements

For many, technology is not just a source of entertainment but a necessary tool for work. Disconnecting from email, messaging apps, and work-related platforms can feel impossible when your job demands constant connectivity. This barrier is especially hard for those working in fast-paced environments or jobs requiring real-time communication.

- **Example**: You may feel that taking time away from your phone or email could affect your work performance or cause you to miss important deadlines, meetings, or messages from colleagues.

Habitual Use of Technology

Many of us are so used to checking our phones or computers regularly throughout the day that it becomes almost second nature. The compulsion to check notifications, emails, or social media is deeply rooted in our routines, making it difficult to stop without feeling a sense of withdrawal.

- **Example**: You may catch yourself reaching for your phone automatically when you feel bored or anxious, even though you know you're supposed to be detoxing. This habitual behaviour can be hard to break.

Uncertainty About What to Do Without Technology

Some people worry that without their devices, they won't know how to fill their time. Technology has become a primary source of entertainment, news, and even relaxation for many, so stepping away from it may feel uncomfortable or even boring at first.

- **Example**: You might feel uneasy or anxious when you have no access to your phone, unsure of how to spend your free time without checking social media or catching up on the news.

2. Tips for Staying Committed During the Detox Period

Set Clear Boundaries and Goals

It's important to have a clear idea of why you're doing the detox and what you hope to achieve. Setting specific goals for your detox, such as limiting social media time to 30 minutes a day or designating certain hours as tech-free, will help keep you motivated and focused on your goal.

- **Example**: Set a clear goal like, "I'll only check social media for 30 minutes in the evening," or "I will not look at my phone during meals." This way, you create realistic boundaries that are easier to follow, and you'll feel more in control of your digital habits.

Communicate with Others

If work or social obligations make it hard to disconnect, communicate with others about your detox. Let your colleagues or family members know that you'll be offline or limiting your tech use for a while. By setting expectations with others, you can avoid feeling guilty or worried about missing important messages.

- **Example**: If you need to be available for urgent work matters, inform your colleagues that you'll be taking a short digital detox but will check your email once in the morning and once in the evening. This way, you're still reachable when necessary but without constantly being plugged in.

Replace Technology with New Activities

One of the best ways to combat the discomfort of a detox is to replace digital habits with enriching, tech-free activities. Try hobbies like reading, cooking, painting, or spending time outdoors. The more you find enjoyable, screen-free activities, the less you'll miss your devices.

- **Example**: Replace your evening screen time with a relaxing walk, or instead of scrolling through social media, pick up a good book. Engaging in these activities will fill the space left by technology and help you feel more present.

Take Small Breaks

If going fully offline is too overwhelming, you can ease into your digital detox by starting small. Set aside specific times during the day when you completely disconnect, such as during meals or before bed. Gradually increase these tech-free periods over time until you feel comfortable with a longer detox.

- **Example**: Begin by designating 30 minutes each day as a tech-free time to unwind. As you become more comfortable, extend that time to an hour or two, eventually working your way to a full digital detox day or weekend.

Practice Self-Compassion

It's important to be kind to yourself during the detox process. If you slip up and check your phone or email when you're not supposed to, don't be too hard on yourself. Digital detoxing is a practice, and the goal is to reduce your dependence on technology, not to be perfect. Acknowledge the slip-up, and get back on track without guilt.

- **Example**: If you accidentally check your social media during your detox, rather than feeling frustrated, remind yourself that breaking the habit takes time. Recommit to your detox goals and move forward with a positive attitude.

Real-Life Example

Let's take the example of *Ritu*, a working professional, who was constantly glued to her phone for work-related emails and social media updates. Ritu decided to do a digital detox to improve her mental health and focus on her personal life. However, she initially struggled with FOMO, and the thought of missing work updates or social media interactions made her anxious. To overcome this, she set boundaries by checking her work email only twice a day, and she also communicated with her team that she would be offline during weekends to focus on her family. Slowly, she replaced her phone time with walks and journaling. Over time, she noticed an improvement in her relationships and felt more productive at work. By practicing self-compassion and taking gradual steps, she successfully completed her digital detox and established healthier habits for using technology in the future.

The Journey Continues

The digital detox journey doesn't have to be a one-time event. Instead, it should be an ongoing process that helps you maintain a healthier, more balanced relationship with technology. As you move forward, it's essential to periodically reassess your technology use and make adjustments where necessary. Technology will continue to evolve, and so will your relationship with it. The key is to stay mindful of how it affects your well-being and make intentional decisions about how and when to engage with it.

Encouragement to Periodically Reassess Technology Use

As we move through life, our relationship with technology can shift. Sometimes, we may find ourselves slipping back into old habits, spending more time on screens than we intend. This is natural, but it's important to take a step back from time to time and assess your digital habits. Reassessing your use of technology regularly allows you to remain aware of how it's impacting your life and adjust accordingly.

- **Example**: In many households across Punjab, families have started setting up monthly "Digital Check-Ins," where they reflect on their screen time, discuss their tech habits, and set new goals for reducing screen time if necessary. These check-ins help them stay on track and ensure they're not falling back into unhealthy habits.

Just as you would check your physical health regularly, it's crucial to check in with your digital health. Make it a habit to evaluate your digital habits weekly, monthly, or even quarterly. Ask yourself questions like:

- How much time am I spending on my phone, computer, or social media?
- Do I feel stressed or distracted by digital devices?
- How is my screen time impacting my relationships, sleep, and productivity?
- Am I using technology mindfully, or is it controlling me?

Emphasizing the Importance of Maintaining a Balanced Relationship with Digital Tools

In today's world, it's impossible to completely disconnect from technology, and that's not the goal of a digital detox. The aim is to maintain a balanced relationship with digital tools. Technology can be incredibly beneficial for work, learning, and staying connected with loved ones, but it's essential to ensure that it doesn't dominate your life or prevent you from engaging in real-life experiences.

Balance comes from conscious decisions about how and when to use digital devices. This means being intentional with your screen time, setting boundaries, and ensuring that technology enhances rather than detracts from your life.

- **Example**: Take the example of a family in Kapurthala who adopted a simple rule: No phones at the dinner table. This small habit has created more meaningful connections and conversations during meals. They also set aside one day a week as a "Tech-Free Sunday" to spend quality time together without distractions. It's a balance that works for them, allowing them to enjoy the benefits of technology while fostering deeper family bonds.

Key Tips to Maintain a Balanced Relationship with Technology:

- **Set daily tech limits**: Decide on a specific amount of time you want to spend on social media, checking emails, or watching TV. Once you hit the limit, step away and engage in something else.
- **Create tech-free zones**: Make certain areas of your home, like the bedroom or dining room, tech-free zones where you can disconnect from screens and be present in the moment.
- **Practice digital mindfulness**: Be intentional about your use of technology. Before you pick up your phone or open your laptop, ask yourself: "What is my purpose for using this device

right now?" This will help you stay focused and avoid mindless scrolling or aimless browsing.

Maintaining a balanced relationship with technology allows you to stay productive, informed, and connected, while also preserving your mental and emotional well-being. With time and practice, you'll find that you can enjoy the best of both worlds—leveraging technology for its benefits without letting it take over your life.

Key Notes on Digital Detox

1. **Digital Detox Defined**: A digital detox is the practice of disconnecting from technology for a set period to reclaim time, reduce stress, and improve overall well-being. It involves stepping away from digital devices like phones, computers, and social media.

2. **The Need for a Detox**: In today's tech-driven world, constant screen time and digital engagement can lead to mental overload, stress, and even physical issues like eye strain and disrupted sleep. A digital detox helps break these patterns and promotes a healthier relationship with technology.

3. **Identifying Digital Overload**: Recognizing when technology is negatively impacting your mental health, relationships, and daily life is the first step toward a detox. Common signs include feeling distracted, anxious, or unproductive due to excessive screen time.

4. **Benefits of a Digital Detox**:
   - **Improved Mental Clarity and Focus**: Disconnecting from distractions allows the mind to rest, improving productivity and concentration.
   - **Enhanced Relationships**: Spending quality, uninterrupted time with loved ones fosters deeper connections.
   - **Better Sleep and Well-being**: Reducing screen time, especially before bed, leads to improved sleep quality and overall health.

5. **Strategies for a Successful Detox**: Setting boundaries around screen time, designating tech-free zones, and engaging in non-digital activities like reading, hobbies, or spending time outdoors can make the detox easier and more effective.

6. **Staying Committed**: Overcoming barriers like fear of missing out (FOMO), work-related tech needs, or the temptation to check notifications is essential. Setting goals and making the detox a group activity can help maintain motivation.

7. **Maintaining a Balanced Relationship with Technology**: After the detox, periodically reassessing technology use is important. The goal

is not to avoid technology completely, but to use it in a way that enhances your life without taking away from real-life experiences.

Actionable Insights for Readers to Implement in Their Lives

1. **Schedule Regular Digital Detox Days**: Dedicate one day a week or a weekend each month to completely disconnect from screens. Use this time to engage in offline activities that nurture your mind and body, such as walking, reading, or spending time with family.

2. **Set Tech-Free Zones**: Create tech-free zones in your home, such as the dining table or bedroom, where you can engage in real-life conversations and activities without distractions from devices.

3. **Limit Screen Time**: Use built-in phone or computer features to track and limit screen time on apps like social media or entertainment platforms. Aim to reduce your usage gradually, with the goal of having more focused and productive time.

4. **Practice Mindful Technology Use**: Before reaching for your phone or computer, ask yourself whether you really need to use it at that moment. Set intentions for how much time you want to spend on digital tasks.

5. **Create New Tech-Free Habits**: Replace digital habits with healthier alternatives. For example, instead of scrolling on your phone before bed, try reading a book or meditating for a few minutes. These habits can help you wind down and improve sleep quality.

6. **Engage in Offline Activities**: Reconnect with hobbies or activities that don't involve screens. This could be anything from cooking a new recipe to playing a sport, gardening, or crafting.

7. **Start a Group Detox Challenge**: Encourage friends or family to join you in a digital detox. Share your experiences and support each other in staying off screens for a set time. This can make the detox more enjoyable and effective.

8. **Reflect and Adjust**: After your digital detox, take some time to reflect on how it made you feel. Did you feel more relaxed? Did you have better conversations? Use these insights to adjust your relationship with technology moving forward.

By following these actionable insights, you can create a healthier, more balanced life that allows technology to complement your well-being instead of overpowering it.

In today's fast-paced, digital-driven world, a digital detox is not just a luxury—it's a necessity. Constant exposure to screens and digital distractions can take a toll on our mental health, relationships, and overall well-being. By taking the time to disconnect, we give ourselves the opportunity to reconnect with what truly matters—our thoughts, emotions, and the people around us.

The significance of a digital detox lies in its ability to restore balance to our lives. It allows us to reclaim our time, focus on the present moment, and engage in meaningful, face-to-face connections that often get overshadowed by digital noise. It also offers mental clarity, better sleep, and a more profound sense of peace, helping us lead a healthier, more fulfilled life.

As we continue to live in an increasingly connected world, it's essential to prioritize our time and well-being over mindless scrolling and constant connectivity. Regularly stepping away from technology gives us the space to recharge, reset, and refocus on our personal goals and relationships.

Remember, it's not about eliminating technology altogether; it's about finding a balanced, intentional approach to its use. By implementing regular digital detoxes and being mindful of how we engage with technology, we can navigate the digital age in a way that enhances, rather than overwhelms, our lives.

So, take a moment to disconnect and reconnect—with yourself, with others, and with the world around you. Your mind, body, and relationships will thank you.

Chapter 12

Resilience

Bouncing Back from Hard Times

What is Resilience: What it Means to Bounce Back from Hard Times

Resilience is the mental, emotional, and often physical ability to recover from difficult or challenging situations and to adapt in the face of adversity, trauma, or significant stress. When people describe someone as resilient, they often mean that this person can maintain a sense of stability, optimism, and strength even in tough times. Rather than getting overwhelmed by hardships, resilient individuals find ways to cope, adapt, and ultimately emerge stronger.

At its core, resilience is about "bouncing back." Imagine a rubber band: when stretched, it doesn't break but instead returns to its original shape. Resilience in humans works similarly—when we face hardships or setbacks, resilience allows us to recover, learn, and grow from the experience rather than letting it define or defeat us.

Key Aspects of Resilience

1. **Adaptability:** Resilience involves being flexible and adapting to change. Life doesn't always go according to plan, and resilience allows us to accept and adjust to new realities, challenges, or disruptions. Rather than resisting change, resilient people learn to embrace it and find new ways forward.

2. **Emotional Regulation:** Resilient individuals can manage their emotions well, even in stressful situations. They are able to stay calm, find perspective, and avoid being overwhelmed by negative emotions, which helps them think clearly and make sound decisions under pressure.

3. **Self-Efficacy and Confidence:** Resilience includes a belief in one's own abilities to handle and overcome challenges. This sense of self-confidence fuels resilience, as individuals trust that they can find solutions and make it through tough times.

4. **Optimism and a Growth Mindset:** Resilient people often approach life with optimism. This doesn't mean they ignore challenges or

194

pretend everything is okay; instead, they have a mindset that allows them to look for lessons, find opportunities for growth, and see setbacks as temporary.

5. **Support Systems:** Although resilience is often thought of as an individual quality, having a strong network of family, friends, or community members plays a big role. Resilient people know when to reach out for help and benefit from the encouragement and support of others.

Why Resilience is Important

Resilience is essential because adversity is an inevitable part of life. Everyone faces challenges—whether it's a difficult job, health issues, relationship troubles, or unexpected crises. Resilience doesn't make these difficulties disappear, but it makes handling them easier and less overwhelming. It empowers us to keep going, to find meaning in hardship, and to emerge with a greater sense of purpose and strength.

Resilience is the skill that helps us not only survive but thrive in the face of adversity. It's about learning, growing, and ultimately becoming stronger from our experiences.

Types of Challenges People Face

Adversity comes in many forms, affecting different areas of our lives. Here are some common types of challenges people encounter:

- **Personal Challenges:** These may include health issues, relationship difficulties, family conflicts, or struggles with self-esteem. Personal challenges often impact one's sense of identity and well-being.
- **Professional Challenges:** At work, people may face challenges like job loss, career stagnation, difficult colleagues, or high-stress projects. Professional challenges can affect one's career growth and financial stability.
- **Emotional Challenges:** Mental health issues, such as anxiety, depression, and stress, are common emotional challenges. Dealing with loss, trauma, or sudden life changes can also affect emotional stability.
- **Financial Challenges:** Financial difficulties, such as debt, unemployment, or unexpected expenses, can lead to stress and insecurity. Financial setbacks can impact many areas of life and make it harder to focus on personal or professional goals.

Recognizing That Setbacks Are a Natural Part of Life

Everyone faces challenges at some point, and experiencing setbacks is part of the human experience. Recognizing this can help us approach adversity with a mindset of acceptance and resilience, rather than seeing it as a personal failure. Life's challenges teach valuable lessons, shape our character, and offer opportunities for growth. By understanding that setbacks are normal, we can learn to handle adversity with strength, patience, and optimism.

Increased Mental Strength and Adaptability

Building resilience helps strengthen the mind, enabling us to face challenges with courage and composure. When we're resilient, we're more adaptable, which means we can adjust to new situations and unexpected changes more easily. This mental flexibility makes it easier to stay positive and keep moving forward, even when things don't go as planned.

Improved Problem-Solving Skills

Resilience enhances our ability to solve problems effectively. When we encounter obstacles, a resilient mindset encourages us to look for solutions rather than dwelling on the difficulties. This approach helps us break down complex challenges into manageable steps, making it easier to find ways forward and tackle issues head-on.

Greater Sense of Control and Reduced Stress

With resilience, we feel a stronger sense of control over our lives. Rather than feeling overwhelmed by challenges, we gain confidence in our ability to manage them. This sense of control helps reduce stress, as we learn to respond to setbacks calmly and view them as opportunities to grow. In the long run, resilience not only strengthens our mental health but also enhances our overall well-being by reducing feelings of anxiety and frustration.

Optimism: Staying Positive During Tough Times

Resilient people tend to stay hopeful, even when facing challenges. Optimism doesn't mean ignoring difficulties but rather choosing to focus on possibilities and solutions. This positive outlook helps them maintain motivation and look for silver linings, even in hard times.

Perseverance: The Importance of Persistence in Overcoming Obstacles

Resilience requires perseverance, which is the ability to keep pushing forward despite setbacks. Resilient individuals don't give up easily; they understand that success often requires hard work and sustained effort. This determination helps them face and overcome challenges one step at a time.

Emotional Awareness: Understanding and Managing Emotions Effectively

Resilient people are aware of their emotions and know how to manage them. They don't let anger, fear, or frustration control them; instead, they take time to understand and process these feelings. By doing so, they're able to make clear decisions and respond calmly, even under pressure.

Flexibility: Being Open to Change and Adapting to New Situations

Flexibility is another key trait of resilience. Resilient individuals are open to change and willing to adapt when necessary. They understand that life is unpredictable and that adjusting to new situations can lead to growth. This adaptability helps them navigate difficult circumstances with ease and turn challenges into opportunities.

Techniques to Build Resilience

Resilience is like a muscle we can strengthen with practice. Here are some simple ways to build it:

1. **Positive Thinking and Self-Talk**
   Positive thinking and self-talk are about shifting your mindset to be more optimistic. When something bad happens, it's easy to focus on the negative. But by practicing positive thinking, you can start to look for solutions or lessons instead. Self-talk means the way you speak to yourself in your head. Instead of saying, "I can't handle this," try saying, "This is hard, but I can find a way through." Reframing your thoughts like this helps you stay strong and keep moving forward.

2. **Developing Coping Strategies**
   Coping strategies are ways to manage stress when things get tough. Examples of coping techniques include taking deep breaths, going for a walk to clear your mind, talking to a friend, or writing in a journal. These strategies help you calm down and feel more in control during difficult moments. Over time, finding what works best for you will make it easier to handle stress.

3. **Practicing Mindfulness and Relaxation**
   Mindfulness is about being fully present in the moment without worrying about the past or future. You can practice mindfulness by focusing on your breathing, noticing sounds around you, or paying attention to how your body feels. Relaxation techniques

like meditation, deep breathing, or even simple stretching can help reduce stress and make it easier to stay calm. These practices can help you bounce back faster when things get challenging.

4. **Setting Realistic Goals**
    During tough times, setting small, realistic goals can keep you focused and give you a sense of accomplishment. For example, instead of trying to solve a big problem all at once, break it down into steps you can tackle one by one. This approach helps you feel more in control and prevents you from feeling overwhelmed. Each small step forward builds your confidence and strengthens your resilience.

5. **Physical Self-Care**
    Taking care of your body has a big impact on resilience. When you eat healthy, exercise, and get enough sleep, your body and mind are stronger and more able to cope with stress. Physical self-care is like building a strong foundation that helps you stay balanced, even when life gets tough. It also improves your energy levels and mood, making it easier to handle challenges.

By practicing these techniques, you can build resilience little by little. These habits can help you face life's difficulties with greater strength, calmness, and confidence.

Resilience in Action: Responding to Setbacks

Resilience truly shows its strength in the way we respond to setbacks. Here's how you can take positive, constructive steps after experiencing a challenging situation:

1. **Steps to Take Immediately After a Setback**
    When you first encounter a setback, it's natural to feel frustrated, disappointed, or even angry. Take a moment to breathe and pause before reacting. Give yourself time to process the situation. Practice calming techniques, like taking deep breaths or going for a short walk, to clear your mind. This initial pause helps prevent impulsive reactions and prepares you to respond with a clear head.

2. **How to Analyse and Learn from Challenges**
    Once you've calmed down, look at the setback more closely. Ask yourself questions like: "What went wrong?" "Is there something I could have done differently?" and "What lessons can I learn from this?" Reflecting on these questions helps you understand the situation and identify patterns or mistakes to avoid in the future. Remember, setbacks are opportunities for growth. Viewing them as learning experiences can make you stronger and better prepared for future challenges.

3. **Creating a Plan to Move Forward**

   After you've analysed the situation, it's time to create a plan to get back on track. Start by setting small, achievable steps that will help you recover from the setback. For example, if you missed a deadline at work, your plan might include organizing your tasks, setting reminders, or breaking large projects into smaller parts to manage time better. Having a clear action plan gives you direction and helps you feel more in control. Moving forward one step at a time allows you to rebuild momentum and regain confidence.

By taking these steps, setbacks become less overwhelming, and you develop the resilience to face challenges head-on. Resilience isn't about avoiding failure but about learning, adapting, and pushing forward.

Resilience and Relationships

Resilience isn't something we have to build alone. Our relationships and connections with others play a huge role in helping us bounce back from tough times. Here's how supportive relationships can boost resilience and how to reach out for help when we need it:

1. **The Role of Supportive Relationships in Building Resilience**

   Having people we can trust and rely on—like friends, family, mentors, or colleagues—makes us stronger during challenging times. These supportive relationships offer comfort, advice, and encouragement, reminding us that we're not alone. Knowing there are people who care about us can be a powerful motivator and help us manage stress more effectively. A supportive network can also offer different perspectives and solutions, which can be valuable when facing difficult situations.

2. **How to Seek Help and Communicate with Others During Difficult Times**

   Reaching out for help can sometimes be hard, especially when we're dealing with personal setbacks. However, communicating openly with those we trust can ease our burden and provide new insights. When you feel overwhelmed, don't hesitate to talk to someone about what you're going through. Be honest about your feelings and what kind of support you need—whether it's just a listening ear, practical advice, or even help with specific tasks. Seeking help is a sign of strength, not weakness, and it can make a big difference in how quickly and effectively you recover.

Building resilience with the support of strong relationships not only helps us overcome adversity but also strengthens our connections with those around us. Resilience is easier to develop when we work together, creating a sense of community and mutual support.

Developing a Growth Mindset for Resilience

1. **Embracing Challenges as Opportunities for Learning and Growth:**

    - **Reframe Challenges**: Instead of viewing challenges as obstacles, see them as opportunities to learn new skills and grow. This mindset helps you remain calm and focused, even when faced with difficulties.

    - **Learn from Experience**: Every challenge presents valuable lessons. Embrace mistakes as part of the learning process and see them as stepping stones toward improvement.

    - **Be Open to Feedback**: A growth mindset encourages the acceptance of constructive feedback. Use it to adjust your approach and improve your performance.

2. **Viewing Failure as a Stepping Stone to Success:**

    - **Redefine Failure**: Instead of fearing failure, view it as an essential part of the journey. Each failure provides insight into what works and what doesn't, helping you make informed decisions going forward.

    - **Develop Resilience**: Resilience comes from learning to bounce back after setbacks. A growth mindset enables you to stay determined and keep trying, knowing that success often follows persistence.

    - **Persist in the Face of Adversity**: Use failures to build emotional strength. With each challenge, your ability to overcome difficulties increases, making you more resilient in the long run.

Developing a Growth Mindset for Resilience

1. **Embracing Challenges as Opportunities for Learning and Growth:**

    - **Seeing Challenges as Learning Chances**: When you face something difficult, instead of feeling upset or scared, try to think of it as a chance to learn. Every challenge can teach you something new, whether it's a new skill or a better way to solve a problem.

    - **Learning from Mistakes**: It's normal to make mistakes when trying something new. Instead of giving up, look at mistakes as a way to get better. Each time you try, you get a little closer to success because you're learning from what didn't work.

- **Being Open to New Ideas**: When you face challenges, it can help to listen to others and get feedback. Sometimes, someone else might have a good idea on how to improve. This openness helps you learn and grow faster.

2. **Viewing Failure as a Stepping Stone to Success:**
   - **Changing How You See Failure**: Many people fear failure, but it's actually an important part of growing. When you fail, you learn what doesn't work, and this helps you figure out what will work next time.

   - **Building Strength Through Failures**: Each time you fail and get back up, you get stronger. Failing is not the end. It teaches you how to try again with more knowledge and experience, and it helps you become more determined.

   - **Staying Determined**: Even when things don't go as planned, keep going. The more you push through challenges, the more you build resilience. This means that the next time something difficult happens, you'll be stronger and better prepared to face it.

Having a growth mindset means always seeing obstacles as chances to learn and grow. It helps you stay strong when things don't go as planned and gives you the courage to keep trying until you succeed.

Overcoming Common Barriers to Resilience

Dealing with Self-Doubt and Fear of Failure:

   - **Understanding Self-Doubt**: Everyone experiences self-doubt at some point, but it's important not to let it control you. Remember, self-doubt is just a feeling, not a fact. It often happens when you're about to try something new or challenging.

   - **Challenge Negative Thoughts**: When you start doubting yourself, ask yourself if those thoughts are true. Often, they are exaggerated or based on fear, not reality. Replace those thoughts with more positive and realistic ones, like "I may not know everything, but I can learn and improve."

   - **Take Small Steps**: When you fear failure, it can be helpful to start with smaller tasks. This allows you to build confidence step-by-step. Over time, these small successes will help you overcome your fear of bigger challenges.

1. **Recognizing and Avoiding Perfectionism:**
   - **Understanding Perfectionism**: Perfectionism is when you expect everything to be flawless, which can be unrealistic and

stressful. It can stop you from even trying because you're too afraid of making mistakes.

- **Accepting Imperfection**: Nobody is perfect, and mistakes are part of the learning process. Instead of focusing on doing everything perfectly, try to do your best and focus on progress. The key is to keep improving, not to reach an unattainable ideal.

- **Set Realistic Goals**: Aim for "good enough" rather than perfect. Set goals that are challenging but achievable, and allow yourself to make mistakes along the way. This can help you stay motivated without feeling overwhelmed.

2. Breaking the Cycle of Negative Thinking:

- **Recognizing Negative Thinking**: Negative thoughts often pop up when things are tough. These thoughts might include things like "I can't do this" or "I'll never succeed." The first step is to notice when you're thinking negatively.

- **Replacing Negative Thoughts**: Once you recognize a negative thought, try to replace it with a positive or more balanced thought. For example, change "I'm terrible at this" to "I'm still learning, and I can improve with practice."

- **Practice Gratitude and Positivity**: Focusing on the good things in your life can help break the cycle of negative thinking. Try to find one thing to be grateful for each day, no matter how small. This shift in focus can help you build resilience and stay optimistic.

Overcoming barriers like self-doubt, perfectionism, and negative thinking is key to developing resilience. By recognizing these challenges and changing the way you think about them, you can become more confident, keep improving, and keep moving forward even when things are difficult.

Real-Life Examples of Resilience

1. Inspirational Stories of People Who Overcame Adversity:

- **Thomas Edison**: Thomas Edison, the inventor of the lightbulb, faced many failures in his career. He failed thousands of times while trying to invent the lightbulb, but instead of giving up, he saw each failure as a step toward success. When asked about his many failed attempts, he famously said, "I have not failed. I've just found 10,000 ways that won't work." His resilience and persistence eventually led to one of the most important inventions in history.

- **J.K. Rowling**: Before becoming the world-famous author of the *Harry Potter* series, J.K. Rowling faced numerous struggles. She was a single mother living on welfare, and her manuscript for *Harry Potter* was rejected by 12 publishers. Many people would have given up, but Rowling didn't. She kept believing in her work and herself, and today, *Harry Potter* is a global success. Her story shows that resilience, persistence, and self-belief can turn dreams into reality.

- **Nelson Mandela**: Nelson Mandela's journey of resilience is one of the most powerful. After being imprisoned for 27 years under apartheid, he emerged as a symbol of peace, forgiveness, and leadership. Instead of allowing anger and bitterness to control him, Mandela focused on reconciliation and justice. His resilience inspired millions around the world to stand up against injustice and fight for equality.

2. Lessons Learned from Resilient Individuals:

    - **Persistence Pays Off**: Resilient individuals like Thomas Edison and J.K. Rowling teach us that failure is not the end. It's just a part of the journey. Success often comes after numerous setbacks, and the key is to keep going, no matter how many times you fail.

    - **Focus on the Bigger Picture**: Nelson Mandela's life shows us that resilience isn't just about personal strength; it's about staying focused on a larger goal. Mandela's focus was not on revenge or anger but on peace, unity, and a better future for his country. In difficult situations, keeping your eyes on your long-term goals can help you push through adversity.

    - **Adaptability**: Bethany Hamilton's story highlights the importance of adaptability. She could have easily given up surfing after her attack, but instead, she adapted her technique and found a way to continue her passion. Resilience often involves changing your approach and adapting to new circumstances.

    - **Self-Belief**: One key lesson from these resilient individuals is the importance of believing in yourself. Even when others doubt you, your own self-belief can fuel your resilience. J.K. Rowling believed in her book when it was rejected multiple times, and her belief eventually turned her into one of the most successful authors in the world.

    - **Resilience is a Choice**: Resilience is not something you are born with; it's something you choose. You can decide to get back up, keep trying, and push through challenges, just as Mandela and

Hamilton did. Even in the toughest times, resilience is about deciding not to quit.

These real-life stories of resilience remind us that adversity is often part of the path to success. Whether it's overcoming personal struggles, professional setbacks, or life-altering events, resilient people show us that we can find strength within ourselves to keep going. The key lessons from these individuals—persistence, adaptability, self-belief, and focusing on the bigger picture—are all important steps in building our own resilience.

Practical Exercises to Strengthen Resilience

1. **Journaling Prompts for Processing Adversity:**

   Journaling is a powerful way to process difficult emotions and gain clarity when facing challenges. Here are some prompts to help you work through adversity and build resilience:

   - **What challenge am I facing right now, and how does it make me feel?**
     Write about the current obstacle and any emotions that arise. This will help you identify the impact of the situation and give you insight into how you're reacting.

   - **What have I learned from this experience so far?**
     Reflect on the lessons you've gained from your struggles. Even in tough times, there's usually something valuable to learn.

   - **What are the things I can control in this situation?**
     Write about the actions you can take to improve your situation. This helps shift focus from what is out of your control to what you can actively work on.

   - **What strengths have I used in the past to overcome difficulties?**

     Remind yourself of the times when you've been resilient before. Write about the qualities and strengths that helped you bounce back.

   - **How can I take care of myself today, even in small ways?**
     Journaling about self-care and small steps of kindness to yourself can promote healing and remind you to nurture yourself during tough times.

2. **Goal-Setting for Recovery and Growth:**

   Setting clear, achievable goals can help you regain focus and build resilience during difficult times. Here's a simple method to guide you through goal-setting for recovery and growth:

- **Start with Small, Manageable Goals:**
  Break down larger challenges into smaller, actionable steps. For example, if you're recovering from a difficult situation, set a goal to take one positive action per day—whether it's taking a walk, talking to a friend, or practicing gratitude. Small wins help rebuild confidence.

- **Focus on the Process, Not Just the Outcome:**
  Resilience is built through effort and persistence. Instead of only focusing on a final outcome, set goals that emphasize the actions you need to take. For example, "I will practice self-compassion for 10 minutes every day" rather than only focusing on the end result of feeling better.

- **Set Short-Term and Long-Term Goals:**
  Set immediate goals that are achievable in a few days or weeks (e.g., writing in your journal each morning) and longer-term goals (e.g., completing a project or achieving personal growth over a few months). Balancing short-term and long-term goals keeps you motivated while you're working toward bigger changes.

- **Review and Adjust:**
  Be flexible with your goals. If something isn't working or if you face setbacks, it's okay to adjust your goals. What matters most is continuing to make progress, no matter how small.

3. **Visualization Exercises to Build Inner Strength:**

Visualization can help you build inner strength and prepare for challenges. It trains your mind to focus on positive outcomes and can be a powerful tool in overcoming adversity.

- **Relax and Focus:**
  Find a quiet space where you can sit comfortably without distractions. Take a few deep breaths and relax your body. Close your eyes and picture yourself in a calm, peaceful place.

- **Visualize Overcoming the Challenge:**
  Imagine yourself facing the difficult situation you're dealing with. Picture yourself navigating the challenge with confidence and resilience. See yourself taking positive steps, staying calm, and using your strengths to overcome the adversity. Focus on how strong and capable you feel.

- **Imagine Your Best Self:**
  Visualize yourself as the person you want to become—strong, confident, and resilient. Picture yourself handling life's obstacles

with grace, learning from each experience, and continuing to grow.

- **Positive Affirmations**:
While visualizing, repeat positive affirmations to yourself, such as "I am strong," "I can handle challenges," and "I grow through adversity." These affirmations can help boost your confidence and reinforce the mindset of resilience.

Strengthening resilience involves both mental and emotional practices. Journaling helps you process emotions, while goal-setting helps you stay focused on recovery. Visualization exercises allow you to mentally prepare for challenges and build inner strength. By regularly practicing these exercises, you can build a resilient mindset that helps you navigate life's difficulties with greater ease and confidence.

Key Takeaways on Resilience

1. **What Resilience Is:**
   - Resilience is the ability to bounce back from adversity, setbacks, or challenges. It's not about avoiding difficulties, but about how you respond and grow from them.
   - Resilience involves maintaining a positive attitude, learning from failure, and adapting to change. It's a mindset that helps you stay strong and keep moving forward, even when things get tough.

2. **Why Resilience Is Important:**
   - **Helps You Overcome Challenges**: Life will always have ups and downs. Resilience allows you to cope with stress, adversity, and change in a healthy way, helping you find solutions and keep going.
   - **Promotes Growth**: Resilience is not just about surviving tough times, it's about learning and growing from them. It encourages you to see challenges as opportunities for growth, which leads to personal development and better problem-solving skills.
   - **Improves Mental and Emotional Health**: By building resilience, you can reduce feelings of helplessness and anxiety. It helps you manage stress, boost your confidence, and develop a more optimistic outlook on life.
   - **Enhances Success and Well-being**: Resilient people are better able to handle setbacks and continue pursuing their goals. Whether in your personal or professional life, resilience makes it easier to stay focused, motivated, and persistent, even when facing obstacles.

3. **Practical Ways to Build Resilience:**

- **Embrace Challenges**: See difficulties as chances to learn and grow. Rather than avoiding hard situations, face them head-on, knowing they are an opportunity to develop resilience.

- **Develop a Growth Mindset**: Understand that failure is a natural part of life and can be a stepping stone to success. Focus on learning and improving, not just on winning or succeeding right away.

- **Practice Self-Care**: Taking care of your physical and mental health helps build resilience. Make time for relaxation, exercise, and connecting with loved ones to recharge when needed.

- **Set Realistic Goals**: Break larger goals into smaller, manageable steps. Achieving small successes builds confidence and keeps you motivated through challenges.

- **Use Journaling and Reflection**: Writing about your experiences and emotions helps you process difficulties and gain clarity. Reflect on your progress and remind yourself of your strengths.

4. **Encouragement to Apply Resilience Techniques:**

- **Incorporate Resilience Practices in Your Daily Life**: Resilience is something you can build over time. Start by making small changes, like adjusting your mindset to embrace challenges, setting goals, and practicing self-care. These small habits can lead to big changes in how you approach difficulties.

- **Stay Persistent and Be Kind to Yourself**: Remember that building resilience takes time and effort. Don't be too hard on yourself if you face setbacks along the way. Celebrate the progress you make and keep moving forward with patience and determination.

- **Seek Support When Needed**: Resilience doesn't mean doing everything alone. Reach out to others for support, whether it's family, friends, or a mentor. Sometimes, sharing your struggles and learning from others can strengthen your own resilience.

Resilience is a vital skill that helps you overcome adversity and grow stronger through life's challenges. By embracing challenges, developing a growth mindset, and practicing self-care, you can build resilience over time. Apply these techniques in your daily life, and remember that resilience is a journey, not a destination. Stay persistent, be kind to yourself, and you'll find the strength to overcome anything life throws your way.

Resilience is not just a temporary trait but a lifelong skill that strengthens over time with practice and experience. Embracing challenges and viewing them as opportunities to grow allows us to build the mental and emotional strength needed to navigate life's ups and downs. Every setback offers a chance to learn, adapt, and emerge even stronger, and by cultivating resilience, we prepare ourselves to face future challenges with confidence. Remember, resilience is about persistence, learning from failure, and maintaining a positive mindset—so, embrace the difficulties you encounter, knowing that they can shape you into a more capable and empowered individual.

Chapter 13

Time Management

Maximizing Your Potential

What is Time Management?

Time management is the ability to effectively organize, plan, and allocate your time across various tasks and activities. It involves setting priorities, making schedules, and creating a balanced approach to handling responsibilities. Good time management is a skill that allows you to make the most of each day, increasing productivity and ensuring you focus on what matters most.

Why is Time Management Important?

Time management is essential because it directly impacts productivity, mental well-being, and success. Managing time well reduces stress by preventing last-minute rushes and unplanned interruptions. It also increases focus and efficiency, helping you complete tasks on time and at a high standard. Proper time management leads to a more organized and less chaotic day, freeing up time for relaxation, personal development, and other important aspects of life.

How Managing Time Well Helps You Achieve More

When you manage time effectively, you can accomplish more in less time, giving you a sense of accomplishment and control. By identifying and prioritizing your tasks, you avoid wasting time on low-priority activities and instead focus on achieving meaningful goals. This approach allows for steady progress, as each planned and completed task brings you closer to your objectives. Good time management creates extra time for personal interests, self-care, and quality time with loved ones, leading to a balanced and fulfilling life.

Understanding Time and Priorities

- **Identifying How You Currently Spend Your Time**
  The first step to managing time effectively is understanding how you currently spend it. Tracking your daily activities helps you see where your time goes and identify any habits or distractions that may be taking up too much time. By examining how you

use your time, you can recognize areas where you could be more productive and make adjustments as needed.

- **The Importance of Setting Priorities**
  Setting priorities is crucial because it helps you determine which tasks and goals are most important and deserve your attention. Without clear priorities, you may find yourself busy with less meaningful tasks while neglecting activities that truly matter. Prioritizing allows you to focus on high-impact tasks that bring you closer to your goals and help you make the best use of your time.

- **How to Focus on the Most Important Tasks First**
  Focusing on the most important tasks, also known as "prioritizing," means tackling activities that have the biggest impact on your goals before moving to less critical tasks. By working on high-priority items first, you ensure that essential tasks get completed even if time is limited. This approach not only improves productivity but also builds momentum, making it easier to tackle other tasks and finish your day feeling accomplished.

Setting Clear Goals

- **How to Set Specific, Achievable Goals**
  Setting goals is an important part of time management, but to be effective, goals should be clear and realistic. Instead of a vague goal like "do well in school," a more specific goal would be "study for one hour every evening." Specific goals are easier to plan for and track. It's also helpful to make goals that you can achieve, so you don't feel overwhelmed. If a goal feels too big, think about what you can realistically accomplish in the time you have.

- **The Difference Between Short-Term and Long-Term Goals**
  Goals can be divided into two main types: short-term and long-term. **Short-term goals** are things you want to achieve in the near future, like completing a project by the end of the week. **Long-term goals** are goals that take more time, like graduating from school or saving money for a major purchase. Understanding the difference helps you plan better, as short-term goals often support your long-term goals. Working toward both types of goals keeps you motivated and moving forward.

- **How to Break Down Big Goals into Smaller, Manageable Steps**

  When a goal is big, it can feel overwhelming. Breaking it down into smaller steps makes it easier to accomplish. For example, if your goal is to complete a big assignment, you could break it into smaller tasks, like researching the topic, creating an outline, and then writing a draft. Each small step is easier to manage and brings you closer to your big goal. Taking one small step at a time makes large goals feel achievable, and checking off each step gives you a sense of progress and motivation to keep going.

Creating a Time Management Plan

- **How to Create a Daily and Weekly Schedule**
  A time management plan begins with setting up a schedule. A **daily schedule** helps you plan each day's tasks and activities, while a **weekly schedule** gives you a bigger picture of what you want to accomplish over the week. Start by listing out your main tasks and deciding when you'll work on each. Be realistic about how much time each task will take, and remember to add breaks. A well-planned schedule helps you stay on track and reduces the stress of last-minute tasks.
  Example: Ritu's Schedule for Better Time Management

Ritu is a homemaker who also runs a small beauty salon from her home. She manages household tasks, takes care of her family, and serves clients at her salon. To balance her responsibilities, Ritu can create a structured schedule to make her day more manageable and efficient.

Ritu's Daily Schedule Example

1. **Morning Routine (7:00 AM - 9:00 AM)**
   - 7:00 - 8:00 AM: Personal time for exercise, meditation, and a quick breakfast.
   - 8:00 - 9:00 AM: Morning household tasks, such as tidying up, preparing breakfast for the family, and organizing the house.
2. **Family and Salon Prep Time (9:00 AM - 11:00 AM)**
   - 9:00 - 10:00 AM: Attend to family needs, ensure children are ready for school, and complete any other important household tasks.
   - 10:00 - 11:00 AM: Prepare the salon space, organize equipment, and check client bookings for the day.
3. **Salon Service Hours (11:00 AM - 2:00 PM)**
   - 11:00 AM - 2:00 PM: Serve clients at the salon. Since she has set these hours, she can work efficiently, focusing solely on clients during this time.

4. **Break and Family Time (2:00 PM - 4:00 PM)**
   - 2:00 - 2:30 PM: Lunch break and a short rest to recharge.
   - 2:30 - 4:00 PM: Time for family activities, helping children with homework, or handling any household chores that need attention.

5. **Second Salon Shift (4:00 PM - 7:00 PM)**
   - 4:00 - 7:00 PM: Continue with salon appointments. By limiting her work hours, Ritu maintains a good balance without feeling overwhelmed.

6. **Evening Routine (7:00 PM - 9:00 PM)**
   - 7:00 - 8:00 PM: Dinner with family and wind-down time.
   - 8:00 - 9:00 PM: Evening household tasks, preparing for the next day, and wrapping up any unfinished salon work (such as cleaning up and organizing).

7. **Night Routine (9:00 PM - 10:00 PM)**
   - 9:00 - 10:00 PM: Time for personal relaxation or unwinding, possibly reading, enjoying a hobby, or watching a favourite show before bedtime.

Tools Ritu Can Use for Better Time Management

- **Planner or Calendar:** Ritu can use a physical planner or digital calendar (e.g., Google Calendar) to note client appointments and personal tasks.
- **To-Do Lists:** She can create daily to-do lists to prioritize tasks, both for home and the salon.
- **Reminders/Alarms:** Setting reminders for appointments or important tasks will help her stay on track.
- By following a structured schedule and using simple tools, Ritu can smoothly manage her time, balance her family and work responsibilities, and reduce daily stress.
- **Tools and Methods to Organize Your Time (Calendars, Planners, Apps)**

   Using tools to organize your time can make planning easier and help you stay consistent. A **calendar** (digital or paper) allows you to see your weekly or monthly schedule at a glance. **Planners** are good for listing daily tasks and setting reminders. **Apps** like Google Calendar, Todoist, or Trello help you set reminders, create lists, and prioritize tasks. Each tool is designed to help you keep track of your time and tasks, making it easier to stay organized.

- **The Importance of Consistency in Following Your Plan**
  Consistency is key to making your time management plan effective. Even the best plan won't work if you don't stick to it. Try to follow your schedule each day and complete tasks as planned. It may take time to develop the habit, but the more consistent you are, the more you'll see positive results. Following your plan daily helps you achieve your goals, avoid stress, and feel in control of your time.

Identifying Activities That Waste Time

Identifying activities that waste time is an essential step in effective time management. Time-wasting activities are those that don't contribute meaningfully to our goals, productivity, or personal growth. Recognizing them helps us reclaim valuable time that can be used for tasks that truly matter.

1. **Frequent Use of social media and Internet Browsing**
   Social media platforms, websites, and apps are designed to keep users engaged for as long as possible. While a little social media can be a break, excessive scrolling often leads to hours lost in content that doesn't add value. Similarly, random internet browsing or falling into "click-holes" on news sites or video platforms can consume a lot of time without achieving anything productive. To identify this, try tracking how much time is spent on social media daily, then decide if it's reasonable or if it needs to be reduced.

2. **Watching TV and Streaming Videos Without Limits**
   Watching TV shows or streaming videos can be a relaxing activity, but it can quickly become a time-waster if left unchecked. Many people watch one episode intending to relax, only to find themselves watching several in a row. Using streaming services without setting limits or without a specific purpose (like watching a particular movie) often leads to excessive time spent.

3. **Unnecessary Multitasking**
   Trying to do multiple things at once, like answering emails while listening to a webinar, may seem efficient but often reduces overall productivity. Multitasking divides attention and can result in both tasks taking longer or being done poorly. Noticing how often multitasking happens, and focusing on doing one thing at a time, can help save time and improve task quality.

4. **Non-Priority Tasks and Overcommitting**
   Some tasks may not align with our priorities but still consume time. For example, small, non-essential errands or unnecessary meetings can pile up and take away time from more important tasks. Similarly,

saying "yes" to every invitation or favour can create extra tasks that don't contribute to personal or professional goals. Identifying these low-priority activities and setting boundaries allows for more time for critical tasks.

5. **Lack of Planning or Goal Setting**
    Without a clear plan or goals, it's easy to drift into time-wasting habits. Time is often wasted on activities that seem urgent but aren't important in the big picture. Creating a daily or weekly schedule, setting clear goals, and checking in on progress can help identify and avoid unproductive activities.

6. **Unorganized and Inefficient Work Environment**
    A cluttered or disorganized workspace can lead to spending extra time looking for documents, files, or tools. Time is wasted in searching for things or trying to remember where tasks left off. Organizing the workspace and setting up a clear system for files, tools, and notes helps minimize time spent on organization during work.

How to Identify Your Own Time Wasters

1. **Keep a Time Log**
    For a few days, track what you do throughout the day and how much time each activity takes. This helps reveal any hidden or unexpected time-wasters.

2. **Notice Patterns of Procrastination**
    If certain tasks are delayed repeatedly, look at what's taking up time instead. Common procrastination methods, like browsing the internet or checking messages, are often big time-wasters.

3. **Reflect on Your Goals**
    Consider which daily activities contribute to your short-term and long-term goals. Activities that don't serve your goals may need to be reduced or eliminated.

By identifying these activities, it becomes easier to make adjustments and focus time on tasks that are genuinely productive or fulfilling.

Reducing Distractions

*   **Limiting social media Use** social media can be a major source of distraction, interrupting focus and taking away from valuable time. To reduce its impact, set specific times in the day to check social media, or use apps that track or limit screen time. Designating "no phone" zones or times, like during work hours, also helps to keep attention on important tasks.

- **Avoiding Multitasking**
  Although multitasking seems efficient, it often leads to reduced productivity because the brain has to switch back and forth between tasks. Instead, try focusing on one task at a time to complete it more efficiently and effectively. Using techniques like the Pomodoro method (working for 25 minutes with a 5-minute break) can help keep focus on one activity at a time.

The Power of Saying No to Unnecessary Tasks

Learning to say "no" can be one of the most valuable time management tools. Often, we take on additional tasks or responsibilities to please others or avoid conflict, but this can lead to overwhelm and less time for important priorities. Politely declining unnecessary requests, Favours, or social commitments can free up time for more meaningful or essential activities. Practice setting boundaries by explaining that you have other commitments or simply need to focus on personal goals. This helps to reduce overload and makes it easier to maintain a balanced schedule.

The Pomodoro Technique and Other Time Management Tools

- **How the Pomodoro Technique Improves Focus and Productivity**
  The Pomodoro Technique is a popular time management method that involves breaking work into short intervals, typically 25 minutes, called "Pomodoros," with a 5-minute break after each session. After four Pomodoros, a longer break of 15–30 minutes is taken. This technique helps improve focus by creating a sense of urgency with a set time limit, making it easier to concentrate without distractions. It also reduces burnout by providing frequent breaks, keeping the mind refreshed and productive over longer periods.
- **Other Effective Methods**
  - **Time Blocking**
    Time blocking is a scheduling method where specific blocks of time are dedicated to different tasks or categories, such as work, meetings, or personal activities. By pre-assigning each hour of the day, time blocking creates structure and minimizes procrastination. For example, one block might be set for answering emails, while another is for focused project work.

- **Task Batching**
  Task batching involves grouping similar tasks together to complete them in a single session. For example, instead of replying to emails throughout the day, set aside a specific time to handle them all at once. Batching tasks reduces time wasted from switching between different types of activities and allows the mind to stay in one mode, improving efficiency and focus.

These tools help create structure in daily routines, making it easier to stay organized and prioritize tasks effectively.

Other Effective Real-Time Techniques for better Time Management:

1. **Time Blocking:**
   Allocate specific time blocks for different tasks or activities throughout your day. For example, dedicate 9:00 AM - 11:00 AM for deep work, 11:00 AM - 12:00 PM for meetings, etc. This helps you stay focused and avoid distractions.

2. **Task Batching:**
   Group similar tasks together and complete them in one go. For example, respond to all emails in one block of time, or do all your phone calls at once. Batching reduces the time spent switching between different types of tasks.

3. **The Eisenhower Matrix:**
   Use this matrix to prioritize tasks based on urgency and importance. Divide tasks into four categories:

   - **Important & Urgent**: Do these first.

   - **Important & Not Urgent**: Schedule these.

   - **Not Important & Urgent**: Delegate these.

   - **Not Important & Not Urgent**: Eliminate these.

4. **2-Minute Rule:**
   If a task can be completed in 2 minutes or less, do it immediately. This avoids small tasks piling up and taking up unnecessary mental space.

5. **Eat the Frog:**
   Tackle the most difficult or unpleasant task first thing in the morning. Once the hardest task is out of the way, the rest of the day feels easier and more productive.

6. **Time Tracking:**
   Track how much time you spend on each task or activity throughout the day. Use apps like Toggl or RescueTime to see where your time goes. This can help identify areas where you waste time and improve efficiency.

7. **The 80/20 Rule (Pareto Principle):**
   Focus on the 20% of tasks that contribute to 80% of your results. Prioritize these high-impact tasks and minimize time spent on less important activities.

   The **80/20 Rule**, also known as the **Pareto Principle**, is a concept that suggests that in many situations, roughly 80% of the results come from 20% of the efforts or causes.

In Simple Terms:

- **80% of outcomes** (like results, rewards, or effects) come from just **20% of the input** (like time, resources, or effort).
- For example:
- **In business**: 80% of sales often come from just 20% of customers.
- **In time management**: 80% of your most important tasks may come from just 20% of what you do.
- **In studying**: 80% of the learning might come from focusing on 20% of the most important concepts or topics.

How It Works:

The 80/20 Rule helps you focus on the **vital few** things that make the biggest difference, instead of spreading your time and energy too thin across less important tasks. By identifying and focusing on the key 20% that will give you the greatest return, you can work more efficiently and achieve better results with less effort.

Example in Daily Life:

If you spend time on many tasks, you might find that only a few are really driving your success. For instance, in studying, you might discover that reviewing 20% of the material (the key points) leads to 80% of your grade.

The Pareto Principle is a powerful tool for prioritizing efforts, improving productivity, and making better use of your time and resources.

1. **Set SMART Goals:**
   Set specific, measurable, achievable, relevant, and time-bound goals. Break them down into smaller, actionable steps and track your progress.

   Real-Time Example of Setting SMART Goals for an Individual:

Individual: *Pratham*, a software developer, wants to learn a new programming language (e.g., Python) to improve his career skills and increase job opportunities.

Setting a SMART Goal:

- **Specific:** *Pratham wants to learn Python programming in the next 3 months to build better coding skills for career growth.*

- **Measurable:** *He will complete one online Python course and build 3 small projects by the end of 3 months.*

- **Achievable:** *Pratham will dedicate 1 hour every day to study Python and work on coding exercises to ensure steady progress.*

- **Relevant:** *Learning Python is directly relevant to his job as a software developer, as it will enhance his ability to work on web development projects.*

- **Time-bound:** *Pratham will finish the course and complete the projects within 3 months.*

Breaking the Goal into Actionable Steps:

1. **Week 1-4:** Complete the first 4 modules of the Python course (1 hour per day).

2. **Week 5-8:** Start building the first Python project (e.g., a simple calculator app).

3. **Week 9-12:** Finish the next modules of the course and build two more small projects (e.g., a to-do list app and a weather app).

4. **End of 3 Months:** Review the projects, test the skills learned, and get feedback from peers or mentors.

Tracking Progress:

- **Daily Check-in:** Track time spent studying and completing exercises on an app or notebook.

- **Weekly Review:** Review completed modules and make sure the projects are progressing.

- **End of 3 Months:** Assess the knowledge gained, the completion of projects, and how it's helping his job.

Result:

By following the SMART framework, Pratham is more likely to stay focused, motivated, and organized, helping him achieve his goal of mastering Python programming in a specific time frame.

1. **Delegation:**
   If possible, delegate tasks to others to free up your time for more important responsibilities. Focus on what you do best and let others handle tasks that don't require your expertise.

2. **Saying No:**
    Learn to say no to non-essential tasks or activities that don't align with your goals or priorities. Saying no helps keep you focused on what truly matters.

3. **Mind Mapping:**
    Use mind maps to visually organize tasks and ideas. This can help you see the bigger picture, prioritize tasks, and stay organized.
    (This topic is covered in this book as a separate chapter)

By implementing these techniques, individuals can improve focus, reduce distractions, and optimize how they manage their time, leading to greater productivity and less stress.

Staying Motivated and Overcoming Procrastination (Postponement)

- **How to Stay Motivated While Working**
  Motivation can dip, especially during long or challenging tasks. To stay motivated, break large tasks into smaller, manageable steps, which makes the work feel more achievable. Celebrate small wins to keep momentum going, and remind yourself of the bigger goal or reason behind each task. Setting up a rewarding break or activity after completing a task can also help you stay motivated.

- **Tips to Stop Procrastination and Get Started on Tasks**
  Procrastination can make even simple tasks feel overwhelming. One effective way to overcome it is to use the "Two-Minute Rule" — if a task will take two minutes or less, do it right away. For longer tasks, set a timer for just five minutes and promise yourself you'll work on it for that short time; often, the hardest part is getting started, and once you begin, you'll likely keep going. Creating a list of specific, prioritized tasks each day also helps clarify what needs to be done, making it easier to dive into work without delay.

Managing Stress and Avoiding Burnout

- **How Overworking Can Lead to Burnout**
  Constantly working without rest or downtime can lead to burnout — a state of physical and mental exhaustion. When we overwork, stress builds up, making it difficult to stay focused and enjoy our tasks. Burnout can cause a loss of motivation, increased irritability, and even health problems. Recognizing that rest is

essential helps prevent this cycle and keeps productivity and well-being balanced.

- **The Importance of Taking Breaks and Relaxing**
Regular breaks improve concentration and reduce fatigue. Short breaks during the day, like a quick walk or stretching session, help refresh the mind. Taking longer breaks on weekends or vacations gives deeper relaxation, helping to recharge and return to work with renewed energy. Remembering to relax and enjoy leisure activities is essential for both physical and mental health.

- **Balancing Work and Personal Time for Better Well-Being**
Work-life balance is key to avoiding burnout. Setting boundaries, like establishing "work-free" times or spaces, helps ensure there's time for personal interests and relationships. Spending quality time on hobbies, with family, or doing things you enjoy outside of work not only reduces stress but also brings a sense of fulfilment. Balancing work and personal time allow you to approach both with more energy and a positive mindset.

Review and Adjust Your Time Management Plan

- **How to Review Your Progress Regularly**
It's important to check in with yourself regularly to see if you're meeting your goals. You can set aside a few minutes each week to reflect on what you've accomplished. Ask yourself: Did I complete my tasks on time? Was I able to stick to my schedule? Reviewing your progress helps you see what's working and what needs improvement.

- **Making Adjustments to Your Schedule If Something Isn't Working**
If you notice that your schedule isn't helping you get things done or feels too overwhelming, it's okay to make changes. Maybe some tasks need more time, or certain activities need to be moved around. Adjust your plan to make it more realistic or flexible. Time management is about finding what works best for you, so be open to modifying your approach as needed.

- **Learning from Mistakes and Improving Your Time Management Skills**
Mistakes happen, and that's okay! The key is to learn from them. If something didn't work out, ask yourself why. Maybe you underestimated how long a task would take or got distracted too often. Use this information to improve your future planning. Over

time, you'll become better at managing your time by recognizing patterns and adjusting your methods to work more efficiently.

Keynotes on Time Management

1. **Prioritize Tasks:** Focus on the most important and urgent tasks first. This helps you avoid wasting time on less important activities.

2. **Set Clear Goals:** Break down big goals into smaller, manageable tasks. This makes it easier to stay focused and measure progress.

3. **Plan and Schedule:** Create daily and weekly schedules to organize your time. Use planners, calendars, or apps to track your tasks.

4. **Avoid Distractions:** Minimize distractions like social media, multitasking, or unnecessary meetings. Stay focused on one task at a time.

5. **Use Time Management Techniques:** Try techniques like the Pomodoro method (work in focused blocks of time), time blocking, or task batching to improve productivity.

6. **Take Breaks:** Regular breaks help refresh your mind and prevent burnout. It improves focus and energy levels for better performance.

7. **Review and Adjust:** Regularly review your time management plan. If something isn't working, adjust your schedule or approach.

8. **Learn to Say No:** Avoid taking on unnecessary tasks that could overwhelm you or distract you from your priorities.

9. **Balance Work and Life:** Ensure there is enough time for work and personal activities. Balance is essential for long-term productivity and well-being.

10. **Stay Consistent:** Consistency is key. Stick to your time management plan as much as possible for better results.

Wrap-up

- **The Benefits of Mastering Time Management**
  Mastering time management allows you to accomplish more with less stress. It helps you prioritize tasks, stay organized, and make the most of your time. By managing your time well, you can improve your productivity, reduce procrastination, and maintain a better work-life balance.

- **Encouragement to Apply Time Management Skills in Daily Life**
  Applying time management skills in your daily routine will help you stay focused and organized. Start by using simple tools like

to-do lists, setting priorities, and sticking to a schedule. The more you practice, the easier it will become to manage your time effectively.

- **How Time Management Can Help You Achieve Your Personal and Professional Goals**
Good time management is key to reaching both your personal and professional goals. By setting clear objectives, breaking tasks into smaller steps, and staying organized, you can make steady progress towards your goals. Time management helps you stay on track and ensures you have enough time for important activities, leading to success and personal growth.

Chapter 14

Self-Care

Prioritizing Your Well-Being

What is Self-Care?

Self-care refers to the activities and practices that individuals do to take care of their physical, mental, and emotional health. It involves intentionally engaging in habits that promote well-being and help maintain balance in life. Self-care can include things like eating nutritious food, exercising, getting enough sleep, practicing mindfulness, spending time with loved ones, and taking breaks from stress.

Why is Self-Care Important for Overall Well-Being?

Self-care is crucial because it helps individuals manage stress, improve their physical health, boost mental clarity, and maintain emotional stability. By prioritizing self-care, people can recharge, prevent burnout, and maintain a sense of inner peace. Regular self-care practices also increase productivity and enhance personal happiness, allowing individuals to perform better in daily activities and relationships. Without proper self-care, people may face exhaustion, frustration, and other health issues.

The Relationship Between Self-Care and Mental, Emotional, and Physical Health

Self-care is deeply connected to all aspects of health:

- **Mental Health:** Taking time for mental self-care, like practicing mindfulness or doing activities that calm the mind, can reduce stress, improve focus, and prevent mental fatigue.

- **Emotional Health:** Activities such as journaling, seeking support from friends, or engaging in hobbies can help individuals process emotions, develop resilience, and boost emotional well-being.

- **Physical Health:** Regular physical activity, healthy eating, Skin care and proper sleep are essential for maintaining good physical health, and they also contribute to better energy levels and a stronger immune system.

When these aspects are in balance, an individual can achieve a higher quality of life, feel more energized, and handle life's challenges more effectively.

Understanding Different Aspects of Self-Care

Physical Self-Care: Taking Care of Your Body

Physical self-care involves activities that keep your body healthy and functioning well. It includes:

- **Exercise:** Regular physical activity like walking, yoga, or gym workouts helps keep the body fit, improve mood, and increase energy levels.
- **Nutrition:** Eating a balanced diet full of fruits, vegetables, proteins, and healthy fats provides the necessary nutrients to fuel the body.
- **Skin Care:** Taking care of your skin through proper cleansing, moisturizing, and protection from the sun helps maintain healthy, glowing skin and prevents premature aging.
- **Sleep:** Getting enough sleep is vital for recovery and overall well-being. Quality sleep improves mood, memory, and immune function.

By prioritizing physical self-care, you maintain the foundation for good health, making it easier to tackle other areas of life.

Mental Self-Care: Keeping Your Mind Sharp

Mental self-care focuses on activities that help keep the mind focused, sharp, and resilient. It includes:

- **Mental Stimulation:** Activities like reading, puzzles, learning new skills, or solving problems keep the brain engaged.
- **Stress Management:** Practices such as meditation, deep breathing, or taking short breaks during work can help reduce stress levels.
- **Journaling:** Writing your thoughts and feelings down can help clarify your mind and reduce mental clutter.

Engaging in regular mental self-care helps improve focus, decision-making, and emotional regulation.

Emotional Self-Care: Managing Your Emotions

Emotional self-care involves managing your emotions in healthy ways. It includes:

- **Mindfulness:** Practices like mindfulness meditation or deep breathing help you become more aware of your emotions and reactions in the present moment.
- **Expressing Emotions:** Talking to someone you trust, journaling, or engaging in creative activities helps process emotions.
- **Setting Boundaries:** Learning to say no and setting limits in relationships or work helps protect your emotional well-being.

By caring for your emotions, you enhance your ability to cope with stress and build resilience.

Social Self-Care: Maintaining Healthy Relationships

Social self-care involves nurturing positive connections with others. It includes:

- **Spending Quality Time with Loved Ones:** Connecting with friends and family through shared activities strengthens relationships and provides emotional support.
- **Building a Support Network:** Surrounding yourself with positive, supportive people helps you feel understood and valued.
- **Setting Healthy Boundaries:** Creating space for yourself and maintaining healthy boundaries with others prevents burnout and stress.

Healthy social interactions are crucial for emotional and mental health.

Spiritual Self-Care: Connecting with Your Inner Self

Spiritual self-care helps connect you to something greater than yourself, whether through religion, nature, or personal beliefs. It includes:

- **Spiritual Practices:** Engaging in activities such as prayer, meditation, or reflective thought can bring a sense of peace and purpose.
- **Nature Walks or Time Alone:** Spending time in nature or engaging in solitude helps foster inner reflection and clarity.
- **Personal Beliefs:** Practicing spiritual beliefs, whether through rituals or community involvement, can provide comfort and grounding.

Spiritual self-care helps individuals find meaning, purpose, and strength in life's challenges.

Each aspect of self-care plays an important role in maintaining overall well-being and balance in life. By addressing all areas, you can enhance your quality of life and cope more effectively with daily demands.

Benefits of Practicing Self-Care

1. **Reduced Stress and Anxiety**

   Practicing self-care helps lower stress levels by giving the body and mind time to relax and recharge. Engaging in activities like exercise, meditation, or taking breaks throughout the day can reduce feelings of overwhelm and anxiety. Regular self-care helps manage stress more effectively and prevents burnout.

2. **Improved Mental Clarity and Focus**

   Taking care of your mind through activities like mindfulness, reading, or problem-solving exercises can improve mental clarity. This enhanced focus allows you to make better decisions, stay organized, and be more productive in both personal and professional life.

3. **Increased Energy and Physical Health**

   Physical self-care practices like exercise, healthy eating, and adequate sleep boost your energy levels and improve overall health. Regular physical activity strengthens the heart, muscles, and immune system, while proper nutrition and rest give the body the fuel it needs to function at its best.

4. **Better Relationships and Communication with Others**

   Self-care also involves maintaining healthy social connections. By setting boundaries, spending quality time with loved ones, and engaging in supportive relationships, you improve your communication skills and build stronger, more fulfilling relationships. Healthy self-care helps you be more present and understanding with others.

5. **Enhanced Emotional Well-Being and Resilience**

   Emotional self-care practices, such as journaling, mindfulness, or seeking therapy, help you process and manage your emotions. This enhances your emotional resilience, allowing you to cope better with life's challenges. By regularly addressing your emotional needs, you develop a stronger sense of inner peace and well-being.

Incorporating self-care into daily life not only boosts physical and mental health but also strengthens relationships and emotional resilience, leading to a more balanced and fulfilling life.

Common Barriers to Self-Care

1. **Lack of Time and Busy Schedules**

   One of the biggest challenges to practicing self-care is having a busy lifestyle with work, family, or other commitments. When schedules are packed, it can feel difficult to carve out time for self-care activities. However, it's important to prioritize self-care, even if it's just for a few minutes a day, to avoid burnout and maintain overall well-being.

2. **Guilt or Feeling Selfish About Taking Care of Oneself**

Many people feel guilty when they take time for themselves, especially if they have responsibilities toward others. This feeling of selfishness can make it hard to prioritize self-care. However, taking care of yourself is not selfish—it's essential for being able to care for others and maintain a healthy balance in life.

3. **Stress, Burnout, or Feeling Overwhelmed**

When overwhelmed with responsibilities or feeling burned out, it can be hard to even think about self-care. In these moments, it might feel like there is no time or energy left for anything else. However, taking small breaks and engaging in self-care activities can help reduce stress, recharge your energy, and make it easier to tackle challenges.

4. **Limited Resources or Knowledge About Self-Care Practices**

Sometimes, people may not know what self-care practices work best for them or feel they don't have the resources (time, money, or knowledge) to engage in them. However, self-care doesn't have to be expensive or time-consuming. Simple practices, such as taking a walk, practicing deep breathing, or journaling, can have a significant impact on mental and physical health without requiring many resources.

Recognizing and addressing these barriers can help you find ways to make self-care a regular part of your life, even with a busy schedule or limited resources.

Practical Self-Care Tips

1. **For Physical Health:**

   - **Regular Exercise:** Engage in at least 30 minutes of physical activity most days of the week, such as walking, jogging, yoga, or any form of exercise you enjoy. It boosts energy, improves mood, and supports overall health.

   - **Balanced Diet:** Eat a variety of nutritious foods, including fruits, vegetables, whole grains, and lean proteins. A balanced diet keeps your body strong and helps prevent illness.

   - **Staying Hydrated:** Drink plenty of water throughout the day to stay hydrated. Proper hydration supports digestion, skin health, and energy levels.

- **Prioritizing Rest:** Ensure you get enough sleep (7-9 hours) every night. Quality rest is essential for recovery, mental clarity, and overall well-being.

2. **For Mental Health:**
   - **Journaling:** Write down your thoughts, feelings, and experiences to gain clarity and release emotional stress. Journaling helps in understanding your emotions and can provide a sense of calm.
   - **Meditation:** Practice mindfulness meditation to calm the mind, reduce anxiety, and improve focus. Just a few minutes a day can make a difference in how you feel.
   - **Cognitive Exercises:** Engage in activities that stimulate your brain, like puzzles, reading, or learning new things. This can improve mental sharpness and reduce stress.
   - **Learning New Skills:** Keep your mind active by trying new hobbies or skills, whether it's learning a new language, playing a musical instrument, or cooking new recipes. This fosters a sense of accomplishment and self-growth.

3. **For Emotional Health:**
   - **Therapy:** Seeking professional help, such as counselling or therapy, can provide support when dealing with difficult emotions. Talking to someone can help you work through challenges.
   - **Self-Compassion:** Be kind to yourself, especially during tough times. Treat yourself with the same compassion and care you would give a friend.
   - **Stress-Management Techniques:** Practice relaxation techniques such as deep breathing, progressive muscle relaxation, or mindfulness to manage stress and calm your emotions.
   - **Setting Boundaries:** Learn to say "no" when needed, and set healthy boundaries to protect your emotional well-being. Avoid taking on too much responsibility or allowing others to overstep your personal limits.

4. **For Social Well-Being:**
   - **Regular Social Interactions:** Stay connected with family, friends, or colleagues. Regular social interaction provides emotional support and strengthens relationships.
   - **Nurturing Friendships:** Invest time in meaningful friendships. Reach out to friends, plan catch-ups, or participate in group activities that foster connection.

- **Participating in Community Events:** Join local events or community activities that interest you. This creates opportunities to meet new people, share experiences, and feel part of something bigger.

5. **For Spiritual Care:**
   - **Meditation:** Take time for spiritual meditation or mindfulness. This practice can deepen your connection to yourself and help you find inner peace.
   - **Prayer:** If you follow a particular spiritual or religious practice, set aside time for prayer. This can bring a sense of comfort and direction.
   - **Nature Walks:** Spend time in nature to reflect and rejuvenate. Walking in a natural setting helps clear your mind, reduce stress, and reconnect with yourself.
   - **Reflection Time:** Allocate time for quiet reflection, where you can connect with your inner thoughts and gain clarity on your life's path and purpose.

By integrating these practical self-care tips into your daily life, you can nurture your physical, mental, emotional, and spiritual well-being, leading to a more balanced and fulfilling life.

Creating a Personalized Self-Care Plan

1. **How to Assess Your Current Well-Being:**
   - **Reflect on Your Physical Health:** Think about your energy levels, sleep habits, and any physical discomfort or health concerns. Are you getting enough rest and exercise? Do you feel physically drained or energized?
   - **Evaluate Your Mental Health:** Consider how you're feeling emotionally. Are you experiencing stress, anxiety, or burnout? Are you able to focus and think clearly, or do you feel overwhelmed?
   - **Examine Your Social Life:** Reflect on the quality and frequency of your social interactions. Are you connecting with friends and family? Do you feel isolated or supported?
   - **Assess Your Emotional Health:** Notice how you respond to challenges and difficult emotions. Do you practice self-compassion? Are you managing stress well, or do you feel emotionally drained?

2. **Setting Realistic Self-Care Goals:**
   - **Start Small:** Begin with achievable goals that you can easily incorporate into your routine, such as drinking more water each day, getting 7-8 hours of sleep, or walking for 20 minutes daily.
   - **Make Goals Specific:** Instead of vague goals like "take care of myself," set specific targets, such as "practice meditation for 5 minutes every morning" or "schedule one hour of relaxation time every weekend."
   - **Be Flexible:** Life can get busy, so allow yourself to adjust your self-care goals if needed. It's okay to change your approach if something isn't working or if new priorities arise.
   - **Focus on Balance:** Aim for balance between physical, mental, emotional, and social well-being in your goals. Ensure that you're nurturing all areas of your life.

3. **Developing a Balanced Routine:**
   - **Create a Daily Schedule:** Include time for work, rest, exercise, and personal activities. Set aside time in the morning, afternoon, or evening for self-care, depending on what works best for your schedule.
   - **Include Time for Relaxation:** Make sure to schedule breaks during the day, even if it's just 10-15 minutes for a quick walk, deep breathing, or a power nap.
   - **Prioritize Key Self-Care Activities:** Identify the most important self-care activities for you, whether it's exercising, meditating, spending time with loved ones, or practicing mindfulness. Make these a non-negotiable part of your routine.
   - **Consistency is Key:** Try to follow your routine consistently. While life may get in the way sometimes, aim for regularity so your self-care practices become habits over time.

4. **Overcoming Challenges in Maintaining a Self-Care Routine:**
   - **Time Constraints:** If you're feeling pressed for time, simplify your routine. For example, do a shorter workout or meditate for just 5 minutes. Start small and build up gradually as your schedule allows.
   - **Guilt or Self-Doubt:** Don't feel guilty about taking time for yourself. Remember, self-care is necessary for your overall well-being and helps you be more productive and positive in other areas of your life.

- **Motivation Issues:** If you find it hard to stick to your self-care routine, try setting reminders, getting support from a friend, or tracking your progress to keep yourself accountable.
- **Overcoming Burnout:** If you're feeling overwhelmed by maintaining your routine, consider adjusting your expectations. Self-care should rejuvenate, not add more pressure. Allow flexibility for rest and recharging.

By creating a personalized self-care plan, you can effectively nurture your well-being and build lasting habits that help you feel more balanced, relaxed, and energized.

The Role of Self-Care in Long-Term Well-Being

1. **How Self-Care Contributes to Long-Term Happiness and Fulfilment:**
   - **Promotes Balance in Life:** Regular self-care practices help create a sense of balance, allowing individuals to nurture different aspects of their lives, including physical, mental, emotional, and social well-being. This balance contributes to a greater sense of overall happiness and fulfilment.
   - **Prevents Burnout:** By taking time to rest, recharge, and manage stress, self-care helps prevent burnout, ensuring that you can continue to enjoy life's experiences without feeling overwhelmed or exhausted.
   - **Improves Self-Esteem:** Consistently prioritizing your own needs builds self-respect and confidence, making you more likely to feel content and at peace with who you are.
   - **Increases Resilience:** Regular self-care habits strengthen your ability to cope with challenges, setbacks, and difficult emotions. This resilience contributes to long-term happiness by helping you stay positive and adaptive.

2. **The Impact of Consistent Self-Care on Productivity and Relationships:**
   - **Boosts Productivity:** When you prioritize self-care, you're better equipped to focus, think clearly, and work efficiently. Regular physical activity, healthy eating, and adequate rest improve energy levels, helping you perform better at work or in daily tasks.
   - **Improves Mental Clarity:** Taking time to care for your mind through practices like meditation or journaling helps reduce

stress and improve focus, which enhances decision-making and problem-solving abilities.

- **Strengthens Relationships:** By engaging in self-care, you're better able to nurture relationships. When you feel good about yourself, you're more patient, understanding, and supportive in your interactions with others.

- **Reduces Conflict:** Regular self-care reduces feelings of frustration or stress, which can otherwise lead to conflict in relationships. It helps you manage your emotions and respond more calmly in challenging situations.

3. **Practicing Self-Care as a Lifelong Habit for Emotional, Mental, and Physical Health:**

    - **Builds Long-Term Habits:** When you make self-care a consistent part of your routine, it becomes a healthy habit that contributes to your well-being for years to come. Lifelong self-care can improve your quality of life by keeping your mind and body in optimal condition.

    - **Sustains Emotional and Mental Health:** Taking care of your emotional and mental health through self-care practices like mindfulness, therapy, or hobbies helps maintain emotional stability, even during difficult times.

    - **Enhances Physical Health:** Regular physical self-care, such as exercise and healthy eating, not only improves immediate energy and health but also lowers the risk of chronic diseases, leading to better long-term physical well-being.

    - **Promotes Personal Growth:** Ongoing self-care allows you to keep growing as an individual, encouraging you to explore new interests, learn new skills, and become more self-aware over time, contributing to a fulfilling life.

By making self-care a lifelong practice, you create a foundation for sustained emotional, mental, and physical health, leading to a more balanced and fulfilling life.

Keynotes on "Self-Care – Prioritizing Your Well-Being"

1. Self-care is about nurturing physical, mental, emotional, and social health.

2. Importance: Reduces stress, improves well-being, and boosts productivity.

3. Types of Self-Care:

- Physical: Exercise, nutrition, skin care, sleep.
- Mental: Cognitive activities, relaxation.
- Emotional: Managing emotions, therapy.
- Social: Relationships, socializing.
- Spiritual: Meditation, reflection.

4. Benefits: Reduces anxiety, improves focus, enhances resilience, boosts health.

5. Barriers: Time constraints, guilt, stress, limited knowledge.

6. Practical Tips: Regular exercise, mindfulness, social connections, spiritual practices.

7. Personalized Plan: Assess well-being, set goals, create a balanced routine.

8. Long-Term Impact: Supports happiness, productivity, and healthy relationships.

9. Reminder: Self-care is essential, not selfish. It leads to a fulfilled life.

Conclusion

- **Recap of the Importance of Self-Care:**
  Self-care is vital for maintaining a healthy balance in life. It nurtures not only our physical health but also supports our mental, emotional, and social well-being. Practicing self-care regularly helps reduce stress, boosts productivity, and strengthens relationships, contributing to a happier, more fulfilled life.

- **Encouragement to Prioritize Well-Being Daily:**
  Make self-care a priority every day. Even small actions, like taking breaks, getting enough sleep, or practicing mindfulness, can have a big impact on your overall well-being. Remember, caring for yourself is not a luxury but a necessity for leading a healthy, successful, and fulfilling life.

- **Reminder That Self-Care Is Not Selfish but Essential for Living a Fulfilled Life:**
  Taking care of yourself is not selfish—it's a crucial part of being able to care for others and perform well in all areas of life. By prioritizing your own well-being, you are better equipped to handle life's challenges and maintain a positive outlook. Make self-care a lifelong habit for emotional, mental, and physical health.

Emotional Intelligence

Navigating Your Feelings

What is Emotional Intelligence?

Emotional intelligence (EI) is the ability to recognize, understand, manage, and use emotions effectively—both your own and those of others. It involves being aware of how feelings influence behaviour, making thoughtful choices based on this awareness, and handling social interactions with empathy (understanding) and respect.

There are four main parts of emotional intelligence:

1. **Self-Awareness**: Knowing your own emotions, strengths, and weaknesses.

2. **Self-Management**: Being able to control your emotions and adapt to changing situations.

3. **Social Awareness**: Understanding the emotions and needs of others, which includes empathy.

4. **Relationship Management**: Building and maintaining healthy relationships by effectively communicating, resolving conflicts, and inspiring others.

Emotional intelligence is important in many areas of life, such as personal relationships, work, and social interactions, because it helps improve communication, reduce stress, manage conflicts, and build stronger connections with others.

Why Emotional Intelligence (EI) is Essential for Personal Growth and Healthy Relationships

Emotional intelligence (EI) plays a crucial role in both personal development and the quality of our relationships. When you understand and manage your own emotions, it's easier to make better decisions, handle stress, and stay motivated. EI also helps you navigate social situations, understand others' feelings, and respond to them in a way that strengthens your connections.

Benefits of High Emotional Intelligence in Daily Life

1. **Better Self-Control**: High EI helps you manage stress, anger, and frustration, allowing you to respond thoughtfully rather than react impulsively.

2. **Enhanced Communication**: With strong emotional intelligence, you're better able to express yourself clearly and understand others, leading to more effective and empathetic conversations.

3. **Healthier Relationships**: EI helps you build trust, resolve conflicts smoothly, and develop closer, more fulfilling relationships by being considerate of others' feelings.

4. **Increased Resilience**: People with high EI can handle challenges more effectively because they're able to view setbacks as learning opportunities rather than failures.

5. **Improved Mental Health**: By recognizing and processing emotions constructively, EI can reduce stress, anxiety, and negative feelings, promoting a healthier state of mind.

In essence, emotional intelligence contributes to overall life satisfaction, helping you grow personally and build lasting, positive relationships.

Understanding the Components of Emotional Intelligence

1. **Motivation**: Motivation within emotional intelligence is using your emotions to stay committed to goals, even when obstacles arise. Emotionally intelligent people use their positive emotions, like passion and curiosity, to keep going. They set meaningful goals and stay focused, using setbacks as learning opportunities rather than reasons to give up.

2. **Self-Awareness**: This is the ability to recognize and understand your own emotions as they happen. Being self-aware means noticing how you feel and understanding how these emotions affect your thoughts, behaviours, and decisions. For example, if you're feeling stressed, self-awareness helps you identify that feeling before it influences your actions, allowing you to handle it in a healthy way.

3. **Self-Regulation**: Self-regulation is all about managing your emotions, especially during challenging situations. It involves controlling impulses, staying calm under pressure, and responding to situations thoughtfully instead of reacting emotionally. For instance, if someone criticizes your work, self-regulation helps you respond constructively rather than defensively.

4. **Empathy**: Empathy is the ability to understand and share the feelings of others. It means seeing things from other people's perspectives,

which can help you respond in a caring and supportive way. When a friend is upset, for example, empathy allows you to listen and comfort them, even if you haven't experienced the exact same situation.

5. **Social Skills**: Social skills in emotional intelligence are about interacting well with others, building strong connections, and managing conflicts. Effective social skills involve clear communication, listening actively, cooperating, and resolving disagreements respectfully. For example, if there's a misunderstanding at work, strong social skills help you clarify the issue without creating tension.

Each of these components contributes to emotional intelligence, enhancing your ability to understand, manage, and apply emotions to live a balanced and connected life.

Developing Self-Awareness

1. **How to Identify Your Own Emotions and Their Causes**: Self-awareness begins with recognizing what you feel and understanding why you feel that way. Start by checking in with yourself regularly throughout the day. Are you feeling happy, anxious, frustrated, or excited? Once you identify an emotion, ask yourself what might have caused it. Did something specific happen, or did a memory or thought trigger it? This process helps you see the connection between your emotions and your experiences.

2. **Recognizing Emotional Triggers and Patterns**: Emotional triggers are situations, words, or even people that can create intense reactions in you. For example, you might feel stressed every time you're under a tight deadline, or anger when someone interrupts you. By recognizing these patterns, you can begin to understand which situations tend to bring out strong emotions. Knowing your triggers helps you prepare and respond more calmly in those situations.

3. **Journaling and Mindfulness Practices to Enhance Self-Awareness**: Keeping a journal is a great way to explore your feelings, identify patterns, and reflect on how your emotions affect your life. Set aside time each day to write about your emotions and what caused them. Mindfulness practices, like deep breathing or meditation, also help you tune into your thoughts and feelings without judgment. By practicing mindfulness, you can increase your awareness of emotions as they arise, allowing you to manage them more effectively.

By developing self-awareness, you gain greater control over your emotions, which can improve your overall emotional intelligence and help you make better decisions in all areas of life.

Practicing Self-Regulation

Self-regulation is the ability to manage your emotions, thoughts, and behaviours in the face of difficult situations or challenges. It involves staying calm, in control, and focused, especially when emotions are running high. Developing self-regulation helps you respond thoughtfully rather than reacting impulsively, leading to healthier relationships and better decision-making in both personal and professional life.

Techniques to Manage Stress and Control Emotional Responses

Stress is a natural part of life, but how we respond to it makes a big difference. High emotional intelligence means we can manage stress effectively and not let it control us. There are several proven techniques to manage stress and regulate our emotional responses:

1. **Deep Breathing**: One of the simplest ways to manage stress is by focusing on your breathing. Taking slow, deep breaths activates the body's relaxation response, which helps reduce tension. For example, before an important meeting, deep breathing can help lower anxiety levels and prepare you to be present and calm.

   Real-Life Example: Neeru, a teacher, often felt overwhelmed by the demands of her job. She started using deep breathing exercises before class and during stressful moments. Now, when she feels her stress levels rising, she takes five deep breaths to center herself, which helps her stay calm and focused during the day.

2. **Progressive Muscle Relaxation**: This technique involves tensing and then relaxing different muscle groups in the body. It helps release physical tension and can be done anywhere, anytime. For instance, if you're feeling nervous before a presentation, practice tensing your hands into fists and then relaxing them, and repeat with other muscle groups.

   Real-Life Example: Komal, a software developer, would get tense during client calls. He felt his shoulders and neck tightening, which would increase his stress. He started practicing progressive muscle relaxation before calls, and it helped him feel more relaxed and confident.

3. **Meditation**: Regular meditation helps train your mind to focus and stay calm. Even a few minutes of meditation can provide a sense of peace and clarity, especially during moments of stress. Apps like Headspace or Calm can guide you through short meditation sessions to reduce anxiety and enhance self-regulation.

Real-Life Example: Neha, a busy entrepreneur, found that meditation made a huge difference in how she handled stress. By spending just 10 minutes in the morning meditating, she was able to stay calm and clear-headed even during challenging moments at work.

The Importance of Pausing and Reflecting Before Reacting

In emotionally charged situations, it's easy to react impulsively—whether it's snapping at someone in anger or becoming defensive when criticized. However, taking a moment to pause before responding allows you to reflect on the situation and respond more thoughtfully, which is a key component of emotional intelligence.

1. **The Pause**: The act of pausing creates space between stimulus (the event or comment that triggered you) and your response (how you react). This pause allows you to reflect on how you feel and how you want to respond. In moments of high tension, the pause is often all you need to regain control of your emotions and avoid reacting out of frustration or anger.

   Real-Life Example: Jyoti, a manager in a corporate office, used to get defensive whenever his team members pointed out flaws in his plans. One day, after receiving feedback in a meeting, he decided to pause and count to five before responding. This brief moment allowed him to calm down, listen without reacting, and respond in a constructive way. His team noticed the positive change and appreciated his thoughtful approach.

2. **Reflection Before Reacting**: Pausing allows for reflection. It helps you to ask yourself key questions: "Why am I feeling this way?" "Is my reaction proportionate to the situation?" "What would be the most productive response?" Reflecting on these questions can lead to a more measured and balanced reaction, which is essential for maintaining healthy relationships.

   Real-Life Example: Gagan, a working mother, was often frustrated with her kids' behaviour when they didn't follow instructions. Instead of snapping at them in anger, she learned to take a deep breath and reflect. She realized that her frustration was due to her own stress from work, not the children's behaviour. By reflecting, she could respond with patience and understanding instead of anger.

Tips for Staying Calm in Difficult Situations

Staying calm in stressful or difficult situations can be challenging, but with practice, it becomes easier. Self-regulation is about having a toolkit of strategies to handle stress effectively. Here are some practical tips to stay calm when life gets overwhelming:

1. **Grounding Techniques**: Grounding is a technique that helps bring your focus back to the present moment. When you're feeling anxious or overwhelmed, you can use grounding exercises like focusing on the sights and sounds around you or touching something in your environment to reconnect with reality.

   Real-Life Example: Jashan, a student preparing for his final exams, would often feel anxious about his performance. Before sitting down to study, he would use a grounding technique by focusing on five things he could see, four things he could touch, three things he could hear, two things he could smell, and one thing he could taste. This simple exercise helped him calm his nerves and improve his focus.

2. **Positive Self-Talk**: Your internal dialogue has a big impact on your emotional state. Practicing positive self-talk can help reframe stressful situations and reduce emotional reactions. Instead of saying, "I can't handle this," try telling yourself, "I've handled tough situations before, and I can do this too."

   Real-Life Example: Pratha, a small business owner, used to feel overwhelmed during peak seasons. She started using positive self-talk, saying, "I've managed this before, and I have the skills to get through this." This simple change in mindset made her feel more in control and less stressed.

3. **Practice Gratitude**: Gratitude helps shift focus from what's going wrong to what's going right. Practicing gratitude daily can rewire your brain to focus on the positives in your life, making it easier to stay calm in tough situations. You can start by listing three things you're grateful for each day.

   Real-Life Example: Rakesh, a salesperson, often found himself stressed due to the pressure of meeting targets. At the end of each day, he started writing down three things he was grateful for—whether it was a successful client meeting, a supportive colleague, or good health. This practice made him feel more balanced and less reactive in difficult situations.

Self-regulation is a vital skill for emotional intelligence. By learning how to manage stress, pause before reacting, and stay calm during difficult situations, you can improve your emotional well-being and handle challenges with confidence. Just like any skill, self-regulation takes practice, but over time, it can help you maintain control of your emotions, make better decisions, and build stronger relationships. The key is to use these techniques regularly so that they become second nature when you need them most.

Healing Through Forgiveness – The Power of the Ho'oponopono Prayer

The Ho'oponopono prayer is a Hawaiian practice of reconciliation and forgiveness designed to clear negative energy and restore peace. It involves four key phrases:

I am sorry
Please forgive me
Thank You
I Love You

It's a simple yet powerful practice rooted in the belief that everything in the world is connected, and by healing ourselves, we can also heal our relationships and environment. The basic prayer involves four phrases, each with its own significance in helping us take responsibility for and let go of any burdens, guilt, or negative emotions.

1. **I'm sorry** – Acknowledging the issue and taking responsibility, even if you don't fully understand how you're connected to it.

2. **Please forgive me** – Asking for forgiveness from yourself or from the universe, acknowledging that mistakes were made, whether consciously or unconsciously.

3. **Thank you** – Expressing gratitude for the forgiveness and healing that is taking place, for the opportunity to release, or for lessons learned.

4. **I love you** – Offering unconditional love to yourself, the situation, or those involved, promoting healing and peace.

Each line in the prayer represents a step toward inner harmony. You can repeat it silently or out loud, focusing on a specific situation, relationship, or aspect of yourself you want to heal. The prayer can be deeply personal and is meant to foster forgiveness, love, and compassion for oneself and others. Many find this simple ritual brings emotional relief, clarity, and a sense of well-being.

Building Motivation through Emotional Intelligence

Motivation is a core component of emotional intelligence that drives us to set and achieve meaningful goals. Unlike external motivation, which depends on outside factors like rewards or praise, internal motivation comes from within. Building motivation through emotional intelligence means harnessing your emotions, thoughts, and resilience to stay committed to your personal and professional goals.

Setting Personal Goals That Inspire and Challenge You

To stay motivated, it's essential to set goals that genuinely inspire you. These goals should feel purposeful and align with your values, sparking excitement rather than feeling like a chore. When goals are personal, they become a source of inspiration and create a sense of direction and focus.

1. **Start Small**: Begin with smaller, manageable goals that lead toward a larger vision. Smaller successes provide momentum and make the bigger goals feel more achievable.

   Real-Life Example: Pratham, a recent graduate, set a goal of becoming a data analyst. He broke this larger goal into smaller steps: completing a certification course, practicing skills on data projects, and applying to jobs in the field. With each small achievement, his motivation grew, keeping him on track toward his larger goal.

2. **Visualize Success**: Visualizing the end result of your goal can help maintain motivation. When you picture what achieving your goal will feel and look like, you're more likely to stay excited and driven.

   Real-Life Example: Neetu, a teacher, set a goal to write a book on her teaching experiences. Whenever she felt her motivation dipping, she'd imagine holding the published book in her hands, which re-energized her commitment to writing each day.

The Role of Positive Self-Talk and Resilience

Positive self-talk is a powerful motivator that keeps us going when we encounter setbacks or face difficult challenges. Resilience, or the ability to bounce back from difficulties, is strengthened by maintaining a positive, growth-oriented mindset.

1. **Challenge Negative Thoughts**: Negative thoughts can drain motivation quickly. When you notice thoughts like "I'm not good enough" or "This is too hard," try reframing them. For example, replace "I can't do this" with "This is challenging, but I'll figure it out."

   Real-Life Example: Mukesh, who was training for a marathon, often found himself discouraged by the intensity of his training. He'd catch his negative thoughts and remind himself of how far he'd come. By focusing on his progress, he felt a renewed sense of motivation.

2. **Build Resilience Through Self-Compassion**: Resilience means treating yourself kindly during setbacks. Remind yourself that

challenges are a normal part of growth, and approach them with curiosity instead of self-criticism.

Real-Life Example: Prerna, who ran a beauty parlour, was hoping to expand her business by getting a big contract to style the hair and makeup for a local event. However, she lost out on the opportunity to a competitor. Initially, she felt disappointed and discouraged. Instead of beating herself up, she reminded herself that setbacks are a part of any business journey. Prerna reflected on what she could learn from the experience—perhaps improving her pitch or offering a unique service. With this mindset, she stayed motivated, learned from the setback, and continued to work hard toward growing her business.

How Motivation Supports Self-Discipline and Goal Achievement

Self-discipline is crucial for reaching goals, and motivation plays a vital role in building it. Motivation can help you stick to routines and make choices that support your progress. When we're driven by a goal that means something to us, self-discipline becomes easier because the actions we take align with our purpose.

1. **Create a Routine**: Motivation helps establish routines that make it easier to maintain discipline. When you're motivated by a goal, creating a daily schedule or set of habits becomes more manageable.

   Real-Life Example: Aradhya, who wanted to improve her physical fitness, set a daily goal of exercising in the morning. Knowing her reasons for staying fit and healthy motivated her to stick to her routine, building her self-discipline over time.

2. **Celebrate Small Wins**: Recognizing small successes along the way keeps your motivation high and strengthens self-discipline. Each step forward is a reminder of how much closer you are to your goal.

   Real-Life Example: Neet, an aspiring artist, celebrated every time he finished a piece, even if it was just a small sketch. By acknowledging these small accomplishments, he stayed motivated to practice daily, building his skills and discipline over time.

Building motivation through emotional intelligence is about connecting with your goals on a deeper level, nurturing positive self-talk, and developing resilience. When we set inspiring goals, practice self-compassion, and celebrate small wins, we build self-discipline and create a path toward fulfilling our aspirations. With each step, motivation grows, helping us transform dreams into reality.

Cultivating Empathy

Empathy is the ability to understand and share the feelings of others. It helps you build deeper, more meaningful relationships and allows you to connect with others on an emotional level.

Understanding and Valuing Others' Perspectives

Empathy begins with recognizing that everyone has a unique set of experiences, challenges, and viewpoints. By appreciating and respecting these differences, you can engage more compassionately with others. Valuing someone's perspective doesn't mean agreeing with them, but it involves recognizing their right to feel or think the way they do.

For example, when a team member expresses frustration with a task at work, instead of dismissing their concerns, you could say, "I see how that would be challenging. Can I help in some way?" This approach shows that you acknowledge their feelings and are willing to support them.

Active Listening to Foster Empathy in Conversations Active listening is a critical skill for cultivating empathy. It means focusing fully on the speaker, understanding their message, and responding thoughtfully. Active listening involves:

- Making eye contact and maintaining an open body posture.
- Nodding or giving small verbal acknowledgments like "I see" or "I understand."
- Refraining from interrupting and allowing the speaker to finish their thoughts.

Real-Life Example: Prince, a teacher, often listens to his students carefully when they express concerns or frustrations about schoolwork. He practices active listening by giving them his full attention, asking clarifying questions, and offering feedback. This creates a trusting environment where students feel heard and valued, which strengthens his relationships with them.

Practicing Compassion and Non-Judgmental Communication

Compassion is the ability to feel for others in times of hardship and respond with kindness. Non-judgmental communication ensures that you're not imposing your opinions or assumptions on others but are genuinely open to understanding them.

When communicating with empathy, avoid making quick judgments about someone's feelings or situation. Instead of saying, "You shouldn't feel that way," try responding with, "I understand why you might feel that way. Would you like to talk more about it?" This fosters an environment of compassion where others feel safe to express themselves without fear of judgment.

Real-Life Example: Tanu, a customer service representative, frequently encounters upset customers. Instead of getting defensive or frustrated, she listens to their complaints and acknowledges their feelings, saying, "I understand how frustrating that must be. Let's see what we can do to fix this." By offering empathy and understanding, she not only resolves the issue but builds customer loyalty.

Empathy helps create a supportive and harmonious atmosphere, whether in personal relationships or professional environments, and strengthens your emotional intelligence.

Improving Social Skills for Better Relationships

Social skills are essential for forming, maintaining, and deepening relationships. By enhancing these skills, you can build positive connections in both personal and professional settings. Here's how to improve social skills using emotional intelligence for better relationships:

1. **Importance of Clear and Respectful Communication**

   Clear communication is about expressing your thoughts and feelings openly, yet with respect and understanding. This skill is key to preventing misunderstandings and building mutual respect.

   - **Practice being clear and specific**: When expressing an opinion or request, be concise. Avoid vague statements, and be straightforward about what you want to communicate.

   - **Use respectful language**: Avoid accusatory or confrontational language. Using "I" statements (e.g., "I feel" or "I need") can help express feelings without putting the other person on the defensive.

   - **Real-Life   Example**:
     Rishi and his friend Pooja are working together on a project. Pooja feels that Rishi isn't contributing equally, and instead of building resentment, she decides to address it. She says, "I feel overwhelmed managing most of the tasks on my own. Can we discuss how we can share the workload more evenly?" This respectful approach helps Rishi understand Pooja's feelings without feeling attacked, leading to a more balanced team effort.

   - **Tip**: When communicating, pay attention to your tone and words. Aim to express your needs clearly without sounding accusatory or demanding.

2. **Conflict Resolution Techniques Using Emotional Intelligence**

Conflicts are a natural part of relationships, but managing them with emotional intelligence can turn challenges into opportunities for growth. Emotional intelligence helps you stay calm, listen actively, and find solutions that work for everyone involved.

- **Stay calm and control emotional reactions**: Take a moment to breathe or step away if needed. Remaining calm can prevent conflicts from escalating.

- **Seek to understand before responding**: Listening to the other person's perspective and acknowledging their feelings can diffuse tension and show that you care about resolving the issue fairly.

- **Real-Life   Example**: Harry and her partner, Shiv, often argue over finances. Harry tends to save while Shiv prefers to spend. During one heated argument, Harry takes a deep breath and calmly says, "I understand that you enjoy spending on things we need, and I appreciate that you want us to have a comfortable life. Can we work out a budget that lets us save while still meeting our needs?" This approach shifts the tone from confrontation to cooperation, allowing them to reach a solution together.

- **Tip**: Approach conflicts as a team effort rather than a competition. Using words that promote unity, like "we" and "our," can help build a sense of working together to find a solution.

3. **Building Trust and Strengthening Connections Through Empathy and Understanding**

Trust is the foundation of strong relationships, and it is built over time through empathy, honesty, and reliability. By showing empathy and understanding, you create a safe space where others feel valued and respected.

- **Demonstrate reliability**: Being consistent in your actions and keeping promises builds trust and shows others they can depend on you.

- **Practice empathy regularly**: Acknowledge others' feelings and make an effort to understand their emotions and perspectives, even when they differ from yours.

- **Real-Life Example**: Aditya and his colleague Aarti have different work styles, which sometimes leads to friction. Aditya prefers planning, while Aarti often makes decisions quickly. Instead of letting these differences affect their collaboration, Aditya takes time to understand Aarti's approach. He acknowledges, "I can see that you're very quick with decisions, which can be great for moving things forward. Let's find a way to balance our styles so we can work well together." This builds mutual respect, making it easier for them to collaborate and trust each other.

- **Tip**: Show your support by listening without judgment and being there for others during challenging times. Small gestures of empathy and support can significantly strengthen bonds over time.

Improving social skills is essential for building and maintaining strong relationships. Through clear communication, emotionally intelligent conflict resolution, and fostering trust with empathy, you can connect deeply with others and create lasting, positive relationships. By making these skills a regular part of your interactions, you'll enhance your relationships and enrich your personal and professional life.

Emotional Intelligence in Challenging Situations

Challenging situations, like facing criticism, dealing with conflict, or navigating high-stress environments, test our emotional intelligence. By learning to manage our emotions effectively, we can approach these situations calmly and constructively. Here's how to apply emotional intelligence when dealing with life's tougher moments:

1. **How to Handle Criticism Constructively**

   Receiving criticism can be uncomfortable, but it also offers valuable opportunities for growth. Emotional intelligence helps you listen objectively, separate the message from your emotions, and respond constructively.

   - **Stay open-minded**: Instead of becoming defensive, listen carefully to the feedback. Ask yourself if there's truth in it and what you might learn from it.

   - **Focus on self-improvement**: Look at criticism as a chance to identify areas of growth. Ask clarifying questions if needed and seek advice on how to improve.

   - **Real-Life Example**:
     Neet, a teacher, receives feedback from a parent that her teaching style could be more engaging for younger students. Initially, Neet feels defensive, but she takes a deep breath and acknowledges the parent's concern. Instead of reacting negatively, she says, "Thank you for sharing your thoughts. I'd love to hear more ideas on how I can make my lessons more engaging for the students." This

approach helps her learn and grow while showing the parent she values constructive feedback.

- **Tip**: After receiving feedback, take time to reflect and let emotions settle. Approach the feedback with a problem-solving mindset to make the best use of it.

2. **Staying Emotionally Grounded During Conflicts or Disagreements**

Conflicts and disagreements are unavoidable, but staying emotionally grounded can help you respond thoughtfully rather than react impulsively. Emotional intelligence allows you to approach conflicts with calmness and clarity.

- **Pause and take a deep breath**: Before responding, give yourself a moment to collect your thoughts. This pause can help prevent emotionally charged reactions.

- **Focus on understanding the other person's perspective**: Show empathy by acknowledging their feelings, even if you disagree. This can lower defensiveness and help the conversation stay constructive.

- **Real-Life Example**: Raj and his friend, Arjun, disagree about a business idea they're planning together. Raj wants to invest in marketing, while Arjun prefers saving the money. During a tense meeting, Raj takes a moment to breathe and says, "I see that you're concerned about overspending. Can we explore a way to approach marketing without stretching the budget too much?" By grounding himself emotionally, Raj keeps the discussion respectful and open to compromise.

- **Tip**: Practice active listening. Often, people simply want to be heard and understood, which can diffuse conflict and help resolve disagreements.

3. **Strategies for Managing Emotional Responses in High-Stress Situations**

High-stress situations can trigger intense emotions, making it easy to feel overwhelmed. Emotional intelligence enables you to recognize these feelings, control immediate reactions, and make thoughtful decisions despite the stress.

- **Recognize your triggers**: Identifying what specifically stresses you out can help you manage your response more effectively. Take note of how your body and mind react in these moments.

- **Practice stress-management techniques**: Deep breathing, grounding exercises, and visualization can help calm your nervous system during high-stress times.

- **Real-Life Example**: Divya is a customer service manager who often deals with frustrated clients. One day, a customer calls, angry about a delay. Divya's first instinct is to respond defensively, but she remembers to take a few deep breaths and listen actively. By calmly acknowledging the customer's frustration, she helps de-escalate the situation. She says, "I understand how this delay has been inconvenient for you. Let's see what we can do to resolve it." By managing her emotions, Divya maintains professionalism and helps the customer feel heard.

- **Tip**: In high-stress moments, grounding techniques such as counting to ten, practicing mindfulness, or taking short breaks can be highly effective. These simple practices can help you regain control and approach the situation with a clear mind.

Using emotional intelligence in challenging situations can transform difficult interactions into opportunities for growth and connection. By handling criticism constructively, staying grounded during conflicts, and managing emotions in high-stress scenarios, you can maintain calm and positivity. Developing these skills will not only benefit you personally but also strengthen your relationships with others.

Practical Tips for Enhancing Emotional Intelligence

Emotional intelligence (EI) is a skill that grows with practice and conscious effort. By incorporating specific habits and exercises into your daily life, you can strengthen your ability to understand and manage emotions effectively. Here are practical tips to help you enhance your EI:

1. **Daily Habits and Exercises to Boost EI**

   Developing emotional intelligence takes consistency. These daily practices can help you build self-awareness, empathy, and resilience:

   - **Mindfulness**: Take a few minutes each day to check in with yourself. Notice your thoughts and emotions without judgment. Mindfulness practices, like meditation or deep breathing, can help you stay calm and focused.

   - **Gratitude**: Reflect on things you're grateful for. Keeping a gratitude journal or listing three things each day that you appreciate can shift your focus to the positive, which improves emotional resilience and overall well-being.

   - **Reflection**: At the end of the day, take time to reflect on your emotions and actions. Consider what went well, what didn't, and how you could respond better in future situations. This reflection process strengthens self-awareness.

- **Real-Life Example**: Vipan starts each morning with a short meditation to center himself, then writes down one thing he's grateful for. This daily habit keeps him grounded and emotionally balanced, helping him stay positive and manage stress at work.

2. **Using "I" Statements to Express Feelings Without Blame**

   "I" statements are a powerful tool for expressing your feelings without placing blame. Instead of making others feel defensive, these statements encourage open and honest communication.

   - **How to Use "I" Statements**: Frame your feelings in terms of "I" rather than "you." For example, instead of saying, "You never listen to me," try saying, "I feel unheard when I'm interrupted."

   - **Benefits**: Using "I" statements fosters a non-confrontational approach to communication. It allows you to express your feelings openly, which can prevent misunderstandings and help others understand your perspective.

   - **Real-Life Example**: Neha feels frustrated when her partner, Prince, frequently checks his phone during their conversations. Instead of accusing him, she says, "I feel disconnected when we don't have full attention during our conversations." This statement helps Prince understand her perspective without feeling attacked.

3. **Practicing Patience and Flexibility with Yourself and Others**

   Building emotional intelligence involves patience, both with yourself and those around you. Flexibility and understanding are key in maintaining healthy relationships and staying resilient.

   - **Be Patient with Yourself**: Growth takes time. If you have a moment where emotions get the best of you, don't be too hard on yourself. Treat yourself with compassion and remind yourself that everyone has challenging days.

   - **Stay Flexible**: Life can be unpredictable, and so can people's reactions. By staying flexible, you're more prepared to handle unexpected situations calmly, making it easier to resolve conflicts or adapt to changes.

   - **Tip**: When feeling stressed, take a moment to breathe deeply, remind yourself of the bigger picture, and try to approach the situation with a flexible mindset.

Enhancing emotional intelligence is an ongoing journey. By incorporating daily mindfulness practices, using "I" statements to express yourself, and approaching challenges with patience and flexibility, you can boost your EI.

These skills not only improve your self-awareness and resilience but also enhance your relationships with others, helping you navigate emotions with greater ease and understanding.

Real-Life Examples of Emotional Intelligence in Action

Emotional Intelligence (EI) plays a powerful role in various aspects of life, helping individuals manage emotions, strengthen relationships, and turn challenges into opportunities for growth. Here are some real-life examples that show how EI can make a difference:

1. **Using EI to Improve Relationships**

    Understanding and managing emotions can help foster better communication and empathy within personal relationships.

    - **Example**: Raman and his friend Komal had a disagreement over a business deal. Raman felt hurt and initially wanted to cut ties. However, after reflecting on his feelings, he reached out to Komal with a clear, non-accusatory message. By expressing how he felt and listening to Komal's perspective, they both realized it was a misunderstanding. Using EI allowed Raman to turn a potential conflict into an opportunity to strengthen their friendship through honest communication.

2. **Applying EI for Better Work Performance**

    Emotional intelligence can greatly enhance work performance by helping individuals handle stress, communicate effectively, and work well in teams.

    - **Example**: Madhu, a project manager, often felt overwhelmed with tight deadlines and pressure from upper management. Instead of letting stress affect her interactions, she practiced self-regulation techniques, like deep breathing and taking short breaks to calm herself. When her team missed a deadline, Madhu focused on problem-solving rather than blame. She encouraged her team to discuss what went wrong and explore solutions together. Her ability to manage her emotions and foster a supportive environment helped her team perform better and trust her leadership.

3. **EI as a Tool for Personal Growth**

    Emotional intelligence can transform setbacks into learning opportunities, allowing people to grow stronger and more resilient.

    - **Example**: Sandhya faced a major setback when her startup business struggled to gain traction. She initially felt disappointed and questioned her abilities. However, using self-awareness and self-compassion, Sandhya reminded herself that setbacks are part of any journey. She analysed her business approach and identified areas for improvement. By staying motivated and learning from her mistakes, Sandhya adjusted her strategies and eventually achieved her business goals. Her resilience and emotional intelligence turned her failure into a valuable learning experience.

4. **EI in Transforming Conflict into Growth Opportunities**

Emotional intelligence is essential for managing conflicts constructively and finding solutions that satisfy all parties involved.

- **Example**: Vipan and his colleague, Neet, had different opinions on how to handle a client project. Tension rose, and they struggled to find common ground. Rather than escalating the conflict, Vipan took a step back and practiced empathy, considering Neet's perspective. He invited her to a calm discussion where both could voice their opinions. They realized they shared the same goal and brainstormed a compromise. Vipan's emotional intelligence helped them resolve their differences and strengthen their professional relationship.

The Long-Term Benefits of Emotional Intelligence

Emotional Intelligence (EI) offers profound benefits over a lifetime, impacting mental health, career growth, and overall satisfaction. Here's how EI contributes to long-term well-being and success:

1. **EI and Mental and Emotional Well-Being**

High EI can significantly enhance mental and emotional health by providing tools to manage stress, cope with challenges, and maintain a positive outlook.

- **Emotional Balance**: By understanding and managing emotions, individuals experience less anxiety, frustration, and mood swings, which helps promote a stable, positive state of mind.
- **Resilience in Tough Times**: Emotional intelligence helps people face setbacks with a growth mindset, making it easier to bounce back from difficult situations.

Example: A person with high EI, like Neeru, who experiences stress at work, may use techniques like self-awareness and self-regulation to prevent burnout. Instead of feeling overwhelmed, she's able to recognize her stress signals early, take breaks, and seek support, maintaining both her mental health and productivity.

2. **EI's Role in Career Success and Personal Satisfaction**

    In professional life, EI is a key factor in career advancement and building strong work relationships. Employers value EI skills, such as teamwork, communication, and leadership, which directly contribute to job success.

    - **Enhanced Work Performance**: Emotionally intelligent people are more likely to manage deadlines, handle feedback, and work well with others.
    - **Leadership Potential**: Leaders with high EI tend to inspire and motivate their teams, create positive work environments, and handle conflicts effectively, making them valuable to any organization.

3. **EI as a Lifelong Skill for Happiness and Resilience**

    Emotional intelligence is not a one-time skill; it's a lifelong asset that supports lasting happiness, resilience, and fulfilling relationships.

    - **Lasting Relationships**: EI promotes empathy and effective communication, which are essential for maintaining healthy relationships with family, friends, and colleagues.
    - **Adaptability to Life's Changes**: Life comes with constant changes and challenges. Emotional intelligence helps individuals adapt, manage emotions during transitions, and maintain a sense of purpose.

    Example: As Divya navigates a major life change—such as moving to a new city—her EI skills help her adjust to her new surroundings and make friends. Her empathy and open communication allow her to form connections quickly, making the transition smoother and less stressful.

The long-term benefits of emotional intelligence are profound. EI enhances mental health, career success, and relationship satisfaction, equipping individuals to handle life's ups and downs with resilience and optimism. It is a skill that grows with time, making it invaluable for achieving a fulfilling, balanced, and happy life.

Keynotes on Emotional Intelligence – Navigating Your Feelings

- **Emotional Intelligence (EI)**: Ability to understand, manage, and use emotions positively.
- **Importance**: Enhances relationships, resilience, and decision-making.
- **Core Components**:

- **Self-Awareness**: Recognize own emotions.

- **Self-Regulation**: Control responses to emotions.

- **Motivation**: Stay focused on goals.

- **Empathy**: Understand others' feelings.

- **Social Skills**: Communicate and resolve conflicts well.

- **Building EI**:
  - Practice mindfulness, journaling, and active listening.
  - Use "I" statements for clear, responsible communication.
  - Set personal goals and show self-compassion.

- **Benefits**: EI boosts mental health, career success, and happiness.

Final Thought: EI is a lifelong tool for personal growth and fulfilling relationships.

Emotional intelligence is a powerful tool that helps us understand, manage, and grow from our emotions. This chapter has explored the essential components of EI—self-awareness, self-regulation, motivation, empathy, and social skills—and how they play a crucial role in our personal and professional lives. Developing emotional intelligence allows us to connect more deeply with others, handle challenges with resilience, and pursue our goals with a clear and focused mind.

Actively cultivating and applying EI skills can transform the way we experience the world. Whether it's managing stress, improving communication, or building empathy, each step toward greater emotional intelligence brings us closer to a fulfilling life filled with positive relationships and a strong sense of purpose. By navigating our emotions with intelligence and compassion, we unlock the potential to lead happier, healthier lives while building stronger connections with those around us.

Chapter 16

The Ultimate Life Toolbox

Putting It All Together

In *"The Ultimate Life Toolbox: Discover the Secrets to a Confident and Peaceful Life "* the journey begins with discovering your life's purpose (IKIGAI) and setting clear goals (Vision to Reality). The book encourages self-reflection, helping you understand yourself better, while journaling helps track growth. It focuses on cultivating gratitude, mindfulness, and prayer for a balanced life. The book explores how gut health impacts mental well-being and emphasizes the power of positive affirmations. Embracing imperfections (Wabi Sabi) and accepting change (Anicca) are key to personal growth. It highlights the importance of taking digital breaks (Digital Detox) and building resilience in tough times. Time management and self-care are essential for well-being. Emotional intelligence and mind mapping help with decision-making and improving relationships. The final chapter ties everything together, guiding you on how to use all these tools for a fulfilling life. The book is about taking small steps toward big changes, balancing self-growth, emotional health, and effective living.

Here is the Summary of all Chapters: "The Ultimate Life Toolbox"

The book begins by introducing the concept of a "Life Toolbox," a metaphorical collection of tools designed to help individuals navigate life's challenges, achieve personal growth, and foster well-being. It emphasizes that personal growth is a continuous process and that these tools can be used as guides for improving both the mental and physical aspects of life.

Chapter 1: IKIGAI – Finding Your Purpose

In this chapter, the Japanese concept of *IKIGAI* is explored, guiding readers to find their unique purpose in life. Understanding your purpose is fundamental to all personal growth, as it sets the direction for everything you do. The chapter delves into discovering what brings you joy, what you are good at, and how to contribute to the world in a meaningful way. Finding your *IKIGAI* creates a sense of fulfilment and aligns your actions with your true desires.

Chapter 2: Vision to Reality – Mapping Your Success

Once you discover your purpose, this chapter helps you map out your goals to create a clear vision of your future. It discusses the importance of setting actionable and realistic goals while breaking them down into smaller tasks to achieve success. The process of turning a vision into reality requires persistence, adaptability, and focus. Readers are encouraged to create a plan and stay committed to achieving their dreams.

Chapter 3: Self-Reflection – Understanding Yourself

Self-reflection is an essential tool for personal growth. This chapter emphasizes taking the time to reflect on your actions, thoughts, and feelings. By understanding your strengths, weaknesses, and patterns of behaviour, you can make more informed decisions that align with your goals. The chapter suggests practices like journaling and meditation to promote regular self-reflection and continuous improvement.

Chapter 4: Journaling – Reflecting on Your Journey

Building on the idea of self-reflection, this chapter explores the power of journaling as a tool for personal growth. Writing down thoughts and experiences allows for better understanding and clarity. Journaling helps track progress, process emotions, and uncover new insights. It is an effective way to document your journey and ensure you're on the right path toward self-improvement.

Chapter 5: Gratitude – The Power of Appreciation

Gratitude shifts your mindset toward positivity and appreciation. This chapter demonstrates how practicing gratitude, whether through daily affirmations or simple acts of thankfulness, can enhance mental well-being. It also explains the benefits of gratitude on physical health, emotional stability, and overall happiness. By focusing on the positive aspects of life, individuals can overcome negativity and improve their outlook on life.

Chapter 6: Gut and Mind Connection – Gut Health & Mental Well-Being

The mind-body connection is explored in-depth, with a specific focus on the gut-brain axis. This chapter explains how gut health impacts emotional and mental well-being. Imbalances in the gut microbiome can affect mood, stress levels, and mental clarity. By nurturing gut health through proper diet and lifestyle changes, individuals can improve their mental health and enhance their overall quality of life.

Chapter 7: Positive Affirmations – Building a Positive Mindset

Positive affirmations are a powerful tool for cultivating self-belief and a positive mindset. This chapter introduces the practice of affirmations and how they can reshape thought patterns. By repeating empowering statements, individuals can challenge negative beliefs and rewire their minds for success. The chapter emphasizes consistency and repetition for effective results in building a positive outlook on life.

Chapter 8: Mindfulness and Prayer – Connecting with Your Inner Self

Mindfulness and prayer are presented as practices that connect you to your inner self and the present moment. This chapter explores the benefits of mindfulness in reducing stress, increasing focus, and improving emotional regulation. Prayer, whether spiritual or secular, is highlighted as a way to seek inner peace, strength, and clarity. Both practices help individuals remain grounded and aware in their daily lives.

Chapter 9: Wabi Sabi – Embracing Imperfection and Transience

Inspired by the Japanese philosophy of *Wabi Sabi*, this chapter teaches the art of embracing imperfection and transience. Life is not always perfect, and learning to accept imperfections can foster personal growth and peace. *Wabi Sabi* encourages finding beauty in the natural cycle of life, including its changes, flaws, and moments of impermanence. This mindset helps cultivate gratitude for the present moment and acceptance of life's unpredictability.

Chapter 10: Anicca (Impermanence) – Understanding and Accepting Change

This chapter delves into the Buddhist concept of *Anicca* (impermanence), teaching readers to accept and embrace the inevitable changes in life. Understanding that nothing lasts forever can help you adapt to life's fluctuations. By accepting change, you can grow and evolve more effectively, making peace with the fact that life is ever-changing.

Chapter 11: Digital Detox – Reclaiming Your Time and Focus

In today's fast-paced digital world, a digital detox is necessary for maintaining focus and mental health. This chapter guides readers on how to disconnect from screens, reduce digital distractions, and reclaim precious time for personal growth. It encourages readers to set boundaries around technology use, prioritize real-world connections, and practice mindfulness in their daily routines.

Chapter 12: Resilience – Bouncing Back from Hard Times

Resilience is the ability to recover from challenges and adversity. This chapter explores the key traits of resilient individuals, including perseverance, adaptability, and optimism. It discusses strategies to strengthen resilience, such as fostering a growth mindset, seeking support, and learning from failures. Resilience is crucial for overcoming setbacks and emerging stronger from difficult situations.

Chapter 13: Time Management – Maximizing Your Potential

Effective time management is essential for achieving success and maintaining balance. This chapter teaches practical strategies for managing time wisely, such as prioritizing tasks, setting deadlines, and eliminating distractions. By mastering time management, individuals can maximize their productivity, achieve their goals, and create more time for self-care and personal development.

Chapter 14: Self-Care – Prioritizing Your Well-Being

Self-care is fundamental for maintaining mental, emotional, and physical health. This chapter emphasizes the importance of taking time for yourself, setting boundaries, and engaging in activities that promote well-being. Self-care routines, such as exercising, eating nutritious foods, and resting, help individuals sustain energy levels and stay resilient in the face of challenges.

Chapter 15: Emotional Intelligence – Navigating Your Feelings

Emotional intelligence (EQ) is the ability to understand and manage emotions. This chapter explores the five components of EQ: self-awareness, self-regulation, motivation, empathy, and social skills. It teaches readers how to improve their emotional intelligence for better relationships, decision-making, and overall well-being.

In conclusion, **"The Ultimate Life Toolbox"** provides a holistic approach to personal growth, equipping readers with practical tools for building a fulfilling life. Each chapter serves as a valuable resource for developing essential skills, from finding your purpose to managing time and emotions. The book offers timeless principles that empower readers to navigate life's challenges, embrace change, and create a life of happiness and success.

Books:

1. **Ikigai: The Japanese Secret to a Long and Happy Life** by Héctor García and Francesc Miralles – This book explores the concept of Ikigai and how it can help find a fulfilling life.

2. **The Power of Now** by Eckhart Tolle – This book emphasizes the importance of mindfulness and living in the present moment, which aligns with several chapters in this book.

3. **The Subtle Art of Not Giving a F*ck** by Mark Manson – A modern take on personal growth, focusing on resilience and emotional intelligence.

4. **Atomic Habits** by James Clear – Discusses time management, self-care, and building habits that contribute to a better life.

Web Resources:

1. Mindful.org – Offers articles and resources on mindfulness practices: https://www.mindful.org

2. Psychology Today – Articles on emotional intelligence, resilience, and self-care: https://www.psychologytoday.com

3. Healthline – A comprehensive resource for gut health and its impact on mental well-being: https://www.healthline.com

Podcasts:

1. **The Tim Ferriss Show** – Tim Ferriss often discusses productivity, mindfulness, and personal growth.

2. **The Minimalists Podcast** – Offers advice on decluttering your life and focusing on what truly matters.

3. **The Daily Stoic** – Focuses on philosophy, self-reflection, and resilience.

4. **Ram Verma's Podcast** – Focuses on personal growth, mindfulness, and mental wellness. Specially on the topic "Gut & Mind Connection"

Websites:

1. **Brain Pickings** – A site with thought-provoking articles on self-improvement, mindfulness, and the human condition: https://www.brainpickings.org

2. **Mindful Schools** – Offers courses and resources on mindfulness: https://www.mindfulschools.org

I hope you've enjoyed reading the ideas, tools, and strategies shared in this book. Each chapter was written with the aim of helping you build a life full of meaning, balance, and happiness.

Remember, the chapters are not just words on a page—they are tools to help you change and grow. By adding them to your daily life, you can create the life you want and deserve. Take your time, follow what feels right for you, and see how small changes can bring big results.

Happiness is not a final goal—it's a journey shaped by the choices we make and the habits we build. I hope this book becomes a guide on your journey, helping you face challenges, grow stronger, and find peace along the way.

Thank you for letting me be part of your story. Wishing you a life full of positivity, growth, and lasting happiness.

Warm regards,

Vipan Kapoor

Use this space to reflect on your thoughts, ideas, or inspirations after reading this book.

www.ingramcontent.com/pod-product-compliance
Lightning Source LLC
Chambersburg PA
CBHW032011150726
47990CB00005B/1925